JOURNAL FOR THE STUDY OF THE OLD TESTAMENT
SUPPLEMENT SERIES

56

Editors
David J A Clines
Philip R Davies

JSOT Press
Sheffield

The
PURIFICATION OFFERING
in the
PRIESTLY LITERATURE

Its Meaning and Function

N. Kiuchi

Journal for the Study of the Old Testament
Supplement Series 56

Copyright © 1987 Sheffield Academic Press

Published by JSOT Press
JSOT Press is an imprint of
Sheffield Academic Press Ltd
The University of Sheffield
343 Fulwood Road
Sheffield S10 3BP
England

Typeset by Sheffield Academic Press
and
printed in Great Britain
by Billing & Sons Ltd
Worcester

British Library Cataloguing in Publication Data

Kiuchi, N
    The purification offering in the priestly
    literature : its meaning and function.—
    (Journal for the study of the Old Testament
    supplement series, ISSN 0309-0787; 56).
    1. Bible. O.T. Leviticus—Criticism,
    interpretation, etc.
    I. Title   II. Series
    222'.1306   BS1255.2

    ISBN 1-85075-103-X
    ISBN 1-85075-102-1 Pbk

CONTENTS

PREFACE

This work is based on my thesis entitled 'The Meaning and Function of the *Ḥaṭṭā't* Offering', which was accepted in 1986 for the Ph.D. degree of the British Council for National Academic Awards.

In producing the work I enjoyed supervision by Dr G.J. Wenham for four years in Cheltenham, and I should especially like to record here my sincere gratitude to him for having guided me with great insight, academic candour and patience. I also wish to express my indebtedness to Prof. J.R. Porter, Rev. J.A. Motyer and Dr R.P. Gordon, without whose assistance the thesis would not have been brought to completion. My special thanks also go to the editors of the *Journal for the Study of the Old Testament* for accepting the work into their Supplement Series and for their helpful suggestions.

Needless to say, I alone bear responsibility for the views expressed in the book.

ABBREVIATIONS

AB	Anchor Bible
AV	Authorized Version
BDB	F. Brown, S.R. Driver, C.A. Briggs, *A Hebrew and English Lexicon of the OT*, Oxford, 1929
BM	*Beth Miqra*
BS	*Bibliotheca Sacra*
CBQ	*Catholic Biblical Quarterly*
DB	*Dictionary of the Bible*, edited by F.C. Grant and H. Rowley, 2nd edn; Edinburgh, 1963.
DBS	*Supplément au Dictionnaire de la Bible*
EI	*Eretz Israel*
EJ	*Encyclopedia Judaica*, 16 vols.; Jerusalem, 1971
EM	*Encyclopedia Miqrait* (Biblica), 8 vols.; Jerusalem, 1950-1982
EQ	*Evangelical Quarterly*
ET	*Expository Times*
FS	Festschrift
GK	*Gesenius' Hebrew Grammar*, 2nd edn; Oxford, 1910
HDB	*Hastings' Dictionary of the Bible*
HUCA	*Hebrew Union College Annual*
IDB	*Interpreter's Dictionary of the Bible*
IDBsup	*Supplement to Interpreter's Dictionary of the Bible*, 1976
JAOS	*Journal of the American Oriental Society*
JBL	*Journal of Biblical Literature*
Joüon	P. Joüon, *Grammaire de l'hébreu biblique*, Rome, 1923
JQR	*Jewish Quarterly Review*
JSS	*Journal of Semitic Studies*
JThS	*Journal of Theological Studies*
KBL	Koehler, L., Baumgartner, W., *Hebräisches und aramäisches Lexikon zum Alten Testament*, Leiden, 1967–

LXX	Septuagint
MT	Masoretic Text
MTZ	*Münchener Theologische Zeitschrift*
NASB	New American Standard Bible
NEB	New English Bible
OTS	*Oudtestamentische Studiën*
OTWSA	*Ou-Testamentiese Werkgemeenskap van Suid-Afrika*
P	Priestly Source
PAAJR	*Proceedings of the American Academy for Jewish Research*
RB	*Revue Biblique*
RIDA	*Revue Internationale des Droits de l'Antiquité*
RSV	Revised Standard Version
Sam	Samaritan Pentateuch
SBL	Society of Biblical Literature
Shnaton	*An Annual for Biblical and Ancient Near Eastern Studies*
ST	*Studia Theologica*
SVT	Supplements to *Vetus Testamentum*
TB	*Tyndale Bulletin*
TDNT	*Theological Dictionary of the New Testament*, edited by G.F. Kittel; translated and edited by G.W. Bromiley; Grand Rapids, 1964–1977
THAT	*Theologisches Handwörterbuch zum Alten Testament*, edited by E. Jenni and C. Westermann; München, 1971.
TWAT	*Theologisches Wörterbuch zum Alten Testament*, edited by G.J. Botterweck and H. Ringgren; Stuttgart, 1970–
VT	*Vetus Testamentum*
ZAW	*Zeitschrift für die alttestamentliche Wissenschaft*
ZThK	*Zeitschrift für Theologie und Kirche*
'ה	Tetragrammaton

INTRODUCTION

The *hattat* offering is the sacrifice in the OT most prominently associated with atonement. While atonement is generally considered to be one of the major theological issues in the OT, the scholarly debate on it has often resulted in a stalemate. It is the belief of the present writer that any discussion of atonement should be preceded by an independent inquiry into expiatory sacrifices such as the *hattat*. This study aims at clarifying the meaning and function of the *hattat* offering in the priestly literature of the Pentateuch[1] in the hope of contributing to the discussion of atonement theology in the OT.

Since the last century the *hattat* offering has been studied in connection with various theological issues. There are three major contexts in which the *hattat* has been discussed by theologians and exegetes. Firstly, since the *hattat* like the אשם has commonly been regarded as an expiatory sacrifice, the differences between these two sacrifices have been vigorously discussed mostly within the particular context of Lev 4.1–5.26.[2] Secondly, being an animal sacrifice like the עולה and שלמים, the *hattat* has been discussed in connection with substitution, the symbolism of blood, the imposition of hand(s) and so on. Thirdly, the *hattat* has been most often taken up in the discussion of 'atonement', 'expiation', and 'propitiation'. This is understandable since the term *kipper*, which has by and large been translated 'expiate for' or 'atone for', is most frequently mentioned in connection with the *hattat*.

However, although these theological issues are closely related to the question of the function of the *hattat* and indeed constitute part of the *hattat* problem, it is surprising that the *hattat* has rarely been studied in its own right. Indeed there are various views about the above theological issues and the texts related to the *hattat*, yet as far as the basic function of the *hattat* itself is concerned, there is little discussion; its function is seen either as expiatory or purificatory, or

both. Setting aside detailed arguments about the individual elements
of the *hattat* or of its ritual for later discussion, we shall briefly
delineate below how the major function of the *hattat* has been
seen.

In the LXX of the Torah the term חטאת (offering) is consistently
translated ἁμαρτία, except in Num 8.7 (ἁγνισμός); 19.9 (ἅγνισμα),
17 (ἁγνισμός). This deviation is ascribed by S. Daniel to the
circumstance that in the eyes of the Greek translators this agent of
purification, i.e. a red heifer, had nothing in common with the
sacrificial animals prescribed in contexts such as Lev 4, which are
more associated with expiation.[3]

With regard to the Rabbinic tradition it has been noted by J. Milgrom
that some sages made a distinction between the *hattat* for expiation
(Lev 4; Num 15.22, 31) and the *hattat* for purification (e.g. Lev 12),
but that the majority of rabbis held the function of the *hattat* to be
purificatory.[4]

In the NT a clear idea about the function of the *hattat* in the OT
ritual is expressed by the author of Hebrews, as follows:

> For if the blood of goats and bulls and the ashes of a heifer
> sprinkling those who have been defiled, sanctify for the cleansing of
> the flesh, how much more will the blood of Christ, who, through
> the eternal Spirit offered Himself without blemish to God, cleanse
> your conscience from dead works to serve the living God? (Heb
> 9.13-14, NASB)

Thus the *hattat* on the day of Atonement (Lev 16.5) and the ashes
of a red heifer (Num 19.9) are equally assumed to *cleanse the
flesh*.[5]

From the last century till today most Christian theologians have
assumed the function of the *hattat* to be expiatory, not only in
contexts where the verb חטא appears, but also in contexts where
apparently only purification is spoken of. For example, on the nature
of the ritual for the parturient (Lev 12) Keil writes:

> For her restoration to the Lord and his sanctuary, she was to come
> and be cleansed with a sin-offering and a burnt-offering, on
> account of the uncleanness in which the sin of nature had
> manifested itself; because she had been obliged to absent herself in
> consequence for a whole week from the sanctuary and fellowship of
> the Lord.[6]

Thus uncleanness is viewed by Keil as a manifestation of the
nature of sin. Similarly, referring to various kinds of uncleanness
J.H. Kurtz says:

These conditions and functions, the whole of which, with the single exception of conjugal intercourse, were involuntary and to a certain extent inevitable, are not treated in the law as sinful in themselves, or as connected with special sins... Yet by requiring a sin- or trespass-offering for the removal of the higher forms of uncleanness, it indicates a primary connection between them and sin, so far, that is to say, as the processes occurring in the body are dependent upon the influences and effects of the universal sinfulness. And it was this sinfulness... which required sacrificial expiation by means of sin-offerings, in the same manner as sinful acts unconciously performed.[7]

Kurtz's work shows how intensively the symbolic meaning of every component of the *hattat* ritual (slaughtering, imposition of hand(s), blood manipulation etc.) was discussed in the last century, a trait not dominant in recent study of the *hattat*.

An additional circumstance, which has affected the study of the *hattat* even until the present, is the place of Lev 17.11 in the study of sacrificial symbolism. In view of the fact that this is the sole passage which explicitly refers to the meaning of blood manipulation, it would be understandable if a question such as whether the *hattat* is expiatory or purificatory appeared to have only secondary importance for scholars concentrating on the exact meaning of the passage. At any rate, despite the consensus that Lev 17.11 should be applied to other animal sacrifices, it is a fact that the passage has not been meaningfully considered in connection with some specific features of the *hattat*.

On the whole this kind of approach to the function of the *hattat* has not basically changed until today,[8] except for a few dissenters mentioned below, culminating in J. Milgrom's thesis (1970).

In his work on expiation L. Moraldi (1956) pointed out that the terms 'expiation' and 'expiatory', which have judicial overtones, are unsuitable for describing the function of the *hattat* in view of the purely purificatory contexts such as Num 19.9, 17; 8.7; 31.23.[9] However, without abolishing the term 'expiatory' he proposed to retain it on the understanding that it has nothing to do with our modern concept of expiation with judicial overtones.[10]

In 1963 J. Barr contributed an article on 'sacrifice and offering' in which he briefly expressed his view on the *hattat*.[11] According to him the *hattat* (sacrifice for sin) is not directly related to 'sin' in the light of חטא (Lev 8.15; Ezek 43.20-23), which refers to purifying or purging. From this usage the term *hattat* acquired a secondary sense of purification. Barr then concludes that '"purification offering" better expresses to the modern mind the purpose of the חטאת than does "sin offering", with its misleading association'.[12]

In the last fifteen years two new theories on the *hattat* have been proposed by the Jewish scholars, B. Levine and J. Milgrom.

According to Levine[13] there are two types of *hattat*: (1) the *hattat* for safeguarding the sanctuary and its ministering priesthood from contamination (e.g. Lev 4.1-21); (2) the *hattat* for expiating the offences of the individual. This latter is expiatory rather than purificatory. The two types of *hattat* are distinguished by the identity of the donor of the sacrifice: the *hattat* of the priests comes from Aaron or priests and safeguards the sanctuary, whereas the *hattat* of the people comes from the people and expiates them.

This characterization of the two kinds of *hattat* by its donor has been rejected by J. Milgrom[14] (see below) on the following grounds: (1) The sacrificial goat on the day of Atonement is burned outside the camp but it is brought by the people (Lev 16.5, 27). Further in Lev 4.13-21 the sanctuary is purged by a *hattat* but it is brought by the people. (2) The burnt *hattat* is not 'safeguarding', since it has no apotropaic function. Neither does it purify the priesthood, since the purgative element, the blood, is never placed on an individual, not even the priest. (3) The eaten *hattat* cannot be expiatory because it is impossible to assume sin or sinfulness in physical impurity (e.g. Lev 12).

In a series of articles since 1970[15] J. Milgrom has established himself as the leading modern authority on the interpretation of the *hattat*. His basic view of the *hattat* is as follows:

חטאת should be translated 'purification offering' for the following reasons. The term is a derivative of a *pi'el* verb חִטֵּא which means 'to cleanse, expurgate, decontaminate' (Lev 8.15; Ezek 43.22, 26). Moreover 'the *ḥaṭṭā't* is prescribed for persons and objects who cannot possibly have sinned'.[16]

The *hattat* is prescribed for an unclean person (Lev 12-15) and for a sinner (e.g. Lev 4). Yet in the former the uncleanness is removed by ablution whereas in the latter the sinner 'has undergone inner purification'[17] by 'feeling guilty *'āšēm*'.[18] Since the *hattat* blood is applied to the sancta, it must be concluded that the blood purifies the sancta and not the person. This is supported by the prepositions *kipper* takes. When *kipper* is followed by inanimate objects (e.g. Lev 16.16ff.), the prepositions על and ב should be taken literally, whereas when the object of *kipper* is a person the prepositions על and בעד mean 'on behalf of'.[19]

The idea of sin/uncleanness contaminating the sancturay is common to all ancient Near Eastern cultures, and in Israel the defilement of the sancta is envisaged in three stages: (1) The sin of an individual and severe uncleanness pollute the outer altar (Lev 4.25, 30; 9.9ff.). (2) The sin of the anointed priest or the whole congregation defiles the shrine (Lev 4.5-7, 16-18). (3) Wanton, unrepented sin defiles not only the outer altar and the shrine but the *kappōret*, and this uncleanness is purified on the day of Atonement (Lev 16.16-19).[20]

The two kinds of *hattat*, the eaten and the burnt, are both purificatory. The eaten *hattat* purges lower degrees of uncleanness; thus it can be eaten by the priests. By contrast the burnt *hattat* purges higher degrees of uncleanness caused by the sin of the high priest, the whole congregation and wanton sinners. Since the *hattat* flesh is dangerously contagious, it has to be burnt outside the camp.[21]

Lastly, Milgrom holds that Lev 17.11:

> For the life of the flesh is in the blood, and I have given it to you on the altar to make atonement for your souls; for it is the blood by reason of the life that makes atonement (NASB).

refers only to the שלמים: he excludes its application to the blood manipulation of other sacrifices.[22]

Z. Weinberg[23] agrees with Milgrom that the function of the *hattat* is purification. Like Milgrom he emphasizes those contexts in which the notion of sin is unlikely to be present, such as Lev 12.6-7; 15.14-15, 29-30; 14.19, 22, 31; Num 6.10-11, 14. He therefore infers that the term *kipper* in those contexts is unlikely to be related to 'expiation'. Weinberg points out, however, that Milgrom's view fails to explain the *hattat* of the Nazirite, offered on the day of completing the vow (Num 6.13ff.), which is associated neither with 'purification' nor with 'forgiveness'. For this kind of context he suggests the idea of 'renewal of right relationship' between God and the offerer.[24]

In his recent exhaustive work on *kipper* B. Janowski includes some criticisms of Milgrom's major theses on the *hattat* and *kipper*.[25] Janowski argues against Milgrom that it is insufficient just to point out that חִטֵּא means 'to cleanse, expurgate, decontaminate' (Ezek 43.22, 26; Ps 51.9) to establish the translation of the *hattat* as 'purification offering'. It should not be overlooked, he says, that חִטֵּא is a privative denominative verb of חַטָּא which means 'de-sin' (Exod 29.36; Lev 8.15; 14.49, 52; Num 19.9; Ezek 43.20, 22, 23; 45.18; Ps

51.9). Indeed Janowski admits that purification is the function of the
hattat in contexts such as Ezek 43.26 (כְּפֶּר//מִחֵר), Lev 12.7ff. and
Num 6.10ff. But he argues that if, as Milgrom says, atonement
consists in the purification of the sanctuary from material uncleanness, that notion is incompatible with the notion of a man being
guilty. With regard to the cultic *kipper* Janowski consistently
translates it 'sühnen',[26] by which he envisages 'eine stellvertretende
Lebenshingabe' achieved by application of blood to sancta, as is
summarized in Lev 17.11.[27]

The Problem

As the above brief delineation of the various views of the *hattat*
shows, the central problem regarding the function of the *hattat* is
whether it is expiatory or purificatory. However in view of the fact
that *hattat* has tended to be unquestioningly translated 'the sin
offering', the observation that it appears in contexts in which the
notion of sin is unlikely to be present seems to be of vital
importance.

Nevertheless, whether the *hattat* is expiatory or purificatory is the
question that arises from observing only the occasions of the *hattat*
ritual; for instance Lev 4 concerns 'expiation', whereas Lev 12
concerns 'purification'. That this definition may be misleading or
superficial is indicated by the following considerations.

Firstly, in both contexts the *hattat* ritual involves the same blood
manipulation and the disposal of the *hattat* flesh. Unless a historical
change in the symbolic meaning of these acts is assumed, the rituals
in both contexts must concern essentially the same thing.

The same inference may be drawn from the usage of *kipper*. It
appears in both expiatory and purificatory contexts. If the sense of
kipper were invariable in those contexts, the function of the *hattat*
could be the same, which must be something more essential than
'expiation' or 'purification'. Even at this level, though, there remains
the problem of translating the חטאת.

Another problem with the *hattat* lies in the circumstance that its
ritual varies with different occasions. Although this circumstance
itself may not affect the basic function of the *hattat*, it calls for an
explanation why, for instance, the blood is brought into the shrine in
Lev 4.1-21 but not in Lev 4.22ff., or why the *hattat* flesh is on one
occasion eaten by the priests but on another burned outside the camp
(Lev 6.17-23).

It is clear then that every aspect of the *hattat* offering requires reassessment. However, we judge that, correct or not, Milgrom's contribution to the *hattat* is of paramount importance because he offers the most systematic view of the *hattat* offering. Therefore our discussion will constantly interact with his view.

Method and Procedure

Most modern critics, especially those in Germany, have tended to show a great deal of interest in the formation of the present text of Leviticus. While this approach is in itself justified, it is rather one-sided where it has not been coupled with an equal amount of interest in the meaning of the rituals, above all, the *hattat* ritual.[28]

In this study we do not intend either to support or to reject, in principle, any particular literary analysis such as those of G. von Rad, K. Koch, R. Rendtorff, K. Elliger and B. Janowski.[29] But with Milgrom[30] we take the present text of Leviticus as the starting point for our inquiry into the *hattat* symbolism.

This approach is justified, we believe, for the following reasons. Firstly, source-critical judgments often presume the intention of a final editor. However the variety of interpretations of the present text of Leviticus, which will be shown in this study, indicates that the intentions of the final editor have not been firmly grasped by modern critics. Thus though we do not intend to devalue traditional disciplines such as source-, form- and redaction-criticism, we hold with Milgrom that these methods will not be meaningful until we know the intention of the final editor, and hence the importance of the present text.

Secondly, source-critical judgments are often based on unevenness of style and ideology. But how one should evaluate the phenomenon is itself a great problem and raises numerous questions concerning the criteria for distinguishing literary strata. Yet conventional source- and form-criticism have operated without a thorough reexamination of those criteria.[31]

Practically, then, it seems more sound to start from the present text because to enter into the history behind the present text involves, at the present stage of scholarship, too many extra problems, and particularly for any study of the meaning of a sacrifice like this one source-criticism is unlikely to be fruitful.

This book mainly concerns the symbolism of the *hattat*. And herein lies a great difficulty. Because the text rarely mentions explicitly the symbolic meaning of ritual acts, we know very little about the meaning of the ritual. Whereas, as modern anthropologists and some biblical scholars have emphasized,[32] it is unlikely that the ancient Israelites performed their ritual acts without being aware of their symbolic meaning; rather the meaning of the ritual acts are rarely spelled out because they were self-evident to them. Nevertheless, we shall endeavour to point out some hints in the text itself. In the case of multiple interpretations the criterion for choice will be whether a suggested interpretation can be coherently applied to the same acts in other contexts. It is hoped that the use of this criterion will reduce any arbitrariness or guess-work to a minimum.

It is not only the meaning of the *hattat* and various ritual acts in the ceremony that we know little about. A series of studies by Milgrom on cultic terms[33] has shown how inadequately we presume their meaning, whereas a subtle difference in the meaning of a single cultic term can affect one's way of looking at the cultic text and even a whole cultic theology (e.g. *kipper*). Thus the importance of detailed rigorous exegesis is obvious. So we shall devote a good deal of space to discussing the meaning of words, phrases and sentences which appear in relevant texts, interacting with medieval Jewish commentators, nineteenth-century writers such as Kurtz and more recent commentators.

It is hoped that our exegesis of particular sections of Leviticus will contribute, in a small way, to the future discussion of the formation of the book.

Our discussion of the *hattat* divides into the following chapters. Chapter 1: The *hattat* offering in Lev 4.1–5.13; Chapter 2: The *hattat* offering in other sources; Chapter 3: Lev 10 and Lev 16; Chapter 4: The *kipper* problem; Chapter 5: Some components in the *hattat* ritual; Chapter 6: The *hattat* offering in Lev 16.

Chapters 1–2 investigate the relevant *hattat* sections in an attempt to discover the basic function of the *hattat* with special reference to Milgrom's view. In Chapter 2 special emphasis is laid on the exegesis of Lev 10.17 which links the function of the *hattat* with *kipper*. On the basis of the interpretation of Lev 10.17, Chapter 3 attempts to clarify the enigmatic episode in Lev 10.16-20, in which Moses argues with Aaron about the people's *hattat* mentioned in Lev 9.7, 15. The interpretation of this incident as well as the Nadab and Abihu incident (Lev 10.1-7) lead to a reassessment of the nature of the ritual in Lev 9 and also to a discussion of the relationship between Lev 10 and Lev 16. Chapter 4 is devoted, first of all, to the clarification of the concept of *kipper*, and the various prepositions it takes. Drawing on the conclusions of Chapter 2 we shall discuss whether the notion of 'purification' is foreign to 'bearing guilt', seeing that each is related to *kipper*. Then Lev 17.11, which is the only explicit clue to the symbolism of blood manipulation, is discussed with reference to Milgrom's restriction of the passage to the שלמים. Chapter 5 discusses three components of the *hattat* ritual: the imposition of hand(s), the blood manipulation and the disposal of the *hattat* flesh. The first and the third concern the question whether the *hattat* flesh becomes unclean or not, while the second is related to the problem of the variety of ritual types created by the sprinkling (הזה) and daubing (נתן) gestures. Chapter 6 addresses the function of the *hattat* in the day of Atonement ceremony, based on the conclusions of all the previous chapters. The central question here is how the Azazel-goat ritual is related to the *hattat* which purifies the sancta. The solution of this question will confirm the inferences drawn in the previous chapters about the relationship between uncleanness and guilt (chs. 2, 4), the relationships between Lev 10 and Lev 16 (ch. 3) and between Lev 4.3-21 and Lev 16.14ff. (ch. 5). Lastly a suggestion will be made about how this atonement ceremony should be seen in relation to other atonement ceremonies.

Limitations

For the reasons stated above we shall not enter into the literary analysis of the texts related to the *hattat*. This task is beyond the scope of the present work.

In addition there are several areas of research which we touch upon in the course of discussion but which we cannot investigate thoroughly, because of the limited scope of this work. They are: (1) the אשם offering and its relationship with the *hattat*; (2) cleanness-uncleanness regulations; (3) the relationship between sancta and the people; (4) the scope of purgation of the *hattat*; (5) the material of the *hattat* sacrifice. Each of these issues requires separate investigation and is germane to a deeper understanding of the *hattat*.

Nevertheless we believe that our approach to the *hattat* is urgently needed in view of the superficial treatments of the Israelite sacrifices in the past. We suggest that similar studies should be made of each of the other four major sacrifices (עולה, מנחה, שלמים, אשם) in ancient Israel with a view to producing a comprehensive interpretation of the sacrificial system of each.

Chapter 1

THE *HATTAT* OFFERING IN LEV. 4.1-5.13

Introduction

We begin our study with Lev 4.1-5.13,[1] the fullest set of regulations dealing with the *hattat*, because this pericope prescribes exactly why and when the sacrifice is to be brought to the sanctuary. At this stage we aim to clarify some of the general principles implied in this passage. We shall leave some of the more difficult problems about the differences between the rites for later discussion.

Lev 4 deals with the so-called inadvertent violation of a divine prohibition,[2] and its expiatory ritual is classified according to four cultic representatives, viz. the anointed priest,[3] the whole congregation,[4] a tribal leader and a lay individual.[5] The ritual for the anointed priest is the same as that for the whole congregation. The main elements of the ritual include bringing the blood into the shrine, sprinkling it towards the *pārōket* veil, daubing the horns of the incense altar with it and burning the flesh outside the camp. The fact that only Lev 4.3-21 and Lev 16.12-17 prescribe the bringing of blood into the shrine suggests some relationship between the two sections. By contrast the ritual for a tribal leader is essentially the same as that for a lay individual. An important feature of the normal *hattat* ritual is daubing the horns of the altar of burnt offering with the blood. Though nothing is prescribed for the *hattat* flesh, it is generally assumed from Lev 6.17-22 that it is consumed by the officiating priest. The above two types of ritual have in common the imposition of a hand, slaughtering, pouring the rest of the blood at the base of the altar of burnt offering and the burning of fat.

Lev 5.1-4 deals with four particular sins, the exact nature of which will be discussed below. The ritual assumed in v. 6 could be the same as that of Lev 4.32ff.[6] However it is followed by two concession-sacrifices (vv. 7-13) taking account of the economic status of the sinner.

At first sight it appears that the function of the sacrifice is reflected
in the ritual itself. And it may well be so. But the complex of ritual
details may be related to the concept of *kipper* which appears at the
end of the sacrificial ritual. On the other hand, in Lev 4–5 differences
in ritual procedure appear to vary with the kinds of sin. These
considerations suggest that the ritual elements should be dealt with
separately and that the protases (Lev 4.2-3, 13-14a, 22-23a, 27-28a;
5.1-4) and their relationship with the ritual as a whole must first be
investigated to approach the essential function of the *hattat*. The
study thus looks first at the overall structure of the protases (A), then
at the concepts of שגג (B) and *'āšēm* (C), and finally at the
consequence of sin (D).

A. *Overall structure of the protases*

The protases in question include Lev 4.2-3, 13-14a, 22-23a, 27-28a;
5.1-4. We shall discuss first the structure of the first four protases and
then Lev 5.1-4.

Formally the law in Lev 4 begins with נפש כי (v. 2) followed by
four sub-cases with אם (v. 3), ואם (v. 13), אשר (v. 22)[7] and ואם (v. 27).
Conceptually, however, v. 2 has been regarded as almost the same as
vv. 13, 22, 27.[8] This view does not seem correct when v. 2 is looked at
more closely. It reads:

v. 2a נפש כי תחטא בשגגה מכל מצות ה' אשר לא תעשינה
v. 2b ועשה מאחת מהנה

The exegetical problem in v. 2 centres on the meaning of מן, which
appears three times. Though there is no problem about the third one,
which is clearly partitive, the first two have been basically taken as
either partitive[9] or 'against'.[10]

The first view, that the first two מן are partitive, seems to be based
on the assumption that the whole chapter deals with the violation of
one divine prohibition.[11] Though this is correct, it is not until v. 2b
that the breach of only one command is mentioned. Thus to take the
first two מן as partitive will make v. 2b virtually redundant. But since
הנה in v. 2b refers back to כל מצות, it is clear that v. 2b, and not v. 2a,
expresses the idea of 'part', and that therefore there is no redundancy
between v. 2a and v. 2b. Hence the first מן is unlikely to be partitive.
Further the second one is also unlikely to be partitive because the
third one is enough to express the idea of 'part'.

The second view that מן marks the object of sin, thus 'against', is more likely. The same usage seems present in Lev 5.13. If so, מן should be connected with חטא rather than with בשגגה.

However if the above interpretation of מן is correct, the general meaning of v. 2 is still ambiguous simply because the passage appears to speak of the violation of one prohibition, and not all the prohibitions.[12] If there is no redundancy between v. 2a and v. 2b there appears to be no alternative but to assume that v. 2b explains v. 2a; *wāw* in ועשה being explicative (cp. vv. 13, 22, 27). Thus the general meaning of the passage should be: 'if anyone sins inadvertently against all the divine prohibitions in that he does one of them'. Therefore the passage seems to assume that even the violation of one divine prohibition is equal to that of the whole.[13]

This idea is not, however, expressed in vv. 3, 13, 22 and 27. Therefore v. 2 presents a principle covering all the four sub-cases, not only formally but conceptually. Nevertheless it could be observed that vv. 13, 22, 27 use the same expressions or expressions similar to those found in v. 2, whereas v. 3 is much shorter than vv. 13, 22, 27. This could well have been caused by the distance of vv. 3, 13, 22, 27 from v. 2; vv. 13, 22, 27, being distant from v. 2, remind a reader of v. 2 by using the same or similar expressions whereas v. 3 could afford to be shorter, coming immediately after v. 2.

Lev 5.1-4 gives an impression entirely different from Lev 4 in that it presents four particular sins, and though it begins with ונפש כי, it is not followed by an אם-clause introducing sub-cases. Traditionally the four cases have been regarded as protases independent of one another. A. Spiro[14] and M. Noth[15] have, however, proposed that vv. 2-4 hinge on v. 1, which 'enjoins a potential witness to give testimony against a man whom he has seen commit a sin or of whom he has knowledge that he has committed a sin. Verses 2-5 bid the observer, the witness of verse 1, to tell or remind his fellow man that he finds himself in a situation where he is liable to commit a sin'.[16] According to Spiro והוא ידע ואשם (vv. 3, 4) refers to the witness in v. 1, while either והוא טמא in v. 2 should be emended to והוא ידע as in vv. 3-4, or v. 2b as a whole should be omitted as in the LXX.[17] In addition ואשם is understood by Spiro to mean 'failure to do [tell] so is a sin'.[18]

The nature of the sins and the clause ונעלם ממנו והוא ידע will be discussed below at length. But even in other respects the above view seems quite unlikely.

Firstly, vv. 2-4 are introduced by או which appears to present alternatives to v. 1 as a whole,[19] but which can hardly serve to present possible instances of witnessing in v. 1.

Secondly, מאחת מאלה in v. 13 appears to disprove the interpretation because the phrase most naturally refers to the four independent cases in vv. 1-4.

Thirdly, to assume 'the failure to tell the fact' between והוא ידע and ואשם seems forced particularly in view of the fact that והוא ידע is missing in v. 2 (see below).

Thus Spiro's proposal, though ingenious, is unlikely. As stated above the particle או functions to present sentence-level alternatives. Now the peculiarity of this section lies in that the alternatives in vv. 2-4 begin in forms rather similar to ונפש כי (v. 1); או נפש אשר (v. 2), או כי (v. 3) and או נפש כי (v. 4). These introductory terms suggest the cases are independent. However Chapman and Streane suggest that 'all four verses should be taken as forming one long protasis to which v. 5 is the apodosis'. In view of this proposal, which appears highly plausible, ונפש כי תחטא in v. 1 could be taken as subsuming four particular cases.[20] In other words, conceptually vv. 2-4 correspond to ושמעה onwards in v. 1. This type of relationship between a main case and sub-cases has been noted above in Lev 4. A possible explanation of the similar beginnings in vv. 1-4 is that, contrary to Spiro's proposal each verse emphasizes its independent character by imitating the beginning of v. 1.

In a word, the four independent cases are conceptually subsumed under ונפש כי תחטא (v. 1) and followed by v. 5.

Another question is how Lev 5.1-13 is related to Lev 4. The widespread view[21] that Lev 5.1-13 is a continuation of Lev 4, particularly vv. 27-35, has been rightly corrected by Milgrom for the following reasons:[22] (a) The introductory formula ונפש כי (Lev 5.1) signifies the beginning of a new law. (b) The law of Lev 5.1-13 concerns any of the four cases enumerated in vv. 1-4 (see vv. 5, 13). Further, as Milgrom notes, there are definitive differences in the nature of sins between Lev 4 and Lev 5.1-4. But the above two reasons seem sufficient to prove that Lev 5.1ff. deals with a new law.

To summarize: in Lev 4, verse 2, which says that the violation of one divine prohibition is equal to that of the whole, covers the four sub-cases in vv. 3, 13, 22, 27, while Lev 5.1-4, a section distinct from Lev 4, presents the four independent cases, subsumed under ונפש כי תחטא and followed by v. 5.

B. שגג (שגה)

Having clarified the structure of the protases in Lev 4.1–5.13 we must now examine the use of the key term שגג in this section. It is important to clarify this term to discover the nature of the sins the *hattat* atones for. Are they done consciously or not?

The general term for sin, חטא, is often modified by the root שגג both in the חטאת and the אשם pericopes (Lev 4.2, 13, 22, 27; 5.15, 18). As we shall see the root שגג (שגה) is important for understanding the nature of sin in Lev 4–5 and the meaning of *'āšēm*. The verb שגג (or שגה) is generally rendered 'go astray, err'.[23] As Milgrom notes,[24] one important aspect inherent in the root throughout its occurrence is that the root expresses the idea of motion. With Milgrom and others the English term 'inadvertence' is adopted in the following discussion.

While the notion of 'unintentionality' constitutes the basic element of the meaning of שגג, a specific problem has been raised by Milgrom when he argues that the root שגג or שגה presumes the notion of consciousness about an act.[25] He reasons that all the *hattat* cases assume that the sacrifice should be brought only after the sin becomes known to the sinner either by his own realization or by others pointing it out. But the term *'āšēm* itself excludes the notion of 'consciousness of an act'. This means that the consciousness of an act must be presumed in the previous phrase בשגגה. Thus the *hattat* pericope deals with 'conscious acts' which were later realized to be sinful. The absence of the root שגג in Lev 5.1-4 is due to the fact that those sins are deliberate.[26]

R. Knierim claims, however, that this theory is untenable, and holds that in most cases where the term appears the consciousness of a sinner is hardly reflected, and that, even if it is, each case should be observed contextually. In principle he assumes that the concept designates the objective result of an unpremeditated act or involuntary error, irrespective of the consciousness of a sinner.[27]

Janowski,[28] following Knierim, opposes Milgrom's view that the sins in Lev 5.1-4 are deliberate, and maintains that they are caused by ignorance. In support of this view Janowski refers to the root עלם in Lev 5.2, 3, 4; 4.13; Num 5.13; Lev 20.4. With K. Elliger, Janowski judges those sins as a 'Mischung von Irrtum und Verantwortlichkeit', and assumes that the whole section of Lev 4.1–5.13 deals with sins which begin unconsciously.[29]

In comparing these two opposing views it is important to note that *'āšēm* is translated 'feel guilt' by Milgrom, whereas it is translated 'be, or become guilty' by Knierim and Janowski, and that Milgrom emphasizes that an unintentional act can be performed consciously. Why Knierim and Janowski cannot accept Milgrom's view may be traced partly to the former's understanding of *'āšēm*. If the term describes the objective status of a sinner 'become guilty', no need arises to inquire about a subjective element in the previous phrase בשגגה. By contrast Milgrom's suggestion on שגגה focuses on the subjective situation of a sinner who has become aware of his offence, either by feeling guilty or by having his sin drawn to his attention (vv. 22-23a, 27-28a).[30] It is logical to hold that if a sin comes to be known to a sinner, he must have been conscious of his act. Does the phrase בשגגה, then, contain the notion of consciousness, as Milgrom insists?

Two basic considerations are in order at this point. Firstly, there is a consideration about the definition of the meaning of a word. Though Milgrom does not explicitly say that the consciousness of an act forms part of the meaning of שגגה, in principle the meaning of a word (including denotation and connotation) should be distinguished from information or situation inferred from the context. Thus when the consciousness of an act is said to be contained in the phrase בשגגה, it is questionable whether it constitutes the meaning of the phrase or whether it is simply inferred from the situation.[31] Secondly, and more importantly, the very meaning of שגג, 'going astray, erring' suggests the existence of norm or rules, which are divine prohibitions in the context of Lev 4. It is only in the context of rules that an act can be known as sinful. However it is clear from the context of vv. 13-14, 22-23, 27-28 that when a person commits an inadvertent sin he is not aware of it. This situation already suggests that if שגג presumes something, it is unconsciousness of sin and not consciousness of an act.[32] The latter appears too self-evident to be at issue. As will become clear in the arguments below the distinction between consciousness of an act and consciousness of the act's being a sin is crucial to the understanding of שגגה.

With these considerations in mind we examine below the concept of שגגה and its related expressions, והוא לא ידע and נעלם מן in the order of Lev 5.17-19; 4.13; 5.1-4; the first and second passages include שגג, whereas the third one does not.

Lev 5.17-19.[33] —The clauses ולא ידע and שגגתו...ידע in vv. 17-18 deserve close scrutiny. First of all, the crucial exegetical problem with ולא ידע in v. 17 is what the offender does not know. Some traditional Jewish exegetes have assumed that the clause means that a sinner did not know whether he sinned or not, but he suspects that he may have.[34] Ibn Ezra, followed by Shadal, assumes that the offender did not know that what he did was prohibited.[35] It seems that the interpretative gloss 'suspect' is unwarranted. But the view adopted by the majority of exegetes that the clause refers to sinning without realizing it seems correct.[36] For it appears most natural that the clause refers to the preceding sentence ועשתה ... תעשינה *as a whole* which expresses nothing but the concept of תחטא. Thus ולא ידע is unlikely to mean unconsciousness of an act. Moreover it must be argued that the ignorance of having committed a sin does not necessarily mean the unconsciousness of the act.

Secondly, the clause שגגתו אשר שגג והוא לא ידע deserves attention. For it will be reasonable to assume that the object of ידע is שגגתו, and that the whole clause is a combination of שגגתו אשר שגג and שגגתו אשר הוא לא ידע. If so, it follows that the root שגג itself does not refer to the self-consciousness of an offender (והוא לא ידע).[37] In the light of this interpretation the widespread assumption that ולא ידע in v. 17 corresponds to בשגגה in Lev 4.22[38] may be misleading. However, seen as a whole Lev 5.17-19 appears to deal with the same situation as in Lev 4: inadvertent sin.[39] Some linguistic peculiarities of Lev 5.17-19 should be noted; the term שגגה comes instead of חטאת in Lev 4; the *qal* form שָׁגַג (v. 18) appears only here in Lev 4–5; in Lev 4 the same situation is expressed by using בשגגה and not ולא ידע.

Therefore from Lev 5.17-19 it may be tentatively concluded that שגג itself is unlikely to refer to the subjective consciousness of the offender.

In Lev 4.13 the fact that all the congregation has erred (ישגו) is followed by ונעלם דבר מעיני הקהל. The subject of נעלם (be hidden)[40] is not the fact of ישגו but דָּבָר; although the usage of the article in biblical Hebrew is not consistent, the word דבר means 'something' rather than 'the matter' or 'the thing'.[41] Then the word (דבר) appears to be explicated by ועשה and following. Therefore ונעלם and following explicates the concept of ישגו. In other words, this passage indicates that the concept of שגה is made of two elements, the violation of a divine prohibition and the hidden nature of the act. At any rate, it is clear that the passage concerns the question where and what the fault is, and not whether the people are conscious of a certain act.

We now return to Lev 5.1-4, where the root שגג is missing, to see what sort of sin is envisaged in this section. We have already suggested that there are four separate cases here. Verse 1 appears to deal with withholding witnessing. Verses 2-3 deal with the contraction of uncleanness and presuppose something like the cleanness-uncleanness regulations in Lev 11–12; 15. Verse 4 appears to deal with a rash oath. Though each verse is somewhat obscure, the crux of the section for our present purpose lies in vv. 2-4, particularly the clause ונעלם ממנו והוא ידע in vv. 3-4.

The following three approaches to this clause have been proposed.

1. An act (contraction of uncleanness or a rash oath) was performed consciously and was forgotten (ונעלם ממנו), but it was later discovered (והוא ידע).[42]

2. An act was performed unconsciously (ונעלם ממנו) but it was later discovered (והוא ידע). This view is adopted by most exegetes who translate 'āšēm 'be guilty', in which case והוא ידע is translated 'when he knows it'.[43]

3. An act was performed knowingly (והוא ידע) but it was forgotten.[44] Unlike the above two views this one assumes that the contraction of uncleanness is a deliberate act.

First of all, the subject of נעלם is clearly the acts that are mentioned before it. The problem is the meaning of נעלם מן. In 1 and 3 it is taken to mean 'forget', '(the fact) escape' whereas in 2 'be hidden'. This difference in meaning is significant; 2's interpretation, 'be hidden', is a correct literal translation. But the more essential problem is whether the meaning 'be hidden' makes sense in the context. For since the sin, whatever it may be, becomes known in the end (התודה, v. 5), it is unlikely that the initial act was performed unconsciously. Moreover the very term בטא, 'speak rashly or thoughtlessly' (v. 4), indicates that the act is unlikely to be an unconscious act despite its thoughtless nature. Thus ונעלם cannot be taken as circumstantial to the foregoing as it is in Lev 4.13; it must follow the foregoing consecutively, meaning 'and (the fact) was hidden from him'. Then this meaning is not essentially different from 'he forgot it' or 'the fact escaped him'.[45] The question then becomes whether והוא ידע is linked with the foregoing or the following, since obviously נעלם ממנו cannot be simultaneous with והוא ידע (cp. נעלם and נודע in Lev 4.13-14).[46] In other words, does והוא ידע refer to the initial act or to an act *after* נעלם ממנו? The latter possibility, represented by approaches 1 and 2, seems unlikely for the following reasons.

Firstly, Lev 4.13-14, 22-23, 27-28 show that the root ידע does not come *before* 'āšēm. This implies that in Lev 5.3-4 והוא ידע is not followed consecutively by ואשם.

Secondly, if knowledge of an act precedes *'āšēm*, the assumption cannot explain the present text of v. 2, where והוא טמא appears instead of והוא ידע as in vv. 3-4. Indeed scholars have either omitted v. 2b as in the LXX or emended והוא טמא to והוא ידע in conformity with vv. 3-4.[47] Overlooked by such emenders is the fact, however, that in the MT והוא טמא is resumed in v. 3a in the form of אשר יטמא בה. If v. 2b were not original, אשר יטמא בה would refer only to human uncleanness, which is unlikely. Therefore the MT in v. 2b must be retained. In that case, by syntactic analogy with והוא טמא, והוא ידע in vv. 3-4 could be taken as a circumstantial clause[48] and translated 'though he had known it'. This means that v. 2, though it lacks והוא ידע, presumes the consciousness of the act.

To sum up: vv. 2-4 deal with the cases in which an act was consciously performed (והוא ידע) but it was forgotten (ונעלם ממנו). Here we concur with Milgrom. But what sort of sins are envisaged in this passage?

With regard to the sins in vv. 2-4 traditional Jewish interpretation has held that vv. 2-3 refer to 'the unlawful eating of sacrificial food or eating in the sanctuary while unclean, while v. 4 refers to the violation of the oath'.[49] The majority of modern scholars assume that vv. 2-3 refer to the omission of a purification ritual, while v. 4 speaks of 'the pronouncing an oath rashly and thoughtlessly but subsequently realizing that it was impossible of fulfilment'.[50] But as Spiro rightly says, vv. 2-3 mention no act except the contraction of uncleanness, which cannot be a sin.[51] Spiro argues further that if the failure to undergo purification rituals were the main concern of the law, the clause ונעלם ממנו would be entirely superfluous.[52] To this could be added a question: If eventually a person performed his purification ritual or carried out his oath, is he free from sin? Spiro also rightly judges both traditional and modern assumptions with regard to the rash oath as meaningless or groundless. However it has been argued above that Spiro's own proposal is also unlikely.[53] Milgrom has proposed that the acts in vv. 2-3 are deliberate,[54] but that since the prolongation of the impurity, being caused by forgetfulness, is not deliberate it is expiable by a *hattat*.[55] That the acts in vv. 2-3 are deliberate does not seem to conform to our exegesis of והוא ידע, which holds that though the sinner was conscious of his action he was not aware that it was sinful; 'deliberately' is different from 'consciously'. At any rate Milgrom assumes that the prolongation of impurity constitutes a sin.[56] But this too seems unlikely in that it postulates the omission of a purification ritual. Rodriguez has recently proposed that vv. 1-4 all deal with 'the intentional concealment of a sinful act', by translating ונעלם ממנו 'it is hidden *by* him'.[57] This interpretation does not appear, however, to be warranted by any occurrence of נעלם מן.

It seems then that throughout the history of the interpretation of these passages there has been a persistent preconception that forgetting the contraction of uncleanness is itself not enough to constitute a sin. We rather suggest that the sins in vv. 2-4 lie in 'forgetting' the initial acts, because 'forgetting' the contraction of uncleanness or an oath is, however unintentional, tantamount to disregarding the cultic and judicial order.

Now what is the sin in v. 1?[58] Though it is clear that the sin lies in not testifying, various interpretations have been proposed as to the situation envisaged in ושמעה קול אלה. Noth assumes that someone unlawfully utters a curse and someone else who is the witness of it fails to report the matter.[59] This is difficult. Clearly the notional subject of שמעה is the witness (עֵד). In addition there is nothing in the text to suggest that the curse is unlawful. The majority of scholars assume from Prov 29.24 and Judg 17.1-3 that this passage concerns a witness, who has heard a solemn adjuration to testify and does not.[60] However A. Phillips argues that the text does not suggest קול אלה was addressed to the witness.[61] Rather it was a curse pronounced on the wrongdoer. Hence he assumes that v. 1 deals with 'the witness who had heard the public proclamation of the curse on the unkown thief, and subsequently fails to testify'.[62] This last interpretation seems to be most satisfactory. The sin in v. 1 lies not just in 'withholding the testimony', but 'neglecting or defying אלה', i.e. denying divine justice.

In sum the sins in vv. 1-4 could be characterized, if put abstractly, as 'neglect of judicial and cultic order'. They are all concerned with people showing indifference to divine norms.

So why does not the root שגג appear in Lev 5.1-4? Milgrom says that it is because the sins described are deliberate in nature.[63] But on our interpretation v. 1 may well speak of a deliberate sin, whereas vv. 2-4 deal with unintentional sins. Thus it may be inferred that the intentionality of sin played little part in bringing together these four cases. Two reasons may be put forward to explain the absence of שגג in this section. First, the root implies that the sinner is conscious of his act though not that it is a sin, whereas here acting unconsciously (vv. 2-4) or not acting (v. 1) itself constitutes a sin. Second, the root is inherently related to the notion of 'movement', as in violation of a prohibitive commandment, but here no act in its primary sense is mentioned. In short the nature of the four cases is in conflict with the root meaning of שׁגג.

From the above examination of Lev 5.17-19; 4.13; 5.1-4 the following conclusions could be drawn with regard to שׁגג (שׁגה).

(a) The root meaning of שׁגג is 'to move in error'. It presumes the unconsciousness of a sin more immediately than the consciousness of an act, which Milgrom argues for. But the latter is indeed presumed in all the protases examined above.

(b) On the above interpretation of Lev 5.17-19 and 4.13 the root שׁגג (שׁגה) does not refer to the self-consciousness of a sinner who does not know that he is sinning. Rather the term describes an objective situation of an inadvertence, as Knierim assumed.[64]

C. *'āšēm*

In discussing the meaning of שׁגג we have already noted different understandings of *'āšēm* which go together with different interpretations of שׁגג.

In the word-group of אשׁם the verb אָשֵׁם poses the most crucial problems in understanding both the protases of the -חטאת and the אשׁם-offerings and the function of the חטאת offering. These problems are the meaning of *'āšēm* and its relationship with the sacrifice. In this section the former problem is discussed on the basis of the above conclusions on the שׁגג, while the latter will be dealt with in the next section.

Over against the standard translation of *'āšēm* 'be, become guilty'[65] Milgrom, partly anticipated by various exegetes, has recently proposed a new and systematic interpretation of *'āšēm*.[66] According to him the term refers to punishment in general, and particularly in the cultic realm it refers to the 'self-punishment of conscience'. Hence his preferred translation is 'feel guilt'.[67] He states:

> Thus, contrary to usual translations, *'šm* without an object does not refer to a *state* of guilt, but in keeping with its consequential meaning, denotes the *suffering* brought on by guilt, expressed now by words such as qualms, pangs, remorse, and contrition. *'šm* would then mean to be conscience-smitten or guilt-stricken... [the emphasis is Milgrom's].[68]

The appropriateness of this interpretation is supported by the following considerations.

Firstly, in Lev 5.21-22 it is reasonable to assume that the sinner is conscious about his act and its sinful nature even while planning it since the sin envisaged is not an inadvertence. Then the term *'āšēm* in v. 23 must definitely refer to an element distinct from consciousness of sin. The rendering 'be conscience-smitten' seems to fit the context (but see below).

Secondly, if 'be guilty' were the meaning of *'āšēm*, the protases in Lev 4-5 would lose much of their prescriptive function. For, when should one bring the sacrifice, if *'āšēm* is simply an objective declaration? Since the term usually comes just before the mention of bringing the sacrifice or of the confession (e.g. Lev 5.5, 17), it is most likely that the term refers to the existential situation of a sinner.[69]

Nevertheless there seem to be two problems latent in Milgrom's solution 'feel guilt', viz. his exclusion of 'consciousness of sin' from *'āšēm* and the pure subjectiveness of 'feeling guilt'. In the following discussion we concentrate on the former problem, assuming provisionally 'feel guilt'. Our own proposal for *'āšēm* will come at the end of the discussion.

The exclusion of 'consciousness of sin' from *'āšēm* is inferred from Lev 5.23 and 5.17. In Lev 5.23, Milgrom argues, the consciousness of sin and guilt exists in the sinner before *'āšēm*. Therefore *'āšēm* cannot simply mean 'be guilty'. Whereas in Lev 5.17 the act in question is said to be ולא ידע, i.e. an unconscious act: only later does the sinner *'āšēm*.[70] Hence, according to him, only the element of contrition is expressed by *'āšēm*. One wonders, however, whether the realm of conscience can be separated from that of consciousness so neatly.[71] That *'āšēm* excludes the consciousness of sin, however, does not appear to fit the contexts of Lev 5.23, 17 and Lev 4.13-14a, 22-23a, 27-28a as the following examination shows.

First of all, a sinner in Lev 5.21-22 may well be aware of his sin and guilt before feeling guilty. But it would be reasonable to assume that when he is conscience-smitten (*'āšēm*), he is *then* acutely conscious about his sin and guilt (cp. Gen 4.11-13; 2 Sam 12.1-13; 24.10). Therefore Milgrom's presupposition that 'even while planning his crime the wrongdoer is fully aware of his guilt'[72] seems to be erroneous. It seems, then, unnatural or artificial to make a clear distinction between conscience and consciousness in such a context.

By contrast Lev 5.17 is taken by Milgrom to mean that the offender did not know even his act. In this passage *'āšēm* is construed by Milgrom as 'suspecting that he has done wrong'.[73] But how can one even suspect that he has done wrong, if he is not conscious of his own act? Indeed, as A. Dillmann and P. Heinisch[74] contemplate, a situation could be envisaged where the offender, though he remembers his act *vaguely*, cannot pinpoint what the sin was, and suspects that he has done wrong.[75] But this view appears to be in conflict with ולא ידע, which does not mean 'suspect', but 'did not know at all'. Another possible way of retaining the view that ולא ידע refers to the unconsciousness of an act is to suppose that the offender started to feel guilty because he was suffering physically.[76] But this view too seems to assume what is not explicitly mentioned in the text.

In fact Milgrom, with L. Moraldi, suggests that in this case it is the ancient fear of unknown sins rather than the above two possibilities that is contemplated.[77] On this view the offender knows that he is suffering mentally or physically or both and therefore concludes he must have sinned somehow. So the nature of the whole passage is described by Milgrom 'as the legal formulation of the psychological truth that he who does not know the exact cause of suffering imagines the worst: he affronted the Deity. . . '[78] However despite the ancients' fear of unknown sins, this view seems fallacious in respect of Lev 5.17. For the law presupposes as an objective fact that a person has committed a sin.[79] In other words, the law does not envisage a case in which the person suspects either unnecessarily or wrongly that he has done wrong. Rather *since* he has done wrong, he feels guilty: when he feels guilty, he knows what the sin was. The inference is inevitable, then, that '*āšēm* includes in it the consciousness of sin.

Lastly the above arguments also affect the interpretation of Lev 4.13-14a, 22-23a and 27-28a. First of all, the presence of או in vv. 23, 28 has been suspected[80] because in v. 14 *wāw* appears instead of או and that '*āšēm* has been taken to mean 'be, become guilty'. Now that the translation is proven to be erroneous, there is no need to emend או to *wāw*. או can be taken as introducing an alternative to the preceding ואשם.[81] If, however, the consciousness (or knowledge) of sin were excluded from '*āšēm* it would have to be assumed that a sinner feels guilty without knowing his sin. Since the root שגג presumes the unconsciousness of sin, the consciousness of sin must be included in '*āšēm*. Verses 13-14a present a more complicated problem. If אשמו in v. 13b presumes the consciousness of sin as we argue, why should the same be repeated by נודעה? The relationship between v. 13b and v. 14a is unlikely to be consecutive; if it were, it would follow that the congregation is still in the dark as to the offence when they feel guilty. So the most plausible interpretation is that אשמו is explicated by נודעה.[82]

From the above examination of the passages it could be concluded that *'āšēm* includes the consciousness of sin. Now in our discussion on Lev 5.17, 21-22 it has also become clear that since the sinner is guilty, he feels guilty. In other words the meaning of *'āšēm* has both objective and subjective aspects. Therefore we propose that *'āšēm* means 'realize guilt', rather than 'feel guilt'.

In sum the protases in Lev 4.1-5.13 mean in general that the *hattat* ought to be brought to the sanctuary when the sinner realizes his guilt or is informed by others.[83]

D. *Consequence of sin?*

Now that the various problems of the protases in Lev 4.11-5.13 have been discussed it is possible to consider the relationship between the protases and the sacrificial ritual.

In general, sins have consequences. Texts outside sacrificial contexts make it abundantly clear that sin is, or ought to be, followed by its consequence, e.g. physical or spiritual suffering. This relationship had been widely understood in terms of divine retribution, until K. Koch proposed that the relationship represents 'schicksalwirkende Tatsphäre'.[84] Unfortunately, though this term properly describes the inseparable nature of sin and its consequence, his whole argument in support of what the term describes has tended to give an impression that it excludes both the idea of 'punishment' and divine intervention in the relationship. There have been various criticisms against Koch's view, most of which point out its one-sidedness.[85] Knierim,[86] for instance, emphasizes that what Koch calls 'schicksalwirkende Tatsphäre' *is* the act of God and that the two are in fact one. Indeed the recognition of this fact leads to an important question: how can God, who is holy by nature, intervene in the process of sin and its consequence? At any rate, the correctness of Knierim's view is assumed in the following arguments.

However in the *hattat* pericope it is not clear, first of all, what constitutes the consequence of sin. Has the consequence of sin in this case anything to do with the guilt-feeling, or with what the sacrifice deals with, or with something else?

As already mentioned[87] Milgrom sees in the guilt-feeling the punishment of sin. But more significantly this view appears to be an important assumption in his theory of the *hattat* offering. Milgrom writes:

The inadvertent offender needs forgiveness not because of his act *per se*—as indicated above, his act is forgiven because of the offender's inadvertence and remorse—but because of the consequence of his act. His inadvertence has contaminated the sanctuary and it is his responsibility to purge it with a *ḥaṭṭā't*.[88]

Whether the central function of the *hattat* is purificatory will be discussed in the next chapter. Here it is more urgent to examine whether Milgrom's understanding of the relationship between the guilt-feeling and the sacrifice is correct. We shall argue that his view is subject to criticism on two major counts.

1. The statement that an inadvertent act is forgiven before the purging of cleanness finds no support in the text.

Sequentially forgiveness (נסלח) is always granted after the *kipper*-acts and never before them (Lev 4.20, 26, 31, 35; 5.10, 13). This fact suggests that it is not the aftermath or the consequence of an inadvertent sin but the very inadvertence that the *kipper*-acts, particularly the *hattat* offering, deals with. This is indicated by the term חטאת (sin) in Lev 4.3, 14, 23, 26, 35; 5.10, 13, which refers unequivocally to the violation of a divine prohibition. This misunderstanding by Milgrom could be caused partly by his use of the term 'an inadvertent *act*'. As argued above in connection with שגגה it is not the inadvertent act but the inadvertent sin that the laws address.

2. It is doubtful whether, as Milgrom assumes, the term *'āšēm* refers to the punishment of sin. According to him the root אשם is similar to עון, פשע, חטא, and רעה in that it connotes both the wrong and the retribution.[89] But as the context of Lev 4 shows, אשם is certainly different from those roots in that it does not stand for the wrong itself, though it presupposes it, whereas those roots can refer both to the wrong and its consequence. In addition there are some reasons to doubt that *'āšēm* in Lev 4–5 refers to the punishment of sin.

a. In Lev 4.23, 28 the case is envisaged that an offender is informed of his sin by others. Since the particle או introduces an alternative to ואשם, it could be argued that on knowing the sin he ought to bring the sacrifice even without the guilt-feeling. In this case it appears that if the term punishment should be retained, it should be related, at least, to what the sacrifice does.

b. In Lev 5.17 the phrase נשא עון appears after *'āšēm*. The phrase appears to *declare* that the offender must bear the legal consequence of his sin.[90] This means that when the offender *realizes his guilt* he has not yet, at least fully, borne the punishment.

c. Milgrom includes in *'āšēm* both spiritual and physical suffering. This seems, however, too broad a definition for the term *'āšēm* which mainly concerns conscience issues in Lev 4–5. It may be that the offender is led to the guilt feeling after he has suffered from disease.[91] In this case it is inappropriate to regard the guilt-feeling alone as punishment.

These two major criticisms of Milgrom's view give rise to the following considerations and implications.

It has been suggested in (1) that what the sacrifice or the *kipper*-act deals with is חטאת (sin) and not merely the consequence of sin. This certainly poses a serious problem; for, as we shall see, the *hattat* in other contexts strongly points to the notion of uncleanness, but here the *hattat* appears, if the above observation is correct, to be related to what moderns would call a sin with moral overtones. But it is a fact that the *hattat* offering deals with חטאת (sin).[92] And even if the notion of uncleanness is meant here, the fact that the *hattat* deals with sins could already disprove Milgrom's thesis that the sin defiles the sanctuary *as its consequence*. Rather it can be shown that Lev 4 pictures both sin and its after-effects as somehow being within the sanctuary, as some older commentators dimly realized, and both being dealt with by the *hattat*.

The view that the sacrificial ritual does not deal with the consequence of sin alone as opposed to the act of sin committed, but with the sin and its consequence, raises the question what constitutes, then, the consequence of sin. However this question cannot be discussed at this stage. Yet at least we shall argue that the consequence of sin is punitive. We have argued above in (2) that *'āšēm* can hardly express the punishment of sin. But this statement requires qualification. For even if the term does not represent punishment of sin in its full sense, it must be admitted that the term *'āšēm* implies the notion of 'punishment' in that it means 'realize guilt'. This suggests that the consequence of sin must be related to punishment. This is also indicated by the phrase נשא עון in Lev 5.1 which is followed by the forgiveness formula (v. 13).[93] Nevertheless exactly what constitutes the punishment of sin depends on the definition of the term 'punishment'. Therefore, without using the term punishment we infer that the ritual deals with both the sin and its consequence, and that the consequence of sin is punitive.

At this point it seems necessary to discuss the formulaic phrase (להם) ונסלח לו, which appears at the end of each prescription. Admittedly it can be translated 'he shall be forgiven'. The clause is constructed in the passive, though the agent of forgiveness is self-evidently God. But since 'God' is not explicitly mentioned in the clause, Noth, assuming the clause as a reflection of a declaration by the priest, inferred that 'in the sin-offering, at least in its formulation, the notion of *ex opere operato* is fairly deeply embedded'.[94] Over against this conception it has been repeatedly argued that the passive form rather emphasizes that forgiveness does not depend on the priest,[95] or that it is not inherent in the ritual.[96] Though these explanations are plausible, they are not totally convincing. For could it happen that a sinner cannot be forgiven after his remorse and the priest's expiatory work? This consideration suggests that the statement 'he shall be forgiven' is, by nature, a promise, and that the use of the passive is not particularly intended to suggest divine sovereignty over the ritual.[97] It appears that the question whether the relation between expiation and forgiveness is automatic or not is one created by postulating too great a distinction between the magical and the monotheistic worlds.[98] It seems, then, to be out of place to argue against the notion of *ex opere operato* from the passive form. The reason for the passive form is not clear. But the fact that the passive form is used despite God's being the agent of forgiveness may, at least, reflect an anthropocentric concern: a sinner being the central concern of the ritual.[99]

This is clearly highlighted by the fact that the text says '*he* shall be forgiven' and not '*his sin* shall be forgiven'. This fact implies that by breaking one divine prohibition the *whole* existence of the sinner is at stake. Thus the inference is inevitable that since the sinner is forgiven because of the expiation of his sin, the expiatory ritual also concerns the salvation of the whole existence of the sinner. This is different from holding that the ritual deals with a sin which is envisaged as being in some sense separate from the sinner.

Our reasoning thus far may be reinforced by recalling the fact noted above that the ritual deals with *sin* and its consequence. This fact itself suggests strongly that the sin and its consequence are envisaged when the sinner stands before the Lord; this would not be the case if the ritual concerned only the consequence of sin.

At any rate the significance of these observations and the question how the ritual deals with both sin and its consequence will be pursued in the following chapters.

Summary

The study of the protases in Lev. 4.1–5.13 has examined two major terms, שגג (שגה) and *'āšēm*. The root שגג has the basic meaning 'to move in error' but it does not contain in it a reference to the subjective situation of the sinner. It presumes unconsciousness of sin rather than consciousness of an act which Milgrom assumes. *'āšēm*, referring to both objective and subjective aspects of guilt, can be best rendered 'realize guilt'.

The sin with which the *hattat* deals is the inadvertent violation of a divine prohibition or the neglect of cultic and judicial order.

Milgrom's view that *'āšēm* expresses the punishment of sin is untenable, though the term implies the notion of punishment. It is thus inadequate to assume that the *hattat* concerns uncleanness alone and not inadvertence. Rather the text says that the *hattat* deals with חמאת (sin). In view of the expressions *'āšēm*, נשא עון, and נסלח, which connote punishment, it was inferred that the *hattat* deals with both sin and its consequence, which is punitive.

All this suggests that if, as Milgrom argues, the *hattat* deals with uncleanness, חמאת (sin) is not essentially different from uncleanness. Thus two major questions are left open: (1) whether the major function of the *hattat* is purification or not, and (2) how purification is related to expiation. To answer these questions we shall turn to other *hattat* texts in the next chapter.

Chapter 2

THE *HATTAT* OFFERING IN OTHER SOURCES

Introduction
In the preceding chapter we examined the *hattat* in Lev 4.1–5.13 and concluded that the rituals there deal with *hattat* (sin). We now turn to *hattat* texts, many of which deal with unique situations or fixed liturgical celebrations.

Apart from Lev 4.1–5.13 the *hattat* also appears in the following priestly texts.

Exod 29.10-14, 36-37	Consecration of priests and the altar
Lev 8.14-17	Consecration of priests and the altar
Lev 9.2-3, 7-15	The eighth-day service
Lev 10.16-20	The *hattat* flesh incident
Lev 12.6, 8; 14.19, 22, 31; 15.15, 30; Num 19.9,17	Purification from natural uncleanness
Lev 16	The day of Atonement
Num 6.11, 14	Purification of the Nazirite
Num 8.7, 8, 12	Purification of the Levites
Lev 23.19; Num 7; 15.22ff.; 28-29.	Festive and unique occasions

The primary aim of this chapter is to discuss the central function of the *hattat* in the above texts and its possible relationship with the *hattat* in Lev 4.1–5.13.

These texts present various literary and theological problems. But we concentrate only on the theological significance of the *hattat* in each ritual, examining these texts as they stand. It will be useful, then, to set out in advance some of the major critical issues relating to the function of the *hattat* and the nature of the texts concerned as a prelude to surveying the variegated material on the *hattat* offering.

Firstly, Milgrom has argued that the *hattat* blood as a ritual detergent purifies sancta from uncleanness.[1] Indeed texts such as Lev

8.15 and Lev 16.14-19 appear to support his thesis that the *hattat*
blood purifies sancta and not its offerer. However Rodriguez has
recently argued that in a context like Lev 12.6 it is rather the offerer
who is purified, and that there is no clear evidence that sancta are
purified.[2] Whether this view is valid will be discussed later, but there
is certainly a problem how the purification of the sancta is related to
that of the offerer.

Secondly, though the *hattat* in the above-mentioned texts is
presumably related to 'purification', it is questionable whether
'defilement of sancta' can always be assumed. For instance, Milgrom
assumes that both in Lev 8.15 and Lev 12.6-7 the same 'uncleanness'
is present in the sancta. However, while it can be easily envisaged
that in Lev 12.6-7 the blood discharge defiled the sancta, it is not
clear what kind of defilement is envisaged in Lev 8.15. Is it really
justified to assume that uncleanness is always present in the sancta
before purification?

Thirdly, there has been a tendency to impose, because of Lev 4.1-
5.13, the concept of 'sin' or 'sinfulness' on *hattat* passages which are
dominated by the idea of purification. By contrast Milgrom has so
strongly stressed that purification is the central function of the
hattat, that sin has been seen by him as something essentially foreign
to uncleanness. Thus how sin is related to uncleanness in the context
of the *hattat* is another moot point.

We shall discuss below these fundamental issues of the *hattat*
under the following headings: A. The *hattat* in Lev 8-9; B. Lev 10.17;
C. Other purificatory occasions; D. Sancta pollution; E. חטאת (sin)
and uncleanness.

A. *The* hattat *in Lev 8-9*

1. *Lev 8.14-17 (Exod 29.10-14, 36-37)*
Lev 8 describes a unique occasion on which the altar was consecrated
and the ordination of the priests was begun. In the course of this
ceremony a *hattat* was offered.

Lev 8.15 describes Moses' cleansing and sanctification of the altar,
preceded by the imposition of hands by Aaron and his sons on the
hattat sacrifice. The unique character of the occasion must be
underlined. Since Aaron and his sons are not ordained, Moses acts as
a priest. But why should Aaron and his sons lay their hands on the
sacrifice, if the purpose of the ritual is sanctification of the altar? In
Lev 4, for instance, it seems to be assumed that he who lays his hand

receives the benefit of atonement (cf. Exod 29.10ff.). On this
principle it follows that the sanctification of the altar leads to, or is
equivalent to, that of priests. Kurtz also wrote:

> That the blood of sacrifice, when brought to the altar, purified the
> altar as well as the person sacrificing, is distinctly stated in Lev
> viii.15.[3]

As will be argued, this theology, far from being restricted to this
passage, constitutes one of the most important aspects in atonement
theology and thus casts some doubt on Milgrom's thesis that the
hattat blood purifies only the sancta.

Now it is obvious that vv. 14–15aβ (ויגש ... באצבעו) finds its parallel
in Exod 29.10-12a. However, how can v. 15aγ (ויחטא את המזבח) and
v. 15bγ (ויקדשהו לכפר עליו) be explained? Elliger and others hold that
these phrases are incompatible with the anointing of the altar in v. 11
because both v. 11 and v. 15 mention sanctification of the altar (קדש),
thus creating redundancy.[4] But they also observe that these phrases
are related to Exod 29.36-37.

Two comments are in order. Firstly, repetitiveness of any kind
could be inherent in the ritual,[5] and in this particular case too there
seems to be nothing strange in the fact that santification (קדש) is
achieved in two different ways, anointing with oil[6] and daubing with
blood. Secondly, in view of the proposed interpretation of Lev 8.15, it
is likely that Lev 8.15 combines and adapts Exod 29.10-12 (consecration of priests) and Exod 29.36-37 (consecration of the altar).[7]

The nature of the *hattat* ritual in Lev 8.15 may be related to the
distinctive nature of the ceremony in Lev 8 as a whole, particularly
in contrast with the ritual in Lev 4.3-21. In Lev 4 atonement of the
anointed priest and the congregation is made by Aaron's entering
into the Tent, whereas here inner sancta such as the adytum and the
incense altar play no part in the ritual. Moreover, while the *hattat* is
a bull both in Lev 8.15 and Lev 4.3 and the burning of the *hattat* is
prescribed both in Lev 8.17 and Lev 4.11-12, in blood manipulation
Lev 8.15 is more similar to Lev 4.25, 30, 34 than to Lev 4.6-7, 17-
18.

Various attempts have been made to explain the incongruity
between the rituals in Lev 4 and Lev 8. The simplest approach is to
assume that in Lev 8-9 the incense altar is not known.[8] But the force
of the argument is slightly weakened by the fact that in Lev 4.3-21
the ritual concerns not only the incense altar but the *pārōket* veil
which appears most important. If the whole ritual in the Tent

concentrated on the incense altar, the presence or absence of it would be significant. But the rite on the incense altar is only part of the ritual in the Tent.

Furthermore opinions are divided among commentators as to the nature of the blood manipulation in Lev 8.15. One stream of interpretation, which is, to some extent, influenced by Lev 4, suggests that the *hattat* was designed for 'a precautionary cleansing of the priests about to be instituted from any "unwitting trespass"'[9] or that it 'originally served as purifying the priests from unwitting sin'.[10] The other stream of interpretation stresses the difference of occasion between Lev 4 and Lev 8. Chapman-Streane comments that 'until they (sc. priests) are consecrated the ritual of the offering is the same as that prescribed in the case of private individuals (cp. iv, 30, 34)'.[11] Similarly Porter observes that since Aaron and his sons are not yet fully priests, they are also not entitled to enter the Tent.[12] Further Noordtzij holds that the situation envisaged in Lev 4 comes after the rituals in Lev 8–9.[13]

The first approach seems to be unlikely for the following reasons. Though the function of purification may be present in Lev 8.15 (חִטֵּא, קִדֵּשׁ), it would be forced to assume that the purification concerns uncleanness caused by particular sins. Nowhere in Lev 8 is there a hint that the purification of the altar was necessitated by particular sins of Aaron and his sons. Since the occasion is the consecration of the altar and priests, could it be that the purification concerns uncleanness which is assumed to be present before the common becomes holy?

The second approach holds that the different occasion on Lev 8 (ordination) prompts different rituals. However, Chapman-Streane's idea that the blood manipulation in Lev 8.15 is the same as that in Lev 4.30, 34 does not prove that would-be priests are regarded as laymen. At least, Chapman-Streane's view is based on a loose comparison of Lev 8 with Lev 4; note the word סָבִיב in Lev 8.15 and the burning of the *hattat* outside the camp in v. 17; both are absent in Lev 4.30, 34. Except for this point, however, it does appear that the difference in ritual between Lev 4 and Lev 8 is caused by the difference of occasion; it is short-sighted to compare them paying attention only to the formal aspects of the rituals and to assume different traditions behind them. Their present contexts ought to be considered first.

So the *hattat* ritual in Lev 8.15 is unlikely to be necessitated by a specific sin like Lev 4. Rather, as suggested above, it is more likely that the ritual here deals with uncleanness which is assumed to be present before the common becomes holy.

2. *Lev 9.7-15*

Another special occasion on which a *hattat* was offered was at the completion of the ordination of the priests, i.e. the eighth-day service.

The purpose of the eighth-day service is theophany (vv. 4b, 7b, 23b-24a). While it is agreed that the eighth-day service is marked off from the seven-day consecration which precedes it, there has been little scholarly discussion about the exact nature of the eighth-day service. However, in view of the theophany which is the purpose of the occasion, it would be reasonable to assume, as Milgrom points out,[14] that the eighth-day service is the climax of the seven-day consecration.

A simple but crucial question is: why should atonement (v. 7) or various sacrifices (vv. 2-4) be necessary for the manifestation of divine glory? It is not sufficient to say that 'cleanness is required because the glory of the Lord was to appear to the congregation';[15] for the congregation is presumed to be ritually clean before atonement (see v. 5b). Moreover, in the case of the priests they are not only clean but holy, having completed the consecration period. Why do the priests require atonement in addition to being holy? The question brings us back to the nature of the occasion i.e. the theophany. But what is the purpose of the theophany? The divine fire in v. 24 and in Judg 6.21; 1 Kgs 18.38; 1 Chron 21.26 seems to suggest that the idea is divine approval or acceptance. Yet the fact that the eighth-day service ends with the joyful response of the people (v. 24b) tends to make one forget the serious nature of the atonement which precedes it. The seriousness of the atonement could be best underlined by the belief that seeing God incurs death.[16] Thus although God obviously does not seek to destroy the people on this occasion, it is natural that atonement is needed to make possible a particular manifestation of divine glory.

Another general comment should be made on v. 7 in which Moses commands Aaron to offer the *hattat* and the עולה both for himself and the people. The LXX seems to translate בעד ביתך instead of בעד העם in the MT. Despite Elliger's suspicion that the LXX is to be preferred,[17] the LXX seems to be harmonizing the phrase in the MT with Lev 16.6, 11, 17. The obvious question is then how the twofold atonement for the people can be explained. Keil comments:

when Moses says in v. 7 that Aaron is to make atonement for
himself and the nation with his sin-offering and burnt-offering, the
atoning virtue which Aaron's sacrifice was to have for the nation
also, referred not to sins which the people had committed, but to
the guilt which the high priests, as the head of the whole
congregation, had brought upon the nation by his sin (ch. iv,3).[18]

But it is misleading to link Lev 4.3 with Lev 9.7 in the way Keil
does, since the latter passage does not speak of any specific sin. Also
it seems problematic to use the term 'sin' in this context. But these
points are discussed below. In spite of the problematic nature of
Keil's comment, however, it has one merit in that it sees a common
principle behind Lev 4.3 and Lev 9.7; Aaron, the high priest, is
responsible both for his own sinfulness (see below) and for the guilt
imputed to the people on account of his sinfulness.[19]

After these two general observations we consider next some
fundamental problems of the *hattat* in this context. As in Lev 8.14ff.
the blood is daubed on the horns of the outer altar (v. 9) and the
hattat flesh is burned outside the camp. In contrast with Lev 8.14-15,
however, Lev 9.8ff. does not mention the imposition of hands nor use
the term סביב (Lev 8.15). In addition the *hattat* blood in Lev 8.15
functioned to consecrate Aaron and his sons as priests, whereas in
Lev 9.8ff. the blood appears to remove some uncleanness in order to
make the divine manifestation possible.

But what does the *hattat* purify, priests and people or the altar?
Rodriguez has asserted that 'here nothing is said about a purification
of the sanctuary or the altar' and that 'the object of the *hattat* is the
priesthood and the people'.[20] This assertion seems simply erroneous.
Daubing of blood in v. 9 should be taken most naturally as a
purificatory rite in the light of Lev 8.15 (see above). However,
against Milgrom we argue, by analogy with Lev 8.15, that the blood
is presumed to purify priests and people as well as the altar.

Now Lev 9 also poses the same question as Lev 8: why does not
Aaron enter the Tent as he does in Lev 4.3-21? One of the reasons
given above, that Aaron and his sons are not yet priests, must now be
excluded, for obviously they were ordained by the end of the
consecration period and became priests in Lev. 9. Moreover judging
from the fact that a similar ritual procedure is prescribed both in Lev
8.15, 17 and Lev 9.9, 11, a similar reason for him not entering the
tent may be operating in both sections, though what that reason is, is
not clear. It is certainly wrong, however, to argue that Aaron and his

sons could not enter because they were not yet priests not only in Lev 9.9, 11 but also in Lev 8.15, 17.

Porter notes that the reference to the outer, and not inner, altar is made 'because Aaron only enters the Tent for the first time in verse 23'.[21] Indeed throughout Lev 8–9 Aaron has nothing to do with the inner sancta. In Lev 8.10 the inner sancta are sanctified by Moses, and only in Lev 9.23 is he said to have entered the Tent with Aaron. Thus if Lev 9 may be seen as the climax of the consecration period, it may be inferred that Aaron and his sons were not entitled to enter the Tent before the manifestation of God's glory which signified divine acceptance of both priests and the people. This means that in a sense all the rituals in Lev 8–9 have the purpose of enabling Aaron and his sons to work in the Tent, and that therefore the eighth-day service marks a stage preliminary to the regular service. In view of this, Noordtzij's view that the situation envisaged in Lev 4 comes after that of Lev 8–9 becomes more likely, because Lev 4 presupposes priesthood (see Lev 4.25, 30, 34).

It should be borne in mind that this view explains why in Lev 8–9 Aaron does not perform rituals in the Tent and why the blood manipulation takes place in connection with the outer altar, but it does not explain why the *hattat* flesh is burned outside the camp. The latter question will be taken up in Chapter 5. At this stage one remark is in order with regard to the meaning of Lev 9.15, which states that the *hattat* for the people was brought or sacrificed as a *hattat*, בָּרִאשׁוֹן. This passage has erroneously been taken by some scholars[22] to mean that this *hattat* was also burned or to be burned outside the camp. Though this passage undoubtedly has a significant bearing on Lev 10.16ff., which we shall discuss presently, Lev 9.15 itself does not warrant this interpretation for two reasons. (a) The verb חִטֵּא in this context refers only to the blood manipulation and is unlikely to refer to the disposal of the *hattat* flesh (see Lev 6.19). (b) 'The burning of the *hattat*' always constitutes part of the ritual and is always explicitly mentioned (see Exod 29.14; Lev 4.11-12, 21; 8.17; 16.27). By contrast the priestly consumption of the *hattat* flesh prescribed in Lev 6.17-22 does not appear to be an essential part of the *hattat* ritual. That is why the consumption of the flesh by priests is not mentioned in Lev 4.22-35 and Lev 9.15[23] In short, nothing is mentioned in Lev 9.15 about the disposal of the *hattat* flesh.

All in all, the reason why the rituals in Lev 8–9 take place in connection with the outer altar lies in the circumstance that the occasions for those rituals are preliminary to the regular service.

Conformably, what the *hattat* in Lev 9 deals with, is not particular sins but rather general sinfulness or uncleanness, assumed in the encounter of man—whether he is a priest or not—with God on any special occasion (see further below).

Milgrom's thesis that the *hattat* blood purifies only sancta and not the offerer, proves unconvincing in respect of the *hattat* ritual in Lev 9 simply because it is difficult to assume 'sancta defilement' in this context.

Thus it may be tentatively concluded that the *hattat* in Lev 9 deals with general sinfulness, and that it purifies sancta as well as priests and people. To be more specific about this it is necessary to investigate a further reference to the eighth-day service in Lev 10.17.

B. *Lev 10.17*

Lev 10.16-20 deals with an episode concerning the eating of the *hattat* which is generally assumed to be the one mentioned in Lev 9.15 (i.e. the *hattat* for the people). Moses expostulates with Eleazar and Ithamar about their not having eaten the *hattat* (vv. 17-18), whereas Aaron, presumably representing the two sons, appears to justify their act (v. 19).

Unfortunately the whole episode is not clear, or rather has been said to be unclear. The section as a whole will be elucidated in the next chapter in connection with its relationship with Lev 10.1-7. Here our major concern lies in v. 17, which appears to give a theological reason for eating the *hattat*.

v. 17 מדוע לא אכלתם את החטאת במקום הקדש כי קדש
קדשים הוא ואתה נתן לכם לשאת את עון
העדה לכפר עליהם לפני ה'

Because of the importance of this passage to the *hattat* ritual we present below a detailed exposition of this *crux interpretum*.

Two widely different approaches to the interpretation of the passage have been proposed. The issue focuses on the philological problem of the preposition *lamed*, a problem which simultaneously has far-reaching theological implications.

One stream of interpretation which has been found since the LXX is that the first *lamed* (in לשאת) expresses purpose, so that the eating of the *hattat* constitutes an essential part of the atonement ceremony.[24] This view has been further elaborated by modern theologians who assume that the *hattat* flesh absorbs iniquity or uncleanness, and that by eating the flesh the sin is removed.[25] This interpretation is connected with a theory which holds that the imposition of hands transfers the sin/guilt to the animal in a quasi-physical way (Lev 16.21).

This rather traditional view has been contested since the last century. The majority of objections seem, however, to concentrate on the conceptual aspect of the *hattat* flesh and not on the meaning of the *lamed* in לשאת. First of all, Kurtz objected to the above view by pointing out that since the *hattat* flesh is explicitly termed קרש קדשים (e.g. Lev 10.17a), it cannot be deemed unclean, having absorbed sin and guilt.[26] Ehrlich,[27] followed by Milgrom,[28] holds that the phrase נשא עון does not mean 'remove sin/guilt' but 'bear responsibility'. So the meaning of v. 17b is, according to Milgrom (*ibid.*), 'and I (*sic*) have given (the *ḥaṭṭā't*) to you for bearing the responsibility of the community by performing purgation rites before the Lord on their behalf' and the eating of the *hattat* 'is the largess granted the priests for assuming the burden, indeed the hazard, of purging the sanctuary'.[29] Milgrom further holds that 'there is no evidence anywhere in the ancient Near East that impurity was removed by eating'.[30] In the same vein Janowski[31] reasons that even if the phrase נשא עון means 'bear guilt', it does not follow that the removal of guilt is achieved by eating the *hattat*. Rather the phrase, being explicated by לכפר (GK § 114o), signifies that the priests are assigned to bear the guilt for the congregation of Israel as mediators by making atonement for them with the *hattat*. The reason why the *hattat* flesh is called קרש קדשים is that it is related to the cultic act which is commanded by God and is significant for the salvation of the people, and not that the sin is transferred into it. Finally, Elliger notes that the idea that atonement depends upon the eating of the *hattat* contradicts the context in which, despite the ritual mistake, the efficacy of the sacrifice is not in doubt.[32]

These criticisms against the view that atonement depends, at least partially, upon the eating of the *hattat* all assume that the *hattat* flesh is a perquisite of the priests. And from a contextual and conceptual point of view there appears to be no doubt about the correctness of this assumption (but see below).[33] However apart from the meaning of נשא עון, which will be discussed later, there remains the question of the meaning of the *lamed* in לשאת. Presumably the second *lamed* (in לכפר) could be translated either 'by' or more preferably 'thus making atonement. . . ', expressing the result. But it appears problematic to translate the first *lamed* by 'for', as Ehrlich and Milgrom suggest, even if the conceptual considerations on the *hattat* flesh seem to require it. This is because when combined with the infinitive construct *lamed* is unlikely to mean 'for'. At any rate, just because of the lack of grammatical discussion on the first *lamed*, the arguments put forth by Ehrlich, Milgrom and Janowski are not conclusive. The first *lamed* appears to mean 'to', expressing purpose. If so, the idea that atonement depends on eating the *hattat* flesh may still be valid, though such an idea does not seem to be expressed anywhere else in the cultic law.

Here we submit an approach totally different from the above two, an approach which focuses on a feature of the term חטאת and the context of Lev 9–10 concerning the *hattat* ritual.

First of all, it may be noted that the term *hattat* normally refers to the sacrificial animal as a whole (see Lev 4.25, 29, 30, 33, 34; 6.18, 20). However, in Lev 6.19, 23 and our passage (Lev 10.17) the term *hattat* appears to refer *practically* to the חטאת *flesh*, because in these passages the term *hattat* appears with the verb אכל.

However, is it adequate to assume that because of the presence of אכל the term חטאת means חטאת *flesh*? If so, it follows that the meaning of חטאת changes with its context; it normally means 'the animal as a whole', but when it is conjoined with אכל it means the flesh of the animal. An examination of the following three passages (Lev 6.19, 23; 10.19), however, seems to show that the term חטאת in אכל חטאת is unlikely to mean the חטאת *flesh*.

Lev 6.19 reads:

הכהן המחטא אתה יאכלנה במקום קדש תאכל בחצר אהל מועד

Here אתה, יאכלנה and תאכל all refer to the החטאת mentioned in the previous verse, which refers to the sacrificial animal as a whole. Moreover, in a single sentence like הכהן המחטא אתה יאכלנה it appears forced to argue that the suffix in אתה is essentially different from the suffix in יאכלנה

Lev 6.23 reads:

וכל חטאת אשר יובא מדמה אל אהל מועד לכפר בקדש לא תאכל באש תשרף

The two verbs תאכל and תשרף refer practically to the flesh. However the suffix in מדמה definitely refers to the whole animal. Thus to determine the meaning of the term חטאת from the viewpoint of the meaning of the conjoined verb creates a contradiction even in a single sentence like this. It may be added that the same problem occurs in Lev 10.18, which reads:

הן לא הובא את דמה—אכל תאכל אתה בקרש

Thus it is unlikely that the term חמאת changes its meaning according to the verbs it is conjoined with (שרף, אכל, שחמ).

On the basis of the above observations we argue that חמאת in Lev 10.17 can be taken in the same way. The חמאת in v. 17a is taken up by אתה in v. 17b. But neither the former nor the latter means 'the חמאת flesh'; both refer to the 'the חמאת'.

This exegetical possibility is strengthened by the literary relationship between Lev 6.18ff. and Lev 10.17ff. It is clear that Moses' theory is based on Lev 6.18ff. not only in topic but also in terminology (cp. Lev 6.18-19 with Lev 10.17, and Lev 6.23 with Lev 10.18). More specifically, the following relationship may be observed. In Lev 6.18 חמאת refers to the whole animal and then in v. 19 the problematic phrase אכל חמאת appears. It may be observed that this order is simply reversed in Lev 10.17; in v. 17a the phrase אכל חמאת appears first and then the חמאת is taken up by ואתה in v. 17b. It is clear then that if the term חמאת is conjoined with שרף, אכל, שחמ it refers to the same whole sacrificial animal.[34]

Thus Lev 10.17b addresses not so much the relationship between the priests and their eating of the *hattat* flesh as that between the priests and the חמאת. In other words, it speaks of the function of the priests in handling the *hattat*!

Now the crucial question is whether v. 17b still refers to the function of eating the *hattat*. As long as the *hattat* flesh is part of the *hattat*, it still appears possible to see v. 17b as referring to the eating of the *hattat*. But this is not the case. For as already hinted, and as will be discussed in the next Chapter, it is unlikely that atonement in Lev 9 was invalidated by the priests failing to eat the *hattat* (see Lev 9.23-24). It follows then that v. 17b cannot refer to the function of eating the *hattat* because the priests' work of 'making atonement for them before the Lord' (לכפר עליהם לפני ה') mentioned at the end of the verse is already completed in Lev 9. In view of the fact that in Lev 9.15 no mention is made of the disposal of the *hattat*, it may rather be inferred that v. 17b actually speaks of the priests' function in their manipulation of blood (and the burning of fat). In other words, v. 17b declares that through the blood manipulation the priests bear the guilt (see below) of the congregation.

This mention of bearing guilt נשא עון demands an investigation of its meaning. To this end we first survey the occurrences of the phrase in the priestly literature in general and then consider its meaning in this passage, Lev 10.17.

The term עון basically means 'iniquity'.[35] But, being a dynamic concept and deep-rooted in Israelite *Ganzheitsdenken*, it expresses the iniquitous *act* and its consequence, or any combination of these ideas. Inevitably it must be translated 'iniquity', 'guilt', or 'punishment', according to the context. For convenience's sake we adopt the translation 'bear guilt' for נשא עון in the following discussions. The phrase can be classified into two categories from the viewpoint of subject-object relationship; in one the offender bears his own guilt (Exod 28.43; Lev 5.1, 17; 7.18; 17.16; 19.8; 20.17,19; Num 5.31) and in another someone bears the guilt of someone else or something else (Exod 28.38; Lev 10.17; 16.22; Num 18.1(bis), 23; 30.16). A problem arises with Lev 5.1, 17, where the offender is to bear his own guilt but simultaneously the law enjoins him to bring a sacrifice. We presume that in these cases the offender is absolved of his guilt by the ritual.[36]

In Exod 28.38; Lev 10.17; 16.22; Num 18.1, 23 the phrase raises the question what specific situation is envisaged by it. But each passage should be examined separately.[37]

With regard to the phrase in Lev 10.17 in particular, Milgrom, following Ehrlich,[38] has heavily criticized a common translation 'remove the guilt/sin' by pointing out:

> Thus the eating of the *ḥaṭṭā't* does not 'remove sin' but is the largess granted the priest for assuming the burden, indeed the hazard, of purging the sanctuary on behalf of the offerer of the *ḥaṭṭā't*.[39]

Thus Milgrom translates the phrase 'bear the responsibility'. We concur with him that נשא means 'bear'. However, it is questionable whether עון means 'responsibility'.

Firstly, as Knierim[40] rightly criticizes Zimmerli[41] who suggested the same translation, the meaning of עון is not as neutral as the modern term 'responsibility' implies.

Secondly, by לשאת את עון העדה Milgrom envisages that the priests make purgation rites on behalf of the congregation who defiled the sanctuary.[42] But as already argued, it is inadequate to assume in the context of Lev 9 that the sanctuary was defiled by the congregation before the purification ritual. Indeed, as Milgrom assumes, it is certainly possible to envisage the idea of purging the sanctuary in

Lev 9.15 behind לשאת את עון העדה in Lev 10.17, though his translation for the latter phrase 'for bearing—' proved to be erroneous. And this becomes probable now on our interpretation of Lev 10.17, according to which v. 17b rather speaks of blood manipulation. Thus, if the notion of uncleanness is envisaged in the *hattat* ritual of Lev 9, the purification of the uncleanness appears to be concurrent with the bearing עון העדה. Therefore it is clearly erroneous to construe עון העדה as 'responsibility of the congregation'. Rather the phrase נשא עון must be taken in a substitutionary sense, in which case it means 'bear guilt'. Yet it must be noted that the term עון in Lev 10.17 cannot simply be translated 'guilt', for 'guilt' has moral overtones which are not necessarily present in the Hebrew term. In this connection Knierim's comment on Isa 6.7 may provide an apposite characterization of the עון in Lev 10.17:

> Die Erkenntnis der Unreinheit und damit des Charakters von עון bezieht sich nicht auf wissentliche oder beabsichtigte Vergehen, sondern auf den—verantwortlich zu tragenden—schuldhaften Zustand, dessen der Mensch infolge der Begegnung mit Gott inne wird. עון wird offenbar, wenn Gott dem Menschen begegnet, gleich, ob der Mensch den עון wissentlich beging oder nicht und ob er sich zunächst die Entstehung des עון erklären kann oder nicht.[43]

Nevertheless, since there is no modern term corresponding exactly to this Hebrew term in such a context, we shall make do with the term 'guilt', bearing in mind the above comment.

Moses' words in Lev 10.17ff. could be further analysed in the following way on the above interpretation of v. 17b. The sentence כי קדש קדשים הוא in v. 17a is not the reason why the *hattat* ought to have been eaten. It is, rather, the reason why the *hattat* ought to be eaten in a holy place. In other words, since the *hattat* is most holy it must be eaten as befitting its holy character. Nor is v. 17b the reason why the *hattat* ought to have been eaten; it explains the priestly function in blood manipulation. Therefore it may be inferred that the reason why the *hattat* ought to have been eaten is given for the first time in v. 18, namely, because its blood was not brought into the Tent.

With regard to the symbolic meaning of eating the *hattat* we do not accept the view that atonement depends on eating the *hattat*, simply because neither v. 17 nor any other passage suggests this.[44] Eating the *hattat* does not belong to the atoning process. Then what about Milgrom's view that the *hattat* flesh is the perquisite of the priests? Again this view is not confirmed by v. 17b because the passage does not address it. Yet the idea may well be reflected in Moses' words in v. 17a. But if so, since those words are imbued with reproachful overtones, the term 'perquisite' cannot perfectly describe the nature of the *hattat* flesh.[45] It seems reasonable to assume, then, that eating the *hattat* is both a privilege and a duty, and that to see the two aspects as contradictory is unnecessary.

Our interpretation of Lev 10.17 throws further light on the nature of the *hattat* ritual in the eighth-day service. It has been stressed that, though the whole ceremony ends on a joyous note, the *hattat* ritual deals with some serious aspect of atonement. This is now confirmed by the presence of the term עון in Lev 10.17. This means that, though the uncleanness or sinfulness of the people is of a general nature, it involves עון (guilt).

By far the most significant corollary arising out of our interpretation of Lev 10.17, however, is the fact that through the blood manipulation assumed in Lev 9.15 the priests bore the guilt of the congregation. If the blood manipulation concerns purification of the altar, thus uncleanness, it could be inferred that the two notions, uncleanness and עון (guilt) are both dealt with by the blood manipulation. Though Lev 10.17 is different in context from Lev 4.1–5.13, this assumption perfectly suits our conclusion in Chapter 1,D that the *hattat* ritual deals with both the act of sin and its consequence. This corresponds to the notion of עון expounded by Knierim.

C. *Other Purificatory Occasions*

The *hattat* also appears on the following occasions.

(1) Purification from natural uncleanness	Lev 12.6, 8: 14.19, 22, 31; 15.15, 30
(2) Dedication of the Levites	Num 8.7, 8, 12
(3) The Nazirite's ritual	Num 6.11, 14
(4) Num 15.22ff.	
(5) Festive occasions	Num 28–29; Lev 23.19; Num 7.

Again, as with the various theological issues set out at the beginning of this Chapter, we approach the central function of the *hattat* on these occasions. An additional problem should be mentioned here, however, namely that the ritual procedure of the *hattat* (handling of blood, fat, flesh etc.) is not prescribed on any occasion in the above list. Does this mean that the ritual procedure is presumed? It is reasonable to assume so, but the question is: what ritual procedure is presumed? On the majority of the occasions mentioned above it is prescribed that the ritual should take place at the entrance of the Tent (Lev 12.6; 14.11, 23; 15.14, 27; Num 8.9; 6.10, 13), i.e. in connection with the outer altar. Since the ritual procedure of the *hattat*, which takes place at the entrance of the Tent, is prescribed only in Exod 29.10-14; Lev 4.22-35; 5.7-13; 8.14-17; 9.7-15, we postulate that those occasions listed above have something to do with these texts.[46]

1. *Purification from natural uncleanness*
The *hattat* is prescribed for a woman after childbirth (Lev 12.6-8), a leper (Lev 14.19, 22, 31), and individuals with serious discharges (Lev 15.15, 30). In these contexts the *hattat* clearly functions to purify some uncleanness, since the purpose of the ritual is purification. However, the question is whether, as Milgrom has forcefully argued, the *hattat* cleanses sancta and not the offerer. As already mentioned, Rodriguez has recently opposed this view by pointing out that Lev 12.7 explicitly states 'she shall be clean from the flow of the blood', and that nothing is stated about the purification of sancta.[47] However does this negative evidence imply that sancta are not purified? The inference cannot be justified, if Lev 12.7-8 as well as Lev 14.19, 22, 31; 15.15, 30 presuppose a certain ritual procedure for the *hattat*.

Presumably the ritual of the bird-*hattat* in Lev 12.7-8; 14.22, 31; 15.14-15, 29-30 would have followed the prescription in Lev 5.7-9,[48] apart from which there exists no prescription for the bird-*hattat* in the whole OT, whereas the ewe-lamb a year old in Lev 14.10, 19 for the *hattat* would have been treated in accordance with the prescription in Lev 4.32ff. In other words, it is reasonable to assume that those texts all presume Lev 4.32ff. and Lev 5.7-9.

In support of this assumption, Lev 14.10, where three sacrificial animals are enumerated, could be adduced. It is not clear which of the three should be assigned for the חטאת and the עולה except that כבם is used for the אשם (v. 12). Ramban noted that this is because the text presumes the knowledge of the עולה and the חטאת in Lev 1 and Lev 4, according to which the עולה must be male (כבם) whereas the חטאת must be female (כבשה).[49]

On the other hand, Rodriguez's emphasis that in Lev 12.7-8 a parturient becomes clean deserves attention. Granted that *hattat* blood purifies the outer altar, does the mention of וטהרה (Lev 12.7, 8) imply that the parturient becomes clean after the purification of the altar? It seems that just as in Lev 4 it is inadequate to separate forgiveness (ונסלח לו) from the preceding ritual, it is also artificial to separate clean status from the preceding ritual and to argue that the *hattat* blood purifies the altar and not the parturient. The mention of 'becoming clean' comes after *kipper* because cleanness is the purpose of the *kipper* act just as forgiveness is. But this does not mean that cleanness or forgiveness is independent of the ritual. Rather the very ritual appears to involve the process of gaining cleanness or forgiveness. Therefore we infer, by analogy with Lev 8.15, that when the altar is purified, so is the offerer in Lev 12.6, 8; 14.19, 31; 15.15, 30.

2. *Dedication of the Levites (Num 8.7, 8, 12)*

In the dedication of the Levites the *hattat* serves as a sacrifice by which Aaron makes atonement for the Levites (v. 12). Since the whole ritual aims to purify the Levites for their task in the Tent (vv. 15, 21), it is reasonable to infer that the *hattat* also functions to purify them by presumably purifying the outer altar. Thus the whole ceremony consists of a series of purification rites (vv. 7, 12, 15). In that the sacrificial animal is a bull and the Levites have no particular cause of defilement, the ceremony resembles that of the consecration of priests (Lev 8.2, 6). However, the fact that while the priests become holy the Levites are never so described[50] suggests that, as the holy status is grounded upon divine calling, the accumulation of purificatory rites does not necessarily make a person holy. This inference may make it inadequate to assume degrees of cleanness in the term טהר.

At any rate, since no cause of sancta defilement is mentioned, it is unnecessary to assume that the *hattat* purifies only defiled sancta and not persons.

3. *The Nazirite's ritual (Num 6.11, 14)*

The *hattat* must be sacrificed (a) when someone dies near the Nazirite (vv. 9-12) and (b) when he succesfully completes his term (vv. 13ff.).[51]

a. When someone dies near him, he defiles his vow (vv. 9ff.). On the seventh day he shaves his hair and on the eighth day he brings either two pigeons or two turtle-doves for the *hattat* and the עולה. On the same day he rededicates his hair and his term, and brings a lamb for the אשם.

Why should the Nazirite bring a *hattat* for expiation? Keil and Milgrom maintain that it is because the Nazirite was defiled by a corpse.[52] However strictly this is not what v. 11 states; it states that the priest makes atonement for the Nazirite's sin (חטא) with regard to the corpse (על הנפש). Normally uncleanness caused by a corpse does not constitute a sin and is purified by the מי חטאת (Num 19.14ff.). The reason why the defilement constitutes a sin (cf. Lev 22.9) may well be that the Nazirite is holy like the high priest (Lev 21.11).[53]

The modern tendency to make a clear distinction between sin and uncleanness must, however, be queried here. For on the one hand v. 9b clearly concerns a purification rite (cp. Lev 14.9) and the ritual in vv. 9b-12 appears to follow the calendrical pattern, which pervades purification rituals, of seven days and then the eighth (Lev 8-9; 12.2-3; 14.9-10, 23; 15.13-14, 28-29). But on the other hand v. 11a deals with the expiation of sin. This is not to say that there was no distinction between sin and uncleanness; but at least the term 'sin' with its moral overtones hardly matches the term חטא here.

If, however, the above inference that the corpse contamination constitutes a sin because of the unusual holiness of the Nazirite is right, it may be inferred, at least in this context, that the sin (חטא) is not essentially different from 'uncleanness', and that a condition is called a sin when it involves a clash of holiness with uncleanness.

Again it is not clear whether the sin defiled the altar, but that the *hattat* blood purifies the altar and resanctifies the person may be inferred.

b. The *hattat* is also required when the Naziritehood is over (vv. 13ff.). Some scholars have seen the nature of the whole ceremony in vv. 14-20a as legitimate desanctification of the Nazirite from holiness to the common (see v. 20a).[54] Though this characterization may be right, two general remarks should be made before considering the *hattat* in vv. 14, 16. Firstly, that characterization indeed fits the character of the occasion as a whole, but it seems doubtful whether it has a direct bearing upon the function of individual sacrifices in the ceremony (שלמים, מנחה, עולה, חטאת).[55] Secondly, since the ceremony takes place at the end of the Naziritehood, it could mark the culminating point of the Naziritehood expressing the special relationship between God and the Nazirite.[56] Thus 'desanctification' seems rather secondary in the essential nature of the ceremony.

Now the question why the Nazirite ought to offer the *hattat* (vv. 14, 16) has puzzled exegetes throughout the ages. While there are no grounds for linking this *hattat* with a particular sin,[57]

Milgrom's thesis that the *hattat* blood purifies sancta hardly answers
the question either. He admits as much when he says that it is
difficult to explain the reason for the *hattat* here.[58] Nevertheless
some scholars including Milgrom prefer to see the motive of bringing
the *hattat* as desanctification.[59] But as stated above 'desanctification'
may not be directly related to the reason for the *hattat*.

We shall suggest that this problem can be resolved by comparing
this ceremony with those related to the priestly installation in Lev
8–9, especially Lev 9. First, the very fact that the status of the
Nazirite is similar to that of the high priest justifies the comparison.
Second, the combination of sacrifices the Nazirite brings resembles
that of the priests in Lev 8–9; they both offer four sacrifices חטאת,
עולה, מנחה and שלמים.

Now given the analogy between this ceremony and that in Lev 9 it
may further be observed that the circumstance prior to the bringing
of the *hattat* is common to both contexts: the priests who have
completed the seven-day ordination and the Nazirite are both holy.
Thus, on the basis of the above discussion of Lev 9 we infer that just
as the priests, who are already holy after the seven-day ordination,
still need expiation/purification when they approach God, so does
the Nazirite who has been holy during the period of his vow. In short,
the Nazirite needs expiation/purification simply because he approaches God (v. 13) just as the priests do in Lev 9, though it is not
said that atonement is made for the Nazirite.

It may be inferred that the *hattat* purifies the altar and thus the
Nazirite, but it seems inadequate to assume that the altar has been
defiled by a particular offence of the Nazirite. Rather the Nazirite
has to offer a *hattat* because he approaches God.

4. *Num 15.22ff.*

The section appears to deal with another version of Lev 4 in that it
prescribes rituals for the expiation of inadvertent sin. Despite some
recent attempts,[60] however, the literary relationship between Num
15.22ff. and Lev 4 has not been satisfactorily clarified. Because of
lack of space the issue cannot be discussed here. However we shall
draw attention to one point which has escaped scholars' attention,
viz. the occasion of the ceremony.

Verse 22 has tended to be taken as introducing a new law, but the
introductory וכי seems to subsume it under v. 18b, which introduces
the law on the חלה (vv. 19-20). Since vv. 17-18 parallel vv. 1-2 and וכי

appears also in vv. 8 and 14, it is useful to see how the laws are presented in this chapter.

וידבר ה׳ אל משה לאמר	17	וידבר ה׳ אל משה לאמר	1
דבר אל בני ישראל	18	דבר אל בני ישראל	2
ואמרת אליהם		ואמרת אליהם	
בבאכם אל ארץ	18	כי תבאו אל ארץ משבותיכם	2
אשר אני מביא אתכם		אשר אני נתן לכם	
והיה באכלכם . . .	19	ועשיתם . . .והקריב	3
וכי תשגו . . .	22	וכי תעשה . . . והקריב	8
והיה אם . . .	24	וכי יגור . . .	14
ואם . . .	27		

Verses 17-18a are the same as vv. 1-2a. A small difference between בבאכם in v. 18b and כי תבאו in v. 2b deserves attention. As rabbis noticed,[61] the beginning of v. 18b (בבאכם) is unique. Verse 2b or similar phraseology is a standard way of introducing laws which take effect in Canaan. The difference between vv. 2b-3 and vv. 18b-19 is that whereas v. 2b gives a general background to vv. 3ff.,[62] the relationship between v. 18b (בבאכם) and v. 19 (והיה באכלכם) is consecutive. This means that בבאכם in v. 18b refers to a specific point of time (entry into Canaan), and that the law of חלה must be observed when the Israelites first eat the produce of the land of Canaan. Verse 20b, though, appears to rule that the law must be observed permanently.

Now it could be argued that just as וכי in vv. 8, 14 is subordinated to v. 2b, וכי in v. 22 is also subordinated to v. 18b; v. 22 parallels v. 19. Thus we infer that the law of inadvertent sin in vv. 22ff. is intended to be observed, at least, upon the Israelites' entry into Canaan.

Why the law of inadvertent sin comes after the law of חלה remains unclear unless the symbolic meaning of the latter is taken into account. From Ezek 44.30b it would be reasonable to infer that the חלה guarantees divine blessing. More specifically, however, the idea may be that, as in offering other first fruits, by dedicating the (best) part of the dough the divine blessing extends to all of it. In view of this symbolic meaning it seems that the law of inadvertent sin is concerned with the purity of the Israelites, at least, at their initial stage of life in Canaan.[63]

That vv. 22ff. is intended for a special occasion could well be reflected in the combination of sacrifices, namely עולה, מנחה, נסך and חטאת, which resembles the combination in Lev 9.3-4; 23.17-20. Furthermore it may be noted that in the *hattat* for the individual a female goat must be *a year old*. There is a possibility that this age qualification, irrespective of the kind of sacrifice, appears on occasions marked by 'newness' or 'beginning' as in Exod 12.5; Lev 9.3; 12.6; 14.10; 23.12, 19; Num 6.12, 14; 7.15.

Therefore we infer that the law in Num 15.22ff. has in mind the time when the Israelites enter the land of Canaan.

As for the nature of sin, the term מצות in v. 22 could include both performative and prohibitive commandments. But vv. 27-31 imply that it refers only to prohibitive commandments (cp. vv. 39, 40).[64] If so, what is the meaning of 'not observing all these commandments' in v. 22? On the basis of our exegesis of Lev 4.2[65] it may be suggested that this non-observance of all the commandments is practically the same as the violation of one commandment. And this appears to be assumed in vv. 27-31.

However, in both vv. 22 and 24 it is not clear whether the law practically deals with the violation of one prohibitive commandment. There are two possible reasons for this ambiguity. First, the law probably presumes Lev 4. Second, and, more immediately, it is the intention of the law to stress the totality of the commandments (see vv. 22-24, 39-40) rather than 'one violation' of all the commandments as in Lev 4. And this intention, we suggest, parallels the symbolic meaning of חלה, which guarantees the overall divine blessing on the Israelites.

5. *Festive occasions*

The *hattat* is also prescribed for festive occasions in Lev 23.15-21; Num 7; 28-29. Why it is required then is not clear. Particularly the function of the *hattat* offered for the dedication of the altar (Num 7) is highly obscure.[66] The rabbinic tradition holds that the *hattat* on festive occasions atones for uncleanness produced in sancta.[67] According to Rodriguez the *hattat* on these occasions expresses 'a recognition of their [the Israelites'] sin/impurity before the Lord and of their dependence on Yahweh's continuous and gracious forgiveness'.[68] Indeed the obscure nature of the *hattat* stems from the fact that no particular sin or uncleanness can be envisaged on these occasions. Yet we rather suggest that the situation could be the same as in Lev 9; some general sinfulness or uncleanness is envisaged when the Israelites encounter with God on special occasions. It may be noted that both in Lev 9 (v. 3) and on those occasions the *hattat* is consistently שעיר (עזים).

Recapitulating: A survey of the *hattat* on various occasions except Lev 4.1-5.13 has led to the following conclusions and implications.

1. There is no doubt that the *hattat* purifies sancta. But contrary to Milgrom's thesis it appears to purify both sancta and person(s). This may be clearly inferred from Lev 8.15 and possibly presumed in other relevant passages as well. The essential question is whether sancta are defiled before purificatory rituals. The possibility is small in the contexts of dedication (Num 8.5ff.), consecration (Lev 8.15) and desanctification (Num 6.14ff.). But in contexts where particular causes of uncleanness are explicitly mentioned, such as Lev 12.6; 14.19; 15.15, 30; Num 6.11; 15.25, 28 it is certainly possible to assume defilement of sancta. Yet in view of the fact that Milgrom tends to assume sancta defilement in all the above contexts they require reexamination.

2. The *hattat* for the people in Lev 9 could be typical of the *hattat* on various festive occasions. In both the *hattat* expiates general sinfulness or uncleanness which is assumed when the people approach God on special occasions.

D. *Sancta Pollution*

That the *hattat* deals with sancta pollution has already been mentioned several times. Now it is time to examine this notion more carefully.

It is J. Milgrom who has insisted that the idea of sancta pollution is central in the *hattat* ceremony. According to him this pollution occurs without any contact with sancta. However, our examination of Lev 8.15 and the *hattat* rituals concerning natural uncleanness casts doubts on the very presence of the sancta pollution, at least in the passages we have examined. Since we need not assume the idea in the contexts of dedication, consecration and desanctification, we shall confine our examination of the idea to the *hattat* for natural uncleanness.

Milgrom asserts:

> Clearly, physical impurity is removed by ablution: 'he shall wash his clothes and bathe in water' (Lev xv, 8 *inter alia*).[69]

The *hattat* is required from an unclean person because he has defiled sancta by his uncleanness. According to this theory, it is not the unclean person but the uncleanness in the sancta that is cleansed by the *hattat* blood. But is this the correct way of looking at the purification ritual which is finalized by the *hattat*? Indeed in the *hattat* rituals in Lev 12–15 an unclean person must be clean before bringing the *hattat*. But it seems misleading to infer from this that the sacrifice does not purify the unclean person. We shall demonstrate this point by taking the leper's case as an example.

In Lev 14.2-20 the leper is declared 'clean' three times: (1) before he enters the camp (v. 8), (2) on the seventh day (v. 9), and (3) after the ritual in the sanctuary (v. 20). It is debatable how one should see the threefold 'clean'. But at least it is clear that the *hattat* in v. 19, even if it purifies sancta, also concerns the uncleanness of the leper (מטמאתו). It seems that here the leper is envisaged to be standing before the Lord as a person who needs purification, and not as one who is clean in himself but requiring purification of the sancta. Indeed one may argue that since the leper is already clean in (2), he himself does not need purification in (3).[70] But the fallacy of this reasoning is obvious because, if so, even (2) would not have been necessary since the leper is already clean in (1).

Then should one assume degrees of cleanness in the three stages? This assumption appears reasonable at first sight; the leper in (2) looks cleaner than in (1) in that he is closer to the sanctuary. However though the assumption may appeal to the modern mind, it also seems one-sided.[71] For a theory of degrees of cleanness implies that at stage (1) the leper is not clean enough. But it seems difficult to assume that the same word טהר expresses various degrees of cleanness.

Thus the most plausible approach seems to be the one that fully admits the repetitiveness of the declaration 'he shall be clean'. This means that the leper is clean enough for stage (1), but that one stage should not be compared with another from the viewpoint of the degrees of cleanness because the declaration 'he shall be clean' itself does not refer to the previous stage.

Therefore the leper stands before the Lord (vv. 10ff.) as a person who needs to be purified. The same applies to other purification rituals as in Lev 12; 15.13-15, 28-30. If so, it is unnecessary to postulate that sancta must have been defiled before a purification ritual in the sanctuary takes place. These rituals serve primarily to cleanse the offerer. Whether they also cleanse the sanctuary will now be addressed.

The recognition that the *hattat* ritual in the sanctuary deals with unclean persons and not with defiled sancta provides a fresh way of looking at the *hattat* ritual in the sanctuary. For the question why a person declared clean needs further purification in the sanctuary is typologically similar to asking why the priests who are already holy (Lev 8) have to be further purified or atoned for on the eighth-day service (Lev 9). And it seems that the purification of the individual in the sanctuary has the same purpose as in Lev 9, i.e. divine acceptance. This would be supported by the calendrical pattern seven days-eighth day both in Lev 8-9 and the *hattat* rituals in Lev 12-15. If a conceptual parallel exists between Lev 9 and the *hattat* rituals for natural uncleanness, it would be even more difficult to assume 'sancta pollution' because, as already argued, the idea is unlikely to be present in Lev 9.

But why does the priest apply blood to sancta, if the sancta are not defiled? At this point it seems necessary to clarify the notion of sancta pollution in terms of its timing. Milgrom assumes that sancta become defiled when a person becomes unclean. Consequently sancta are defiled before the priest undertakes purification rites: since the sancta are defiled, the priest cleanses them. We rather assume that uncleanness is envisaged in the sancta when an unclean person stands before the Lord, i.e. at the entrance of the Tent, and that when the priest purifies the sancta, the unclean person becomes clean concurrently. Thus the *hattat* blood indeed purifies the sancta but not the sancta that have been defiled for a lengthy period.

To understand more fully this parallel between the cultic status of an offerer and what happens on the altar, it is necessary to enquire further into the meaning of purification on the one hand and the substitutionary character of the *hattat* blood on the other. Both will be addressed in connection with Lev 17.11 in Chapter 4.

Contrary to all the above, a few passages do suggest long-term 'sancta pollution'. They are Lev 15.31 and Lev 16.16, 19.[72]

Lev 15.31 could be translated, 'You shall warn the Israelites against uncleanness, that they die not in their uncleanness when they defile my tabernacle that is in the midst of them'.[73] The latter half of the sentence appears to envisage the failure to observe cleanness/uncleanness laws, which results in death. Therefore the passage hardly implies that the uncleanness dealt with in Lev 15.2-30 defiles the tabernacle. Rather what v. 31 says is that when the rules in vv. 2-30 are not kept, that defiles the tabernacle. Thus Lev 15.31 does not contradict our proposal that the *hattat* ritual in Lev 12-15 does not assume sancta pollution in Milgrom's sense. Seen this way Lev 15.31 closely resembles Num 19.13, 20, though in the latter the *karet* penalty is prescribed. As in Num 19.13, 20 it is unnecessary to assume, as the rabbis did, that in Lev 15.31 defiling the tabernacle meant or involved actual entry into the sanctuary in an unclean state.[74] At any rate Lev 15.31 is the first clear reference in Lev 11-15 to the idea of sancta polution.

Lev 16.16, 19 cannot be fully examined here. But they also strongly suggest that the sancta have been defiled for a certain period of time.

Thus we conclude that the *hattat* purifies sancta such as the outer altar, and unclean persons, though the sancta do not appear to be defiled by unclean persons, except in Lev 15.31 and Lev 16.16, 19. And this pollution is caused by failure to undergo the prescribed cleansing procedures, not by the person contracting uncleanness.

E. חטאת *(sin) and uncleanness*

As presented in the Introduction,[75] whether the *hattat* offering is expiatory or purificatory constitutes a major problem of the *hattat* offering. A related question concerns the relationship between sin and uncleanness. However, it becomes complicated not only because the English term 'sin' may not correspond to the Hebrew term חטאת, but because it may well be used with different connotations by different modern scholars. Thus some would conceive the two notions in the cultic text as mutually incompatible, whereas others would take them to be synonymous with each other.

In what follows we shall confine ourselves to discussing the relationship between חטאת (or חטא), which appears in the חטאת context, and uncleanness. For one thing, to discuss a general question like the relationship between sin and uncleanness goes beyond the scope of our inquiry. For another, to use the Hebrew term חטאת rather than the ambiguous term 'sin' reduces potential notional confusion. First we shall briefly address the notion of uncleanness, and then we shall compare it with חטאת (חטא) within the context of the *hattat* offering.

The term unclean(ness) is the translation of טמא. The concept appears repeatedly in the cleanness/uncleanness regulations in Lev 11-15 and Num 19. Questions concerning 'uncleanness' are generally abstruse. Here only one issue which appears most germane to the *hattat* offering is addressed, viz. the symbolic meaning of 'uncleanness'.

The sense of טמא, i.e. 'unclean', can be either tangible or metaphorical. When טמא has a tangible meaning it means 'dirty'.[76]

But it is used metaphorically in almost all its occurrences in cultic law. To ask, then, the meaning of uncleanness is to ask why certain things and conditions are designated as 'unclean'. Indeed this question has perplexed commentators on Leviticus throughout the ages, but we presume that explanations based on hygiene and cultic polemic against pagan cult are only partial and unconvincing, as Wenham has meticulously argued.[77] Here we rather take up the explanation, which has been offered by some scholars[78] and which seems most plausible, that uncleanness is related to 'death'.

This is clear from various uncleanness regulations. For instance, in Lev 11.24ff. uncleanness is contracted by physical contact with animals only when they are dead. In other words only dead animals can convey uncleanness. Num 19.13ff. deals with the contagion of uncleanness produced by human death and is probably presupposed by Num 31.19-24, which speaks of contact with corpses in war. Uncleanness is also accompanied by various diseases: serious skin diseases (Lev 13)[79] and serious male and female discharges (Lev 15.2-15, 25-30). Naturally these diseases could be seen as the manifestation of death.

Furthermore it has been demonstrated by Wenham[80] that an opposition between life and death can explain four categories of animals, reflected in cultic law: (1) animals suitable for sacrifice (holy), (2) suitable for eating (clean), (3) inedible (unclean but not polluting), (4) inedible and untouchable (very unclean and polluting). The same opposition of life and death can also answer why menstruation and emission of semen are defiling; they are regarded as the loss of 'life liquid'. Thus with Wenham we postulate that uncleanness symbolizes an 'aura of death'.[81]

Now in connection with the *hattat* offering these cleanness/ uncleanness regulations pose a basic question why the *hattat* is required on some occasions (Lev 12.6, 8; 14.10, 19, 22, 31; 15.14-15, 29-30) but not on every occasion a person becomes unclean. It seems probable that the defilement on those occasions is regarded as more serious than other cases for which only washing clothes and ablution are required, though the exact criterion of the degrees of uncleanness is debatable.

With the above comments on the cleanness/uncleanness regulations we shall attempt to clarify the relationship between חטאת (חטא) and uncleanness within the context of the *hattat* offering. The following data can be obtained from the foregoing discussion of the sections related to the *hattat*.

A	Lev 4.1–5.13	חטאת		כפר
B	Lev 5.2-3	uncleanness———→חטאת		כפר
C	Lev 12–15	uncleanness		כפר
D	Num 6.9ff.	uncleanness———→חטא		כפר
E	Lev 8.15; 9.9; 10.17	uncleanness*	עון	כפר
F	Num 6.14ff.	uncleanness*		- - -
G	Num 19	uncleanness		- - -

* = inferred

In the first place it may be argued that חטאת (sin) is distinguished from 'uncleanness' in the above texts. For the fact that in contexts C and G the natural defilement, however severe, is never associated with חטאת or חטא suggests that there is a clear distinction between חטאת (sin) and uncleanness.[82] The same inference can be drawn from Lev 15.31 and Lev 5.2-3, that as long as the purification rules are observed, the defilement itself is not regarded as sinful.

Yet does this distinction correspond to the modern distinction between sin with moral overtones and uncleanness, which tend to be regarded as foreign to each other? We shall point out below a possibility that the difference between חטאת (sin) and טמא (uncleanness) is essentially related to the dimension of uncleanness rather than to two mutually exclusive notions as their English equivalents suggests.

(1) As noted above the case in D appears to indicate that sin is regarded as just a more severe or special case of natural uncleanness. This is clear from the fact that the expiatory rite is preceded by the purificatory rite (cp. Num 8.7, 12).

(2) As postulated above, in C the natural defilement for which the *hattat* is required is more severe than other cases for which no sacrifice is prescribed. Thus conversely it may be inferred that because the defilement is more severe, the law demands the *hattat* as well as washing clothes and ablution.

(3) The term חִטֵּא may also shed some light on the relationship between חטאת (sin) and uncleanness. It has been translated either as 'de-sin' or 'purify'.[83] Which meaning is more suitable is difficult to determine in a context like Lev 8.15. However in the contexts of Lev 14.49, 52; it seems difficult to translate חִטֵּא 'de-sin' because חטאת or חטא does not appear. In these contexts there is first something or someone that is unclean. And then this status is transformed to clean status through the act of חִטֵּא. Thus there is no room for 'sin' to come in the process. The term חִטֵּא definitely points to the meaning of

'purge' or 'cleanse'. And there seems to be no particular reason to deny the same meaning in the other occurrences of the term.

All these observations lead to the inference that at least in the examined cases, חטאת (sin) is unlikely to be regarded as a notion essentially incompatible with 'uncleanness';[84] rather it is a kind of uncleanness, produced on a dimension different from that of natural uncleanness, namely by breaking a divine prohibition (Lev 4), neglecting cultic and judicial order (Lev 5.1-4) and the Nazirite's being defiled by a corpse (Num 6.9ff.).

Since uncleanness symbolizes the aura of death it follows that חטאת (sin) symbolizes a more intense aura of death.

But all this implies that the *hattat* offering is simply a higher form of purification agent.

Tentative Conclusions on the Function of the hattat

Our task in this Chapter has been to determine the function of the *hattat*. An examination of the relevant texts except Lev 4.1-5.13 led to conclusions, though still tentative, rather different from Milgrom's view. We agree with him that the *hattat* blood purifies sancta; but otherwise we differ from him on all the crucial issues on the *hattat*.

1. Milgrom's view that the *hattat* blood purifies only sancta is unlikely. The blood appears to purify sancta and by doing so also persons who need purification.

2. It also seems misleading to assume that sancta are defiled by uncleanness in the camp, except in Lev 15.31; 16.16ff.

3. Our study of the nature of the *hattat* in Lev 9 has revealed the hitherto overlooked fact that the presence of 'guilt' is assumed (Lev 10.17) even in a context where a specific sin is not envisaged. This suggests that the *hattat* ritual in Lev 9 concerns both 'uncleanness' and 'guilt', and that the concept of priests' 'purifying' parallels that of their 'bearing guilt' in some way.

4. In the examined *hattat* texts the concept of חטאת (sin) seems to be distinguished from 'uncleanness'. But the comparison of the contexts, particularly Lev 5.2-3; Num 6.9ff.; 8.7-12 suggests that there is no essential distinction between purification and expiation. Thus since the verb חטא is also

deeply rooted in the idea of purification it may be inferred
that חטאת (sin) is a kind of uncleanness. Further, since
'uncleanness' symbolizes an aura of death, so does חטאת
(sin).

5. In the light of points 3 and 4 above it is highly plausible that
    the *hattat* in Lev 4.1–5.13 deals with uncleanness as well as
    guilt. If so, it follows that since the *hattat* in this section
    deals with חטאת (sin), uncleanness and guilt constitute some
    aspects of the חטאת (sin).

Chapter 3

LEVITICUS 10 AND LEVITICUS 16

Introduction

In Chapter 2 we examined the role of the *hattat* on unique occasions such as the climax of the consecration of the priests on the eighth day. We suggested cleansing was necessary to prepare for the theophany. But sadly the divine acceptance of the priests and the people (Lev 9.24) is followed by the death of Nadab and Abihu (Lev 10.1ff.).[1] And this incident is referred to again in Lev 16.1 to introduce the ritual on the day of Atonement. Thus in the present book the death of Nadab and Abihu connects both Lev 9 with Lev 10 and Lev 10 with Lev 16, though this still leaves open how much of each chapter contributes to these literary connections.

The purpose of this Chapter is to discuss the significance of the Nadab and Abihu incident in its relation to Lev 9 on the one hand and Lev 16 on the other, both of which contain much material pertinent to an understanding of the *hattat*.

That this incident is relevant to the *hattat* offering is indicated by Lev 10.16-20, for on our interpretation of v. 17[2] the following observations may be made: 1. In v. 17 the function of the *hattat* is associated with 'atonement'. 2. To judge from Moses' words (v. 18) the problem in the episode concerns two types of atonement ceremony (see Lev 6.17-23). 3. Verse 19 indicates that the reason why Aaron did not eat the *hattat* has something to do with the Nadab and Abihu incident.

Indeed these points appear to be related more to atonement theology or the *hattat* symbolism than to the function of the *hattat* itself. But needless to say, a fuller understanding of the function of the *hattat* cannot be obtained without considering various rituals related to the *hattat*. This is especially true since our interpretation of Lev 10.17 has suggested a close relationship between the *hattat* and the role of the priest in bearing guilt.

Now Lev 10 consists of narrative and laws, and as often in such cases the chapter has been assigned to various literary strata by modern critics.[3] However, though the alternation of narrative and laws may strike the modern mind as odd, it must be underlined that no serious attempt has been made to understand the significance of the Nadab and Abihu incident. This may well be reflected in the modern exegetes' failure to give any satisfactory reason, based on the present context of Lev 10, why Aaron did not eat the *hattat* (v. 19); instead they have assumed the pericope of vv. 16-20 reflects some developments in cultic history.[4]

We shall argue below that this solution is unnecessary if the present text is interpreted accurately, and that the two incidents in Lev 10 (the Nadab and Abihu incident and the *hattat* flesh incident), far from giving merely factual information, illuminate some aspects of atonement theology regarding both the eighth-day service and the day of Atonement.

So the question why Aaron did not eat the *hattat* appears to form a nexus of various literary and ideological questions not only within Lev 10 but possibly with Lev 9 and Lev 16 too. To answer we shall first comment on vv. 1-7 (A) and then interpret vv. 16-20 with reference to vv. 1-7 (B). Based on the interpretation of Lev 10 as a whole we finally ask how Lev 16.1ff. is related, literarily and ideologically, to the Nadab and Abihu incident (C).

A. *The Nadab and Abihu Incident: An Exegesis of Lev 10.1-7*

The episode begins enigmatically:

ויקחו בני אהרן נדב ואביהוא איש מחתתו ויתנו בהן אש
וישימו עליה קטרת ויקריבו לפני ה' אש זרה אשר לא צוה אתם

It is unclear why Nadab and Abihu burned incense on their censers and brought it before the Lord. Yet the phrase אש זרה אשר לא צוה אתם appears to point out the nature of their sin.

Over against the common translation of the phrase אש זרה, 'illegitimate fire', Dillmann and others reason that if the phrase meant 'illegitimate fire', one would expect ויתנו בהן אש זרה, and that therefore אש in the phrase must mean 'fire-offering' like אִשֶּׁה, which also fits in well with the sacrificial term ויקריבו.[5] But two objections can be lodged against this view. First, אש hardly means 'fire-offering'. Second, הקריב could mean 'bring near' and not necessarily 'offer' with sacrificial overtones. The real question on Dillmann's view would be rather why the burning of incense is called אש and not קטרת.

Laughlin and others,[6] calling attention to אשר לא צוה אתם, argue that the sin consists in not taking the fire from the altar. This view is supported by Lev 16.12-13, where the fire was indeed taken from the altar in connection with the incense burning (cf. Lev 6.6), provided that a contrast is intended between Lev 10.1 and Lev 16.12-13. The advantage of this view is that it gives a partial reason why the text says אש זרה and not קטרת זרה. Nadab and Abihu are priests and fully entitled to burn incense. There is nothing wrong in the burning of incense itself. What is wrong is the nature of the fire, that it was taken from some source other than the altar. Another possible reason why the text says אש זרה may be that the author intended to express a talionic principle by the concord of offence and punishment (v. 2).[7]

Thus v. 2 states that 'a fire came out from the Lord and devoured them'. The fact that the same expression is found in Lev 9.24 strongly suggests that fire in both passages is the same fire, though in Lev 9.24 it is the fire of acceptance, whereas in Lev 10.2 it is the fire of punishment.

The next problem is posed by Moses' words in v. 3:

בקרבי אקדש ועל פני כל העם אכבד

They are poetically formulated and appear to be addressed to Aaron as an explanation of the incident. Provisionally the sentence could be translated 'In those who are close to me I am sanctified and before all the people I am honoured'. In what way, however, can these words be a comment on the Nadab and Abihu incident? Ehrlich comments:

> Durch die unparteiische exemplarische Bestrafung dieser beiden privilegierten Personen hat JHVH seine heilige Würde behauptet und somit angesichts des gesamten Volkes seine Ehrenkränkung gerächt.[8]

Ehrlich thus sees in Moses' words an exact description of what happened to Nadab and Abihu. However, though this view is possible, it is doubtful whether it is adequate to restrict the highly general language of Moses to the particular incident of Nadab and Abihu. If Moses' words express some principle, they need not be taken to refer only to the divine punishment, especially because the combination of the roots קדש and כבר appears in contexts other than that of punishment (e.g. Exod 29.43b).

The large majority of commentators have, in effect, adopted the following view of Dillmann:

je näher einer Gott steht, desto sicherer und stärker hat er es zu
erfahren, dass seine heilige Majestät sich nicht ungestraft antasten
lässt, und desto strenger muss er sich zu pünktlichster Beobachtung
des göttlichen Willens verpflichtet halten.[9]

This view may also be possible, but it seems unclear how such an
interpretation can be produced from vv. 1-3.

Earlier exegesis still leaves some points unclarified. Now, if Moses'
words should be taken as expressing a principle, בקרבי אקדש would
mean 'I am sanctified in my priests'.[10] Yet it is clear that Nadab and
Abihu did not sanctify God. Therefore בקרבי אקדש by referring to the
divine punishment that they suffered is insisting that they should
have been holy in approaching God.

However, since Moses' words consist of two parts, בקרבי אקדש and
על פני כל העם אכבד, one must ask first how the two parts are related
to each other before discussing the meaning of the isolated
בקרבי אקדש. This is highlighted by the fact that the second half
(על פני ff.) cannot stand apart from the first half, because, as
על פני כל העם shows, the second half refers to the concurrent effect of
the manifestation of God's holiness on the people. In other words,
the glory of God before the people is contingent upon the fact that
God is sanctified by priests. Thus the whole sentence essentially
means: 'When I am sanctified in those who are close to me, then I am
honoured before all the people'. What is clearly enunciated by Moses'
words is, therefore, the heavy duty of the priests, because the
sentence clearly implies that by failing to sanctify God, the priests
mar the glory of God. On this interpretation Dillmann's view cited
above is indeed right, in that it stresses the heavy responsibility of
priests, though it seems slightly over-subtle.

The third issue raised by this episode concerns the treatment of
the dead priests by their brothers. After the corpses of Nadab and
Abihu are carried away from the sanctuary (v. 4), Moses enjoins
Aaron and his two remaining sons (1) not to mourn for Nadab and
Abihu—that ought to be done by the whole people (v. 6)—and (2) not
to leave the entrance of the Tent of meeting. Apparently the two
injunctions are grounded upon כי שמן משחת ה' עליכם (v. 7aβ).[11] Why
are they forbidden to mourn or leave the sanctuary?

In view of Lev 21.10ff. commentators have rightly taken these two
injunctions to indicate that Aaron and his remaining two sons are
regarded as having the status of the high priest.[12] Yet by looking at
the injunctions only from the viewpoint of Lev 21.10ff., they have

also tended to minimize the impact of the sin of Nadab and Abihu on their family and the people. We shall point out below that it is wrong to see the death of Nadab and Abihu as nothing more than them bearing their own guilt and to see vv. 6-7 simply as the priest's observance of the law in Lev 21.10ff.

Verse 6a states that if the priest mourn, they will die and the divine wrath will fall upon all the congregation. The assumption that the sin of the anointed priest makes the whole people the object of the divine wrath appears to be common with Lev 4.3;[13] but more immediately it leads to the idea expressed in v. 3 (see above). At any rate, v. 6a implies that as long as the priests keep the commandment, they are not at risk and there will be no outburst of divine wrath on the whole congregation. But it must be stressed that all this does not necessarily imply the priests are innocent; v. 6a does not say that Aaron and his remaining sons have nothing to do with the Nadab and Abihu incident.

In v. 6b the mourning is entrusted to the whole house of Israel. Undoubtedly the whole house of Israel is assumed to become defiled by this mourning.[14] However, as Ehrlich notes[15] it is striking that the object of the bewailing (בכה) is הַשְּׂרֵפָה (= the burning), though v. 6b as a whole obviously refers to the mourning for the death of Nadab and Abihu; normally בכה is followed by a personal object (cp. Num 20.29; Deut 34.8). This unusual form may be explained by assuming that the mourning on this occasion is not something natural. Indeed as אשר שרף ה' stresses, it rather bears the character of the after-effect of the divine punishment on Nadab and Abihu.

Yet the unusual form points to an even more significant aspect of the Nadab and Abihu incident: v. 6b is in stark contrast with Lev 9.24. In other words, in contrast with the fact that the whole people rejoiced (וירנו) at the sight of divine fire devouring the sacrifices on the altar (Lev 9.24), they ought this time to bewail (בכה) the divine fire's devouring of Nadab and Abihu. Thus it must be assumed that the situation of Lev 9.24 has been reversed, involving not only Nadab and Abihu but *the whole people*.

Thus from v. 6b it is clear that the sin of Nadab and Abihu involved both their family and the whole congregation. True, Aaron and his remaining sons could escape from death by performing what Moses commanded and by so doing withhold the outburst of divine wrath against the people, but the fact remains that the whole people are *now* far from being accepted before the Lord.

With this background we now tackle the *hattat* flesh incident in vv. 16-20.

B. *Lev 10.16-20 and its Relationship with 10.1-7*

We now turn to Lev 10.16-20 to discuss again the enigmatic *hattat*-flesh incident which appears to be related to the Nadab and Abihu incident. Earlier we devoted much discussion to the interpretation of v. 17. We suggested that v. 17b should be translated: 'and it (the *hattat*) was assigned to you to bear the guilt of the congregation, thus making atonement for them before the Lord', and that eating the *hattat* does not belong to the atoning process. The next crucial verse is v. 19.

Before attempting an exegesis of v. 19, however, we should note one point about v. 18a. Since the reason in v. 18a (הן לא הובא ...) is given in connection with the people's *hattat* mentioned in v. 17b, the *hattat* about which Moses is talking is the people's *hattat* and not the priests'.[16]

Now most problematic is Aaron's reply in v. 19. Obviously here Aaron is justifying the burning of the people's *hattat*. His main argument appears to lie in v. 19a: 'Even though they offered before the Lord their חטאת and their עולה today, things like these have happened to me...' Why did Aaron and his remaining sons not eat the people's *hattat*?

In an attempt to answer this important question we examine v. 19 philologically and ideologically below.

In the first place, which sacrifices do חטאתם and עלתם in v. 19 refer to, to the priests' or to the people's? The context of Lev 10.17-19 suggests that Aaron is *justifying* his sons' act of burning the people's *hattat*. Thus, at least, the pronominal suffixes in חטאתם and עלתם can best be taken as referring to Aaron's two surviving sons, Eleazar and Ithamar.[17] However, against Dillmann,[18] who restricts the pronominal suffixes to Eleazar and Ithamar, it must be argued that since Aaron is referring to what is recounted in Lev 9.8-14, the pronominal suffixes may include Nadab and Abihu as well.

Secondly, it may be admitted that ותקראנה אתי כאלה refers at least to the death of Nadab and Abihu. Yet in view of כאלה it seems better to take the clause as referring to both their death and its consequences, i.e. what is recounted in Lev 10.1-7.

Thirdly, by saying ואכלתי חטאת Aaron appears to be responding to Moses' rebuke. Thus חטאת here refers to the people's *hattat*. As already argued, eating the *hattat* does not belong to the atoning process.[19] Therefore the fact that Aaron did not eat the *hattat* does not imply that the atonement of the people in Lev 9 was invalidated.

It rather implies that Aaron, for some reason, abandoned his right
and privilege of eating the *hattat*.

Thus it may be inferred from the above that in v. 19 Aaron is
contrasting the ritual in Lev 9.8-11 with the Nadab and Abihu
incident in Lev 10.1-7. Yet most remarkable is the fact that in
response to Moses' rebuke Aaron is, first and foremost, pointing and
appealing to the atonement of *priests*, in contrast to Moses, who
refers only to the atonement of the *people* (vv. 17-18). These
considerations also suggest that the reason for Aaron's abandoning
his right and privilege of eating the *hattat* should be sought in his
family situation, viz. how he evaluated the incident in Lev 10.1-7.

Some Jewish exegetes explained the reason for Aaron's not eating
the *hattat* by pointing out that Aaron and his sons were in
mourning.[20] However, as Dillmann noted, this view is inconsistent
with vv. 6-7, where their participation in the mourning is explicitly
prohibited.[21] Another objection to the 'mourning' approach is given
by Ehrlich: if they did not eat the *hattat* on the ground that they were
in mourning the text would have read ואכלתי בקדשים or בקדשי ה'
instead of ואכלתי חטאת because they, being unclean because of
mourning, are to be debarred from all the holy things and not only
from the *hattat*.[22] Ehrlich also infers that Nadab and Abihu died
after they offered their *hattat*, and that therefore Aaron and his
remaining sons knew that the *hattat* was not accepted by God.[23]
These two observations by Ehrlich are criticized and developed
below in reverse order.

First of all, there is no evidence in Lev 9-10 to support the idea
that Nadab and Abihu were killed after they offered the *hattat*.
Rather Lev 9 as a whole shows that the purpose of the eighth-day
service, i.e. the appearance of God's glory, is successfully achieved by
various offerings including the חטאת and עולה (cf. Lev 9.23). There is
no hint in the text itself that something went wrong. Thus it must be
assumed that the glory of God was manifested to the people because
both Aaron and the people were atoned for by Aaron's offering of the
חטאת and the עולה. Indeed one may argue that this may be the
author's (or redactor's) view though not necessarily Aaron's; Aaron
may have misunderstood the meaning of the event in Lev 9. But at
least in Lev 10.17-18 Moses clearly assumes that the people were
atoned for by the *hattat*. And if there were no common understanding
between Moses and Aaron that Aaron and the people were indeed
atoned for by the sacrifices prescribed in Lev 9, Aaron might well
have expressed his view in v. 19. Yet it appears that in saying ואכלתי

חטאת Aaron agrees with, and presupposes, the correctness of Moses' theory in vv. 17-18.

Now the mention of חטאת and עולה in v. 19 is, as Ehrlich noted, highly significant. It has been argued above that Aaron is stressing the atonement of the priests in contrast with Moses who thinks of the atonement of the people. This is clearly observable in the following comparison of Moses' words in v. 17b and Aaron's in v. 19a as well.

> Verse 17b (atonement of the people)
>
> ואתה נתן לכם לשאת את עון העדה לכפר עליכם לפני ה'
>
> Verse 19a (atonement of the priests)
>
> הן היום הקריבו את חטאתם ואת עלתם לפני ה'

It seems likely that the underlined part of v. 19a parallels conceptually *kipper* in v. 17b because the purpose of offering the חטאת and the עולה is to make atonement (see Lev 9.7). If this is admitted, then the contrast between the two passages becomes even sharper in terms of the beneficiary of atonement: in v. 17b the congregation and in v. 19a the priests.

However it may also be noted that the mention of עלתם is superfluous if Aaron's reply is compared only with Moses' words. Moreover חטאת in ואכלתי חטאת (v. 19b) may refer indefinitely to any eaten *hattat*, not particularly to the *hattat* which should have been eaten. From these observations it may be inferred that Aaron is appealing to some definite principle rather than referring to the particular *hattat* Moses is making a fuss about (cp. החטאת in vv. 16-17). Nonetheless in that in ואכלתי ff. Aaron now mentions only חטאת instead of 'their חטאת and their עולה', this implies that Aaron is now referring more directly to Moses' rebuke.

Then the question arises why the חטאת and the עולה are singled out from various offerings offered in the eighth-day service to be contrasted with the Nadab and Abihu incident. As hinted above,[24] we assume that this is because the two sacrifices are expiatory or propitiatory, being related to *kipper* (Lev 9.7). Thus the contrast in v. 19a between the atonement of the priests and the Nadab and Abihu incident can be expressed in the following two ways. Firstly, though Aaron and his sons could avert the wrath of God, they still experienced it in the divine punishment on Nadab and Abihu even on the same day. Secondly, it illustrates the two aspects of bearing guilt: in Lev 9 Aaron bore the guilt of the priests, but in Lev 10.1ff. Nadab and Abihu bore their own guilt and died. But this still leaves it unclear how the atonement of priests in Lev 9 is related to the Nadab and Abihu incident.

In an attempt to pinpoint the exact reason why Aaron did not eat the *hattat*, thereby abandoning his right and privilege to it, it seems necessary to reemphasize that the priests and the people were indeed atoned for in Lev 9. Furthermore it must be borne in mind that the idea that atonement can be annulled or invalidated after it is made is not mentioned in the cultic law, and that more immediately both Moses and Aaron appear to assume in Lev 10.16ff. the validity of the atonement in Lev 9. Therefore one cannot say that the atonement of priests in Lev 9 was invalidated by the sin of Nadab and Abihu. What did Nadab and Abihu's sin do then? Did it create a new need of atonement? In addition it has been argued above that the mourning approach contradicts Lev 10.6.[25] What, then, made Aaron shrink from eating the *hattat*? There are some considerations which may lead to an answer to these questions.

1. Although atonement was indeed made in Lev 9 and could not be cancelled by the Nadab and Abihu incident, as the contrast between הקריבו את חטאתם ואת עלתם and ותקראנה אתי כאלה in Lev 10.19 suggests, the main reason why Aaron did not eat the people's *hattat* appears to lie in the overriding cultic (not emotional) impact of the Nadab and Abihu incident on Aaron. Thus the death of Nadab and Abihu could be compared to the following situation: A man committed a minor crime and it was expiated, but later he committed a murder and suffered capital punishment. In this case if the expiation remains valid and the death penalty is inflicted just for the murder, the expiation of the minor offence may well be regarded as meaningless or insignificant when it is seen in the light of the man's subsequent execution. Is this not the kind of situation Aaron had in mind when he compared the atonement of priests with the Nadab and Abihu incident in Lev 10.19?

2. As noted above, in vv. 6-7 Eleazar and Ithamar are regarded as equal to Aaron in their holiness (Lev 21.10-12). Indeed several texts in Lev 9-10 regarding the relationship between Aaron and his sons rather point to the circumstance that Aaron's sons are included in the person of Aaron. This shows the equal holiness of Aaron and his sons.

In Lev 9.7 Aaron is commanded to make atonement for himself and the people but his sons assist him in the blood manipulation (vv. 9, 12, 18). In Lev 10 acts of Aaron's sons are often attributed to Aaron himself. So in v. 3 Aaron is rebuked for the act of Nadab and

Abihu. In v. 6, as mentioned above, it is assumed that a sin of the anointed priest makes the whole people the object of divine wrath. And in v. 16 Moses rebuked Eleazar and Ithamar for burning the people's *hattat*, but it was Aaron who replied to Moses, which suggests that Aaron's sons acted under Aaron's supervision. This is most clearly reflected in the change of number in Aaron's reply in v. 19; from the third person plural to first person singular. Thus it is reasonable to assume that though Nadab and Abihu died bearing their own guilt, Aaron is held responsible for the incident as the head of the family; so this case should not be confused with the one in Lev 4.3, where the anointed priest himself commits a sin.

As has been argued, the Nadab and Abihu incident put the whole congregation in a situation opposite to that in Lev 9.24. In view of the above assumption that Aaron's four sons are included in the person of Aaron, it can be concluded that in v. 19 Aaron assumes that he caused the whole situation by the sin of Nadab and Abihu; i.e. he is guilty in his capacity as the head of the family.[26]

The same conclusion can also be reached by another route. On the theological postulate that Aaron's atonement reflects the people's atonement (Lev 9.7; 4.3; 10.3), the very fact that the whole people are mourning and are no longer acceptable to the Lord proves that Aaron (thus the priesthood as a whole) is in need of expiation or atonement.

Thus it can be concluded from the above that the sin of Nadab and Abihu is a sin of the priestly family as well as that of Nadab and Abihu, and that Aaron is guilty of it in his capacity as the head of the family.

3. The contrast between priests and the people is found in Lev 10.3 as well as Lev 10.19. In both passages the priority of priestly duties over the people's is emphasized. In the light of this parallel, Aaron appears to be arguing in v. 19 that unless he is atoned for, it is meaningless for him to exercise his right to the people's atonement, or to put it another way, that since he is *now* not atoned for, he is unworthy of enjoying his right to the people's *hattat*. Either way it is clear that Moses' remark in v. 3 is utilized by Aaron in justifying his action. Furthermore it may also be noted that וידם אהרן in v. 3 is contrasted with וייטב בעיניו in v. 20. The latter implies divine approval, which is expressed by the author using the same phrase that Aaron used. And this again forms a contrast with Moses' words in v. 3a, which originated in the Lord.[27]

It is clear, then, that Aaron acted tacitly and even confidently in accordance with the principle uttered from the very mouth of Moses.[28]

4. The twice-mentioned 'today' in Lev 10.19 also deserves note. The emphasis is unlikely to imply that Aaron can eat the *hattat* the next day. Rather the emphatic 'today' seems to imply that the purpose of the eighth-day service (i.e. the divine acceptance of the priests and the people) must not be equivocated. Yet it must be stressed that this motive is shared by both Aaron and Moses. The difference between them was that whereas Moses wished Aaron and his sons to implement their priestly duties concerning the eighth-day service, Aaron held that, being guilty, he could no more exercise his right to the people's *hattat*.

The above four points thus lead to the following conclusions. The reason why Aaron did not eat the people's *hattat* is that Aaron, being in the unatoned-for status in the wake of the Nadab and Abihu incident, thought it inappropriate to enjoy his priestly right of eating the *hattat* on the principle that atonement of Aaron, i.e. of his house, was of paramount importance.

This situation indeed creates a ritual difficulty for Aaron owing to the fact that the day was the eighth day. For the ceremony on the eighth day (Lev 9) is not designed to expiate a particular sin of the priestly house, yet Aaron is still bound by the principle that his (= priests') atonement must take priority (Lev 10.3, 19).

Therefore Lev 10, particularly vv. 16-20, implies that the ritual in Lev 9 is incomplete in view of the sin of Aaron's house, and it demands an atonement system which is different from the one in Lev 9 and which atones for the sin of Aaron's house in an all-sufficient manner.

We shall argue below that all the above arguments are highly relevant to the interpretation of the day of Atonement ceremonies described in Lev 16.

C. *Lev 16 and its Relationship to Lev 10*

The literary character of Lev 16 as a whole has been variously evaluated since the last century.[29] It is a fact that the chapter contains peculiar vocabulary and style which are not found in other parts of the priestly literature. Also from the ideological point of view the chapter presents a highly complicated atonement ritual which has no parallel in other parts of the OT. Thus, with some exceptions, the majority of scholars have seen the chapter as composite, though no consensus has been achieved as to the analysis of the text. Normally the existence of various literary strata in the chapter has been inferred on the basis of unevenness in vocabulary, style and ideology.

A comprehensive evaluation of the literary character of Lev 16.1-28 will not be made in this study. In what follows we limit our discussion only to the literary framework of the chapter (vv. 1-2, 34b), and to the fundamental theme of the ritual set out in vv. 3-28 as it relates to Lev 10 as discussed above. So the central question pursued below is how the prescription of the ritual is related to the historical framework: why the mention of the death of Nadab and Abihu, and the ban on Aaron's entry into the adytum (vv. 1-2) should be followed by various atonement ceremonies by Aaron (vv. 3-28) and the institution of the day of Atonement (vv. 29-34a). Our suggestion on this question will inevitably be tentative until our further discussion in Chapter 6.

Here we shall (1) discuss the meaning and significance of vv. 1-3, (2) make a comparison between Lev 10.1-11 and Lev 16.1ff. and (3) examine the ideological connection between Lev 10 and Lev 16.3ff.

1. *Interpretation of vv. 1-3*
Verse 1 begins with the introductory formula 'And God spoke to Moses' and then refers to the death of Nadab and Abihu. From the fact that the introductory formula is repeated in v. 2 von Rad and Koch[30] infer that v. 2 is an introduction independent of v. 1. The implausibility of this interpretation is well argued by Elliger, who points out that the repetitive introduction in v. 2 in the form of ויאמר instead of the usual לאמר is caused by the historical reference אחרי מות . . . וימתו.[31] Also against von Rad's view that ולא יבא is a second part of God's command, Elliger rightly adduces passages like Lev 22.2; 24.2, in which indirect speech is introduced by *wāw* + jussive.[32] So with Elliger it should be concluded that v. 1, though its syntax is unusual, is naturally followed by v. 2.

The exegetical problems in vv. 1-3 seem to revolve around the two prepositional phrases, בכל עת in v. 2 and בזאת in v. 3, the interpretation of which affects one's approach to the whole chapter. The problems are presented below.

Usually the phrase בכל עת has been translated 'at any time' or 'at all times'. However, whatever meaning the phrase itself has, the more crucial question is whether v. 2a, being a negative sentence, implies a total prohibition against entry, i.e. Aaron should never enter the adytum, or a partial prohibition, i.e. he could not enter the adytum at all times. On the former interpretation it would follow that vv. 3ff. form an exception to the prohibition in v. 2a, since vv. 3ff. appear to show that with proper precautions Aaron may enter the adytum. On the latter interpretation vv. 3ff. explain how Aaron should enter the adytum when he enters.

However the fact that the specific date for Aaron's entry into the adytum is not given until vv. 29, 34a led Dillmann and others to assume that v. 2 originally included fixing a date, which we do not have now; this was later changed or shortened in conformity with later practice on the day of Atonement. This is refleced in vv. 29, 34a.[33]

Benzinger,[34] though he by and large agrees with Dillmann, still hesitates to decide whether the mention of בכל עת necessarily implies the fixing of a date when Aaron may enter the adytum, and suggests the possibility that the phrase explains the gap between v. 2 and v. 3; 'nicht zu jeder Zeit ohne weiteres sondern erst nach der Erfüllung der Bedingungen 1) Sündopfer 2) heiliges Gewand'.[35]

According to Ehrlich[36] the phrase בכל עת is unlikely to be contrasted with 'once a year' in v. 34, firstly, because the two are so far from each other, and secondly because 'once a year' is said not about the entry into the adytum but about the performance of the ritual. Thus Ehrlich holds that בכל עת is contrasted with בזאת in v. 3, according to which the author of v. 2 is not contemplating the fixing of a date for Aaron's entry into the adytum. Consequently he concludes that the exact meaning of בכל עת is not 'zu jeder Zeit' but 'unter beliebigen Umständen'.

These earlier interpretations have therefore left the following questions unresolved.

a. The meaning of בכל עת, particularly when the phrase is found in the negative sentence.
b. The meaning of בזאת in v. 3

a. To begin with, is it right to presume that בכל עת is a temporal phrase in the way it has been taken? Wilch[37] has convincingly demonstrated that עת denotes not only time but also, and more importantly, 'a certain quality or peculiarity' of it. Thus he translates the phrase 'on every occasion'. And this translation seems to reflect the meaning of עת more exactly than the alternative 'at any time' or 'at all times'.[38] In view of this it would be misleading to take the phrase simply as a temporal one.

Furthermore this proposed translation of the phrase may explain the structure of Lev 16. For the fact that עת denotes both time and quality, with more emphasis on the latter, perfectly fits in with the arrangement of the material in the chapter: vv. 3-28 concerns the ritual on certain occasions, whereas vv. 29b, 34a give the date. In the context of Lev 16.1-2, then, the phrase בכל עת implies 'an occasion like the eighth-day service' because, as argued above, v. 2 makes an allusion to the death of Nadab and Abihu on account of the juxtaposition of v. 1 and v. 2.[39]

Thus v. 2a says that Aaron must not enter the adytum on every occasion. This means that there might be one or two occasions on which he can enter it.

b. What, then, does בזאת in v. 3 mean? A common view holds that it means 'with this' or 'with the following'[40] while the LXX understands it to mean οὕτως. However against the former view it must be argued that if ב in בזאת meant 'with' as ב in בפר the text should have read באלה and not בזאת. Rather it seems more likely to connect v. 3b with v. 4 and to put a colon between v. 3a and v. 3b. Indeed various speculations have emerged as regards v. 3b over the fact that a ram for the עולה is unlikely to be brought into the adytum.[41] But this problem disappears if v. 3 is interpreted as above. Then the עולה in v. 3b can refer to the one in v. 24b.[42]

In view of the other occurrences of בזאת (Gen 34.15, 22; Num 16.28-30; Josh 3.10) the phrase in our passage may be translated 'thus' (LXX) or 'herewith' or 'in the following'. It may be added that on this translation v. 3a can refer not just to vv. 3b-4 but even to vv. 3b-24.

With regard to the relationship between v. 2 and v. 3a the following comments are in order.

First, the following chiastic word order in v. 2a and v. 3a implies that v. 3a is formulated in view of v. 2a.

V. 2a	‏ואל יבא בכל עת אל הקרש מבית לפרכת...
V. 3a	‏בזאת יבא אהרן אל הקרש...

Second, since בזאת is not preceded by particles like רק, אך or *wāw*, v. 3a is unlikely to intend to give an exception to the rule in v. 2a; v. 3a marks a new paragraph.[43]

Third, Exod 18.22(26)

ושפטו את-העם בכל-עת והיה כל-הדבר
הגדל יביאו אליך וכל-הדבר הקטן ישפטו-הם ...

is illuminating. Here Moses' judicial burden is, on the advice of
Jethro, allotted to various chieftains of the people. The phrase בכל-עת
can be translated 'on every occasion', but והיה ff. does not in fact
appear to be concerned about the time element. Rather the sentence
והיה ff. can best be taken as explicating, i.e. giving the detail of, the
preceding general principle. And it seems that this general-detail
relationship is also found in Lev 16.2-3.

Thus we propose that the general and allusive rule in v. 2 is
detailed, firstly in vv. 3ff. in terms of the occasion of Aaron's entry to
the adytum and secondly, in vv. 29ff. in terms of its date.

2. *A comparison between Lev 10.1-11 and Lev 16.1ff.*

Because of its connection with v. 1, Lev 16.2 becomes a highly
allusive sentence. Thus it is possible to infer that Nadab and Abihu
even entered the adytum.[44] Furthermore v. 2 appears to imply that
only Aaron can enter the adytum on a definite occasion. Therefore
Lev 16.1-2 adds to אש זרה in Lev 10.1-2 three more pieces of
information on the sin of Nadab and Abihu: their entry into the
adytum, its untimeliness and their trespass on Aaron's right.

In fact Lev 10.9 may add another circumstance to the sin of Nadab
and Abihu: they were drunk.[45] Though this view is not adopted by
the majority of modern exegetes, it seems highly plausible as the
following considerations show.

Lev 10.1-2 mentions only אש זרה as the sin of Nadab and Abihu.
This is probably because the passage intends to pinpoint the
immediate cause of their death. Were other aspects of their sin as in
Lev 16.1-2 mentioned in Lev 10.1-2, the literary effect of presenting a
dynamic contrast between the two 'divine fires' (Lev 9.24; 10.1-2)
would have been greatly weakened.

As for Lev 10.9 it could be observed that if one aspect of the sin is
alluded to, the passage as a whole does not refer specifically to their
sin. However this is fully in accord with the purpose of vv. 8-11,
which is to lay down the priestly duties. This is reflected, firstly, in
the fact that Aaron is addressed as being responsible both for his and
his sons' duties (cp. Num 18.1), and secondly in the mention of
אהל מועד, which suggests that priests in general do their duties there
as well.[46] Thus in the light of the general purpose of vv. 8-11, it
would have been inept for the author to refer explicitly to the entry
into the adytum at this point.

With the above considerations in mind we propose below a kind of 'climactic parallelism' between Lev 10.1-11 and Lev 16.1ff. Firstly, it is striking that Lev 10.9a mentions the entry into the Tent and ends with ולא תמתו while Lev 16.2 concerns the entry into the adytum and also says לא ימות. Secondly, Lev 10.9-11 concern not only Aaron but his sons, whereas the law in Lev 16.2ff. deals exclusively with Aaron's work. And lastly, assuming that Nadab and Abihu were drunk, both Lev 10.1-11 and Lev 16.1ff. are indeed similar to each other in that the two laws enacted (Lev 10.9-11 and 16.2-28) are based on the same actual event, the death of Nadab and Abihu. In Lev 10 the law in v. 9 alludes to the sin of Nadab and Abihu, but it also expresses a general principle. Then this slightly allusive law is followed by the mention of the general priestly duties in vv. 10-11. Similarly Lev 16.2 (parallel to Lev 10.9) alludes to various aspects of the sin of Nadab and Abihu, but can be a law independent of v. 1. Again this allusive passage v. 2 is followed by the prescription of Aaron's work in the adytum (vv. 3ff.), which appears to be remote in topic from the death of Nadab and Abihu, just as Lev 10.10-11 does.

It seems that the above literary-stylistic feature is not accidental but deliberate.

Therefore we conclude that apart from אש זרה various aspects of the sin of Nadab and Abihu are reflected in the law of Lev 10.9 and 16.2, and that Lev 10.1-11 shows remarkable literary-stylistic similarity to Lev 16.1ff. in the relationship between the narrative and the law.[47]

These observations help to clarify the mention of the חמאת in Lev 10.16ff., and the relationship of this episode with the day of Atonement.

3. *An ideological connection between Lev 10 and Lev 16.3ff.*

As already mentioned, the main purpose of our study of Lev 16 in this Chapter is to answer the question why the mention of Aaron's entry to the adytum begins with a ritual prescription and then moves on to the institution of the so-called day of Atonement. In connection with this problem we have suggested three points. Firstly, the question of Aaron's entry is answered in two stages: vv. 3ff. and vv. 29ff. Secondly, there is a literary style common to Lev 10.1-11 and Lev 16.1ff., which lies in a transition from a specific historical event to a general law. Thirdly, we have also suggested that Lev 16.12-13 polemizes against the sin of Nadab and Abihu.

These observations seem to be sufficient for the assumption that Lev 16.1-28 is closely related to Lev 10. Especially Lev 16.1-2, 12-13 may suggest that the relationship is that of type and anti-type, for these passages appear to contrast the incorrect way of entering the adytum and burning incense with the correct one.

However, these observations are made on the basis of certain passages within the two chapters which do not appear to be related to the whole of Lev 10 or Lev 16.1-28.

We suggest here an idea which links Lev 10 with Lev 16 far more closely than scholars have hitherto assumed, namely the atonement theology discussed in Lev 10.16-20. It has been argued that the *hattat* flesh incident in Lev 10.16-20 demands an atonement system in which Aaron can atone for his house in an all-sufficient manner because the atonement ceremony in Lev 9 is not designed to expiate the specific sin of the priestly family like Nadab and Abihu's. When this fact is recalled it would be simple to see the fulfilment of this need in the ritual in Lev 16, the central purpose of which is to make atonement for sancta because of uncleanness and the transgressions of priests and people (vv. 16a, 19).

This seems to be reflected in Lev 16 in the following ways.

a. If vv. 1-3 are read as we have suggested, the historical reference in v. 1 indicates that the author of Lev 16 intends to answer questions raised by the Nadab and Abihu incident. The questions include, in our opinion, the one of entry into the adytum (v. 2) and more importantly how atonement of Aaron's house can be made (vv. 3ff.).

b. For the first time the idea appears in Lev 16 that Aaron makes atonement for *his house* as well as for himself (Lev 16.6, 11, 17b). This may well reflect the posing of the problem in Lev 10.16-20 as we have suggested.

c. The order of the ritual in Lev 16.14-15 confirms the idea expressed in Lev 9-10 that atonement of priests must precede that of the people.

d. In Lev 16 Aaron is the sole agent of atonement except in the problematic v. 10.[48] He is said to make atonement (*kipper*) for himself, his house and the people. However, as noted in Chapter 2, *kipper* may be related to the concept of נשא עון. In view of the above overall literary and ideological relationship between Lev 10 and Lev 16, the same may apply to *kipper* in Lev 16: Aaron bears the guilt of himself, his house and the people. Indeed it may be said that in Lev 10 Aaron could not bear the guilt of his house, which was caused by

84 *The Purification Offering*

the specific sin of Nadab and Abihu. Thus it may be suggested that at least this theological predicament is resolved by the Azazel-goat ritual; the guilt Aaron bears is to be transferred onto the Azazel goat (vv. 21ff.) and removed to the wilderness. This proposal certainly requires further detailed arguments and substantiation, which will be offered in the following Chapters.

However, even if this last point is inconclusive, it seems certain that the ritual in Lev 16.3ff. is prescribed, at least partly, with a view to answering the question implicit in Lev 10.16-20, namely how the sin of Aaron's house is to be atoned for.

Conclusions

1. The crux of Lev 10.16-20, the matter of why Aaron did not eat the *hattat*, can be resolved by observing that Moses thinks of atonement of the people whereas Aaron (on the basis of v. 3) emphasizes that the death of Nadab and Abihu made the atonement ceremony of the eighth-day service virtually meaningless, hence the assumption is being made that Aaron became guilty of the sin of Nadab and Abihu as the head of the house. Thus it is the intention of the author of Lev 10.16-20 to present the above problem. To see the controversy between Moses and Aaron as reflecting historical changes in cultic practice is unnecessary and misleading.

2. Lev 10.1-11 parallels Lev 16.1ff. stylistically in the transition from historical account to stipulation of general laws. In content Lev 10.1-11 stands in a climactic relationship with Lev 16.1ff. in that the former deals with the priests' (including Aaron's) work in general whereas the latter concentrates on Aaron's work in the adytum. Since the two incidents in Lev 10 (the Nadab and Abihu incident and the *hattat* flesh incident) show together the inadequacy of the atonement ceremony of the eighth-day service, they may also imply the inadequacy of the atoning work of the priests in the shrine and the forecourt, in the face of the sin of the priestly family such as Nadab and Abihu's.

3. As stated above, the essential problem posed by the two incidents in Lev 10 is that of atonement for Aaron's house, which is dealt with neither in Lev 4.3 nor in Lev 9.7. In view of the circumstances that *kipper* may be related to נשא עון

(Lev 10.17), and that in Lev 16 the Azazel goat removes the guilt of all the Israelites, the demand in Lev 10.16-20 for a more effective atonement may ultimately be met by the Azazel-goat ritual.

Chapter 4

THE *KIPPER* PROBLEM

The term *kipper* appears frequently in connection with the *hattat*, but so far the meaning of this fundamental term has not been discussed. While forgiveness (ונסלח) or cleanness (וטהר) constitutes the purpose of the *hattat* ritual in Lev 4.1-5.13 and Lev 12-15, the final result of the ritual appears to be expressed by *kipper*. If this term were unambiguous, the *hattat* ritual would have been understood without much ado. However the history of the research into the term has shown various approaches to the term, thus to atonement theology in general.[1]

This Chapter certainly does not intend to resolve all the critical questions regarding the use of the term in the cultic law. Its aim, rather, is to discuss those aspects of the concept of *kipper* that are likely to shed light on the *hattat* ritual, but which have not received sufficient attention from scholars. There are at least two fundamental problems concerning the cultic *kipper*: the meanings of various prepositions which *kipper* takes, and the concept of *kipper*. We shall look at both problems in turn. Our first task (A) is to determine the meanings of those prepositions; but it will be seen that that involves atonement theology, being far from a mere philological task. Then secondly (B) we shall reexamine the concept of *kipper*: this small study does not attempt to propose a new meaning of *kipper*. For convenience's sake we prefer to translate it 'atone for' or 'make atonement for', as we have done thus far. But the term will be considered from various angles. Lastly, we shall discuss in detail the theologically indispensable passage Lev 17.11 in order to supplement and develop the above arguments (C).

A. *Kipper constructions*

Kipper in the cultic law takes the following syntactic relations.[2]

I. כפר (alone) Lev 16.32

    + ב (*beth instrumenti*)   Exod 29.33; Lev 5.16; 7.7; 17.11b(?)[3]; 19.22; Num 5.8.

    + ב   (*beth loci*)   Lev 6.23; 16.17a, 27.[4]

II. כפר + את (*nota accusativi*) + sanctum   Lev 16.20a, 33a; Ezek 43.20, 26; 45.20.

III. כפר + על + sanctum   Exod 29.36, 37; 30.10a; Lev 8.15; 14.53; 16.18.

    כפר + על + sanctum + מן[5]   Exod 30.10b; Lev 16.16.

IV. כפר with personal object

  (a) כפר + על

    (1) על + (alone)   Exod 30.15, 16; Lev 1.4; 4.20, 31; 8.34; 12.7,8; 14.20, 21; 16.30, 33b; 17.11a; Num 8.12, 19, 21; 15.25, 28 (bis); 28.22, 30; 29.5; Ezek 45.15 (Lev 16.10?)[6]

    + על + ב (*beth instrumenti*) Lev 5.16; 19.22, Num 5.8.

    + על + לפני ח'   Lev 5.26; 10.17; 14.18, 29, 31; 15.15, 30; 19.22; 23.28; Num 31.50.

    (2) על + מן   Lev 4.26; 5.6, 10; 14.19; 16.34; Num 6.11.

    (3) על + על   Lev 4.35; 5.13, 18.

  (b) כפר + בעד   Lev 9.7 (bis); 16.6, 11, 17b, 24; Ezek 45.17.

For the sake of convenience we discuss the above syntactic constructions in the order of IV, III and II.

Now when the translation 'atone for' or 'make atonement' is given to *kipper*, nearly all the prepositions in IV acquire the following meanings which have been widely accepted. על or בעד after כפר means 'for' or 'on behalf of'. מן or על after על (IV (2) (3)) refers to motives or reasons for atonement. ב (IV (1)) means 'by means of'.

However it is not clear how כפר על differs from כפר בעד. Milgrom has argued that 'the difference is that על can only refer to persons other than the subject, but when the subject wishes to refer to himself he must use בעד (e.g. Lev 9.7; 16.6, 11, 24; Ezek 45.22)',[7] adducing Job 42.8 as a confirmation.[8] Janowski[9] however demurs at his view on three grounds: a. Passages like Lev 9.7b; 16.17, 24 and Ezek 45.17, where Aaron (or הנשיא) makes atonement, refer to the atonement not only of himself but also of the whole people. b. In Job

42.8 כפר does not appear but התפלל. c. Milgrom's reference to Ezek
45.22 is misleading because it only speaks about the bringing of the
hattat and not about the נשיא making atonement. Janowski thus
concludes that the semantic difference between כפר על and כפר בעד
is not as great as Milgrom assumes.

It seems that Janowski's criticisms are by and large valid.[10]
However the above two arguments by Milgrom and Janowski appear
to be slightly confused by failing to make a distinction between the
two aspects of על and בעד: the meanings of כפר על and כפר בעד, and
their usage, i.e. in what contexts they appear. What Milgrom has
drawn attention to is essentially about the usage of כפר על and
כפר בעד, and not about the meanings of the independent על or בעד. In
this regard it cannot be denied, as Milgrom has observed, that, unlike
כפר על, כפר בעד appears in contexts where its subject is the object of
atonement, though atonement is made for the whole people as
well.

Another syntactic difference between the two phrases is that
כפר בעד is followed only by personal objects whereas כפר על has
personal objects and simultaneously allows the impersonal detail of
the rite (by מן, על and ב) to follow after it.

However the difference in usage between the two phrases is not
purely linguistic or syntactic. While כפר על appears in various
contexts (with subjects such as the priest, the high priest, the נשיא;
with objects such as Israel, its representative, individual), כפר בעד
appears only in the specific contexts where Aaron (or the נשיא) makes
atonement for himself and the whole people. Furthermore these
contexts are related to special occasions, such as the ordination of
Aaron (Lev 9.7), the atonement of Aaron and his house on the day of
Atonement (Lev 16.6, 11, 17b) and the atonement by the נשיא (Ezek
45.17). Although the occurrences of כפר בעד are limited, it could be
suggested that, unlike כפר על, כפר בעד expresses the personal effect
of the atonement made by Aaron and the נשיא upon himself and the
whole people.

Most problematic is the meaning of כפר על in III. Is the meaning
the same as that of כפר על in IV? Unlike על in IV various
interpretations have been proposed to 'כפר + על + sanctum'.

First of all, Milgrom argues that when *kipper* takes a non-human
object in the context of the *hattat*, על means literally 'on, over'.[11] It is
not clear why he has decided to make a distinction between human
and non-human objects. However, as long as the simple על can mean
'on, over', it would be fair to check how far the meaning suits *kipper*

in the *hattat* context. The meaning appears to suit the following passages: Exod 29.36, 37; 30.10ab; Lev 8.15; 16.18. But it seems problematic for Lev 16.16. The interpretation of this passage hinges on the relationship between v. 15 and v. 16. However, it is not correct to assume, as Milgrom does,[12] that the sprinkling of blood before and over the *kappōret* is the meaning of *kipper* in v. 16; for הקדש in v. 16 cannot be identified with the *kappōret*, though the latter is certainly part of the former. Since הקדש should be understood as referring to the entire adytum, it is reasonable to assume that v. 15 and v. 16 deal with two different matters from two different viewpoints. Another objection to the interpretation that על means 'on, over' is that it is not clear what the significance of '*kipper* on the adytum' is. It is still not clear if *kipper* is translated 'purge', as Milgrom suggests. Now it is certainly possible to argue that 'purging on the adytum' or the preposition על (= 'on') does not have to be given any special theological significance whatsoever. Nevertheless the interpretation of על as 'on, over' is not correct. Firstly, there appears a phrase כפר ב in vv. 17a, 27, the preposition of which is undoubtedly locative.[13] What is the difference, then, between '*kipper* on' and '*kipper* in'? Secondly, it would be unreasonable to assume that על means 'on, over', if the adytum (הקדש) were understood as room.[14]

Since 'on, over' is unlikely to be the meaning of על in this passage, it is also dubious whether the general distinction between human and non-human objects can be justified.[15]

In contrast with Milgrom, who translates the phrase כפר על 'purge on', Janowski translates it 'Sühne schaffen für'.[16] Nevertheless Janowski notes the strangeness of the notion that the priest makes atonement *for* sancta just as he does *for* persons.[17] Drawing on I. Benzinger's reference to the parallelism between כפר על and חטא על[18] Janowski calls attention to a close relationship between the blood manipulation and חטא/כפר in Ezek 43.20 (and 45.18b, 19), a passage which he assumes reflects the pre-priestly tradition. For him *kipper* and the synonymous חטא in Ezek 43.20b comprise the blood manipulation on (על) the four horns of the altar of burnt offering, on (אל) the four corners of the ledge and on (אל) the rim round about, all of which result in the atonement of the altar. Hence על in נתן על is the same as על in כפר על in P, meaning 'at, to', or simply expressing dative relation.[19]

Apart from Janowski's assumption that Ezek 43.20 reflects a pre-priestly tradition, the following criticisms may be lodged against his linguistic observations.

Firstly, על in נתן על can mean 'on, over' and not necessarily 'at, to'. Then Janowski's analogy between נתן על and כפר על leaves anyway some room for Milgrom's view that על in כפר על means 'on, over'. In short, Janowski is not consistent because he offers the translation 'Sühne schaffen für' for כפר על in one place, and 'Sühne schaffen zu' in another.

Secondly, the above analogy loses some of its force in view of the fact that Ezek 43.20 does not read כפר על like Exod 29.36 but וכפרתהו. Without the analogy it is questionable whether כפר על is the same in meaning as כפר את. On this point Janowski offers no comment.

In view of the above criticisms of Milgrom and Janowski the question inevitably arises: why should there be any necessity to preclude the notion that Aaron makes atonement *for* sancta? Undoubtedly behind the various proposals for giving a locative meaning to על there exists the presupposition that the *kipper* act by the priest or Aaron affects persons and not *inanimate* sancta. However can this presupposition be warranted? We present below some arguments against the presupposition.

1. The priestly writer(s) hardly distinguishes between human and non-human objects in the contexts of purification and sanctification. For instance, Aaron and the priests ought to be holy just like the altars (cp. Exod 29.33 with 29.37). Also not only Aaron and the priests but also their garments are said to become holy (Exod 29.21). Similarly, the ritual procedure for the leper (Lev 14.2ff.) resembles closely that for a house infected by disease (Lev 14.49ff.).[20] In view of the priestly writer's general view of uncleanness it seems artificial to make a semantic distinction between על in כפר + על + sanctum and על in כפר + על + person.

2. In response to Janowski's translation 'expiate for' for כפר על Milgrom has recently pointed out that not only does the translation imply personification of the sanctum, but it leads to the absurd idea that the sanctum is capable of sinning. Rather Milgrom assumes that '*kipper* is done directly to the sanctum' in contexts where sancta are *kipper*-ed, and translates 'purge on'.[21]

First of all, it must be argued that to translate the על 'for' does not personify the sanctum; 'for' simply refers to the 'beneficiary' of the atonement. The idea of personification may stem from a sharp distinction between human and non-human objects in atonement, coupled with the idea that the object in atonement or expiation must

be human. Thus we are not of the opinion that there is no distinction
between human and non-human objects. There is such a distinction.
Rather we are simply emphasizing that Aaron can make atonement
(or expiate) for sancta. On the other hand, Milgrom's translation
'purge' for *kipper* seems to be problematical as the following
observations show.

As already noted above, it is unlikely that על in Lev 16.16 means
'on, over', because הכפרת in vv. 14-15 cannot be identified with הקדש
in v. 16. The relationship between the two passages is rather as
follows: The sprinkling of blood on and before the *kappōret effects*
the atonement *for* the entire adytum. In other words, vv. 14-16 speak
of the relationship between the *kappōret* and the entire adytum. Now
it should be asked whether the sprinkling of blood on and before the
kappōret (vv. 14-15) can be the meaning of *kipper* in v. 16. The
answer is probably in the negative. Certainly the sprinkling of blood
constitutes an important part of the *kipper* rite. However the
sprinkling of blood, even if its symbolic meaning is taken into
consideration (presumably 'purification', see v. 19), is directed only
to the *kappōret*, whereas the verb *kipper*, whatever the exact meaning
is, deals with a triangular relationship between Aaron, the *kappōret*
and the entire adytum. Therefore it could be argued that the
meaning of *kipper* lies in a dimension different from the symbolic
meaning of the sprinkling of blood. Thus we tentatively infer that
'purge' is the symbolic meaning of the sprinkling of blood but not the
meaning of *kipper* in v. 16.

3. In the phrase כפר את[22] Milgrom seems to find one of the
strongest supports for his contention that '*kipper* is done directly to
the sanctum'[23] and that it means 'purge'. However if our above
argument is correct, it is unlikely that כפר את (Lev 16.20, 33; Ezek
43.20, 26; 45.20) means 'purge'. To discover its right meaning it
seems important to examine the usage of the phrase. Clearly את is
nota accusativi (cp. Ezek 43.20), and this indicates that *kipper* can be
either transitive or intransitive, according to the context.

The most remarkable feature of the phrase is that it is always
followed by sancta. The question is how the phrase is related to
another one כפר על. Lev 16.20a could be compared with Lev
16.16a.

v. 20a   ... וכלה מכפר את-הקדש ואת-אהל מועד ואת־המזבח
v. 16a   ... וכפר על-הקדש מטמאת

Why does *kipper* take על in one case and את in another? There is no obvious reason, except that כפר את is followed *only* by sancta (see III in the table above). But if, as suggested above, the sense of כפר על remains the same whether the phrase is followed by a sanctum or a person, it could be posited that the use of כפר על comprehends that of כפר את. This may be confirmed by Lev 16.33, where כפר את is conjoined by כפר על followed by persons.

v. 33   וכפר את-מקדש הקדש ואת-אהל מועד ואת המזבח
יכפר ועל הכהנים ועל-כל-עם הקהל יכפר

This verse suggests that כפר את excludes any reference to the atonement of persons.

Now one might be tempted to assume from this passage that the *kipper* of sancta leads to the *kipper* on behalf of the priests and the people. But if *kipper* has the same sense in the first and second halves of the passage, that assumption may be erroneous; the sancta *kipper* is somehow equivalent to, or parallel to, the *kipper* on behalf of the priests and the people. The same applies to the relationship between כפר על (Lev 16.16) and כפר בעד (v. 17). Then this same idea would militate against Milgrom's clear-cut distinction that purification is done to sancta and not to persons.

As to the meaning of *kipper*, we have disagreed with the translation 'purge'. Though this translation looks plausible in that כפר את appears along with חִטֵּא and טִהַר in Ezek 43.20, 26, as will be argued fully below these latter terms are neither synonymous with, nor parallel to, *kipper*.

We tentatively draw the following conclusions:

(a) כפר על means 'atone *for*' whether it is followed by a sanctum or a person.

(b) כפר את also means 'atone *for*'. את is required here, simply because it is followed only by sancta and not because *kipper* denotes 'purging'.

Thus the three major prepositions that *kipper* takes appear to have the following relations.

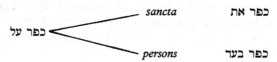

The above discussion of the *kipper* constructions also shows that essentially there exist two types of *hattat* ceremony behind the various constructions. One could be called 'the usual *kipper* rite' in which the priest (or Aaron) makes atonement for himself, the whole congregation, the leader and the individual (e.g. Lev 4). The other could be called 'the special *kipper* rite' in which Aaron (or Moses) makes atonement *for sancta* on special occasions such as the consecration days and the day of Atonement.[24] Each of these two types of ceremony also forms its text-group. The former includes Lev 4.1–5.13 and the relevant sections in Lev 12–15; the latter includes Exod 29; Lev 8–9 (10), 16. How these two types of ceremony or text-groups are related to each other will be discussed in Chapters 5 and 6, on the basis of our investigation in Chapter 3.

B. *The Concept of* kipper

Recent trends in the study of the cultic *kipper*[25] are largely characterized by two divergent approaches to the term. One seeks in *kipper* a concrete meaning such as 'cover', 'wipe off' or 'purge'.[26] The other assumes that the meaning of *kipper* lies in the result of all the priest's work.[27] This latter approach again divides into two views. One holds that since the priest's work consists mainly of the blood manipulation, כפר expresses the symbolic meaning of blood manipulation.[28] The other holds that the blood manipulation by itself does not possess expiatory force but the ritual as a whole does.[29] In addition to these there are a number of scholars who think the connection between כִּפֶּר and כֹּפֶר significant.[30]

However, what has been surprisingly inadequate in all these investigations seems to be the most fundamental inquiry into the alleged synonyms of *kipper* or terms related to it. Indeed it does seem that part of the reason for the existence of the divergent approaches to *kipper* lies in the inexactitude or insufficiency of that inquiry.

Although it is not our intention to determine the exact meaning of the cultic *kipper*, it nevertheless seems necessary to investigate the concept. This is partly because we have demurred at the translation 'purge', and partly because we have found, through the exegesis of Lev 10.17, that the concept of נשא עון is close to *kipper*. Thus even if the following discussion should fail to give a definitive translation for *kipper*, it may help to clarify the concept more fully than before.

After the investigation of the alleged synonyms of *kipper* we ask an additional question: how is *kipper* related to the different kinds of offerings?

1. Kipper *and its semantically related words*[31]

In some contexts *kipper* appears in relation to the following terms.

I	חָטָא -- כפר	Exod 29.36; Ezek 43.20; 45.18, 20
II	טָהֵר -- חָטָא -- כפר	Lev 14.49, 52-53
III	קָדֵשׁ -- כפר	Exod 29.33, 37; Num 6.11
IV	קָדֵשׁ -- טָהֵר -- כפר	Lev 16.18-19.
V	(a) טָהֵר -- כפר	Lev 16.30; Num 8.21; Ezek 43.26
	(b) טָהֵר -- כפר	Lev 12.7, 8; 14.20
V1	נִסְלַח -- כפר	Lev 4.20, 26, 31, 35; 5.13, 16, 18, 26; 19.22; Num 15.25, 26, 28
VII	קָדֵשׁ -- חָטָא -- כפר	Exod 29.36; Lev 8.15
VIII	נָשָׂא עָוֹן -- כפר	Lev 10.17
IX	נִרְצָה -- כפר	Lev 1.4[32]

From these related words it is clear that *kipper* is a positive term. Furthermore it may be observed that the positiveness lies in forming a link not only between the unclean/sinful and the clean/forgiven (II, V, VI) but also between the common and the holy (I(?), III, VII) and even between the unclean and the holy (IV).[33]

The most obvious question is what conceptual relationship exists between *kipper* and juxtaposed words such as חָטָא, טָהֵר and קָדֵשׁ. To answer this question we examine the following problematic passages: Exod 29.36-37; Lev 8.15; 16.14-19, 30; Ezek 43.20.

a. Exod 29.36-37

This passage is important because *kipper* appears to be related to חָטָא and קָדֵשׁ in some way.

v. 36 ... ופר חמאת תעשה ליום על הכפרים וחמאת על המזבח בכפרך
v. 37 ... שבעת ימים תכפר על המזבח וקדשת אתו

The problem in v. 36 is the meaning of threefold עַל. The first one means 'for' and the third, as already argued,[34] also means 'for'. So the problem is חָטָא עַל. Elsewhere חָטָא never takes עַל. In fact, חָטָא usually takes a direct object, and if not, as in Ezek 43.22, 23 the object is self-evident. In this regard חָטָא עַל in our passage appears unique. Now the term חָטָא itself can mean either 'de-sin, purify' or 'bring a *hattat* offering, perform the rite of the *hattat*'. However, the lack of a direct object and the presence of עַל הַמִּזְבֵּחַ suggest that the idea of 'purify/

de-sin the altar' is not the right one.[35] Rather another meaning of
חִטֵּא, 'offer a *hattat*', better suits the context. Then it would be
understandable that the omission of the direct object of חִטֵּא is caused
by the mention of פַּר חַטָּאת at the beginning of the passage. עַל could
be translated 'upon', by analogy with 2 Chron 29.24.

More important is the meaning of ב in בְּכַפֶּרְךָ. It is commonly
translated either 'when'[36] or 'in that'.[37] In view of the meaning of חִטֵּא
here, however, the latter seems unlikely. Thus בְּכַפֶּרְךָ means 'when
you make atonement for it (*sc.* the altar)'.

Since חִטֵּא means 'offer a *hattat* offering', nothing can be deduced
from this passage as to the conceptual relationship between *kipper*
and חִטֵּא (de-sin, purify). But it should be noted that in v. 37a the
consecration (קִדֵּשׁ) of the altar appears to be the purpose of the *kipper*
act.

b. Lev 8.15

Here again *kipper* appears to be related to חִטֵּא and קִדֵּשׁ.

> וישחט ויקח משה את-הדם ויתן על-קרנות המזבח סביב באצבעו ...
> ויחטא את-המזבח ואת הדם יצק אל-יסוד המזבח
> וַיְקַדְּשֵׁהוּ לכפר עליו

It is clear that the daubing the horns of the altar with blood, the
effect of which is described by חִטֵּא, leads to the consecration (קִדֵּשׁ) of
the altar. However the problem lies in the interpretation of ל in לכפר.
It has been understood as either 'in order to'[38] or 'by means of'[39].
However in that the purpose of the rite is in the consecration of the
altar, the former is incorrect. Here again it could be observed that
kipper is the act by means of which the unclean (or common)
becomes holy. This suggests that the concept of *kipper* overlaps with
that of חִטֵּא but is distinct from that of קִדֵּשׁ.

c. Lev 16.14–19

Enough has been said above regarding the relationship between
vv. 14–15 and v. 16. It has been argued that the symbolic meaning of
the blood manipulation in vv. 14–15 cannot be identified with the
meaning of *kipper*. So we comment here on the relationship between
v. 18 and v. 19.

> v. 18   ויצא אל-המזבח אשר לפני-ה' וכפר עליו ...
> v. 19   והזה עליו מן-הדם באצבעו שבע פעמים וְטִהֲרוֹ
> וְקִדְּשׁוֹ מטמאת בני ישראל

Unlike the majority of *kipper*-statements, vv. 18-19, which deal
with the atonement of the altar of burnt offering, begin with the
mention of *kipper* (v. 18) and then give the details of the rite (vv. 18b-
19). Undoubtedly, at least, the purification (טִהַר) and the consecration
(קִדֵּשׁ) of the altar form part of the concept of *kipper*. But it is arguable
whether the concept of 'קִדֵּשׁ + טִהַר' can be identified with that of
kipper. For one thing *kipper* here can be taken as a concept parallel to
'קִדֵּשׁ + טִהַר' and yet simultaneously referring to them. For another,
the ambiguity of the relationship between *kipper* and 'קִדֵּשׁ + טִהַר' is
created by the circumstance that the object (or beneficiary) of the
kipper act is the same as that of טִהַר and קִדֵּשׁ. If it may be assumed,
however, that vv. 18-19 form a chiasmus with vv. 14-16 in *kipper*-
statement and the mention of blood manipulation, *kipper* in v. 18
may well be different in concept from 'קִדֵּשׁ + טִהַר'.

d. Lev 16.30

כִּי-בַיּוֹם הַזֶּה יְכַפֵּר עֲלֵיכֶם לְטַהֵר אֶתְכֶם

The purpose of the *kipper*-act is to purify the people. Similar
constructions are found in Num 8.21 and Ezek 43.26.

e. Ezek 43.2

וְלָקְחוּ מִדָּמוֹ...וְחִטֵּאתָ אוֹתוֹ וְכִפַּרְתָּהוּ

As noted by Janowski[40], de-sinning (חִטֵּא) of the altar is achieved by
putting blood not only on its four horns but also on the four corners
of the ledge and the rim round about. The juxtaposition of חִטֵּא and
כפר tends to create the impression that the two are synonymous with
each other. But really the fact that the two terms are juxtaposed
indicates that they are not exact synonyms; חִטֵּא expresses the
symbolic meaning of the blood manipulation but *kipper* at least
appears to add some new semantic dimension to חִטֵּא.

The above survey of the words related to *kipper* leads to the following
conclusions.

1. *kipper* is a term, the semantic level of which should be
considered separately from those of טִהַר, קִדֵּשׁ and חִטֵּא. But it cannot
be gainsaid that those concepts of טִהַר, קִדֵּשׁ and חִטֵּא are included in
that of *kipper*. These two aspects indicate, then, that *kipper* is
supernym of טִהַר, קִדֵּשׁ and חִטֵּא.[41] In other words, *kipper* expresses
some act which enables progression from uncleanness to cleanness,

from cleanness to holiness and from uncleanness to holiness.

2. The effect of blood manipulation certainly constitutes the central part of the concept of *kipper*. But this effect should not be identified with the concept of *kipper*, at least in the context of the *hattat*. For as Lev 16.14-16 exemplifies, *kipper* deals with a triangular relationship, i.e. sancta–the priest–the beneficiary, whereas the blood manipulation by the priest is directed only to the sancta. In this case the blood manipulation is a part of the *kipper*-act and does not itself stand for the concept of *kipper*. This distinction is of importance in judging the cases in which the beneficiary of the *kipper*-act is the same as the object of purification, i.e. sancta, because in those cases one tends to identify the purifying act (חִטֵּא, קִדֵּשׁ, טִהַר) with the concept of *kipper*.

With the above conclusions in view we turn to the conceptual relationship between *kipper* and נשא עון, which we have noted in Lev 10.17.[42] In this passage not only is *kipper* juxtaposed to נשא עון but, according to our translation, it can be posited that the priest makes atonement for (כפר על) the congregation by bearing their guilt (נשא עון). Apart from the concepts of טִהַר, קִדֵּשׁ and חִטֵּא, which are essentially associated with 'purification', this phrase נשא עון appears to express another significant component of *kipper*. Three other instances, though not explicit, make it likely that the bearing of guilt is constitutive of the concept of *kipper*. Two instances may be found in Lev 5.1 and Lev 5.17. In Lev 5.1 the term אָשֵׁם does not appear. However if v. 1 is to be read consecutively with v. 5, it follows that נשא עונו in v. 1 corresponds to the ritual presumed in v. 6, since in v. 1 the envisaged אָשֵׁם must precede נשא עונו.[43] In vv. 17-18 it could be readily admitted that the bearing of guilt (v. 17) is done by means of the אשם offering. These obvious instances seem to have been neglected partly because the interpretation involves 'penal substitution' and partly because the meaning of נשא עונו has not been clearly defined. To these two instances we add a parallel between Num 8.19 and Num 18.22ff., which Milgrom has established.[44] Both sections speak of the function of the Levites, which is bearing the guilt of the Israelites (נשא עונם, Num 18.23aβ) or making atonement for them (לכפר על בני ישראל, Num 8.19aβ). Furthermore if אָשֵׁם in Lev 4.1–5.13 implies the existence of guilt, as we have assumed, then *kipper* in that section also seems to presuppose the notion of נשא עון.[45]

In view of the circumstance that the above instances come from variegated contexts it may safely be concluded that the cultic *kipper* has נשא עון as a semantic component.

However it appears difficult to determine from the instances adduced above whether נשא עון is synonymous with *kipper*. Yet the fact that the concept of *kipper* includes the notion of 'purification' expressed by טהר, קדּשׁ and חטּא, while the latter is clearly distinct from the notion of 'bearing guilt', suggests that *kipper* is also *supernym* of the concept of נשא עון.[46]

In short, *kipper* is *supernym* of טהר, קדּשׁ and חטּא on the one hand and נשא עון on the other.

נָשָׂא עָוֹן   חטּא, קדֵּשׁ, טהֵר

2. *Offerings related to kipper* [47]

In the above consideration of the concept of *kipper* we have tended to restrict the major data to *kipper* in the *hattat* context. However as the following list shows, *kipper* also appears in connection with other offerings, some of which are not bleeding.

I	חטאת (alone)	Exod 29.36; 30.10b; Lev 4.20, 26, 31, 35; 5.6, 13; 6.23; 8.15; 10.17; 16.6, 11, 16, 18; Num 15.28.
II	עולה + חטאת	Lev 5.10; 9.7; 12.7, 8; 15.15, 30; Num 6.11; 8.12.
III	שלמים + מנחה + עולה + חטאת	Lev 9.3-4 (see v. 7)
	אשם + מנחה + עולה + חטאת	Lev 14.18-20, 21-32; Num 15.25; Ezek 45. 17.
IV	עולה (alone)	Lev 1.4; 16.24.
V	אשם (alone)	Lev 5.16, 18, 26; 7.7; 19.22; Num 5.8.
VI	מלאים—offering	Exod 29.33; Lev 8.34.
VII	Blood or life (נפשׁ) in blood	Lev 17.11.
VIII	The Levites [48]	Num 8.19.
IX	The atoning money (כסף הכפרים)	Exod 30.15, 16.
X	Bird-rite	Lev 14.53.

Thus the following fundamental questions will immediately arise: (1) Is the subject of *kipper* significant for the concept of *kipper*? (2) How far is the concept of *kipper* contingent upon the kind(s) of offerings it is related to?

(1) As regards the subject of *kipper* Janowski asserts that except in Lev 1.4; 17.11b; Num 8.19 and Ezek 45.15, 17 the agent of *kipper*

acts is always the priest.[49] Although in the *hattat* contexts the priest (or Aaron) is nearly always the agent of *kipper* and the *hattat* is the means of the *kipper* act, this assertion by Janowski seems to lack exactness. For the logical subject of *kipper* appears to be indefinite in passages like Lev 6.23; 8.34; 14.21; 16.27, 30; 17.11aγ (?); Num 28.22, 30; 29.5. This is because in these passages the author is concerned not about the agent of the *kipper* act, but simply about the final purpose of the atonement. But it seems to go beyond the grammar and the intention of the relevant passages to assume that the agent of the *kipper* act is the priest.

Now in IV, VII, VIII, IX above, blood, an עולה, the Levites and the atoning money are the agents of the *kipper* act. Clearly in these instances *kipper* appears on a dimension different from the *hattat* context in which the priest is the agent of the *kipper* act. However we see no reason to suppose that whether the object of *kipper* is indefinite, or things or persons other than the priests, the concept of *kipper* changes.

(2) A more important question is whether the concept of *kipper* depends on the kind(s) of offering that *kipper* is related to. Milgrom holds that *kipper* in the context of the *hattat* should be translated 'purge', but that in the contexts of the עולה, מנחה and אשם 'expiate'.[50] This distinction is partly supported by the difference in the mode of blood manipulation that in the *hattat* there appear the sprinkling, the daubing and the pouring of blood, whereas in the other offerings only the pouring of blood around the altar appears. Further Milgrom assumes that the latter evolved from the former.[51]

This classification of the meaning of *kipper* involves serious difficulties. Firstly, this division between *kipper* in the *hattat* and *kipper* in the other offerings is based on blood manipulation, which, as we have argued above, is not central to the term *kipper*. Such a division is particularly difficult when *kipper* is applied to a combination of offerings such as *hattat* + עולה. Moreover even the bloodless *hattat* exists in Lev 5.11. Does the meaning of *kipper* in Lev 5.13 differ from that in Lev 5.10? Secondly, the translation 'purge' does not appear to fit in with *kipper* in the *hattat* context, as it has also been argued above. 'Purge' is rather the meaning of חִטֵּא. Moreover, the inadequacy of the translation 'purge' seems apparent when it is observed that in the *hattat* context *kipper* is also related to the burning of fat. Though important, blood manipulation is part of the whole *kipper* ritual. Indeed there are some cases in which the *kipper* act consists only of blood manipulation. Then the question would be whether the symbolic meaning of 'blood manipulation' means something different from 'blood manipulation + burning of fat', over against the concept of *kipper*.

We thus conclude from the above considerations (1) and (2) that arbitrariness tends to emerge when an attempt is made to classify the meaning of cultic *kipper* either on the basis of the subject of *kipper*, the names of offerings, or individual elements within the rite. Rather the concept of *kipper* is related directly to 'uncleanness' or 'sins'. Therefore we venture to assume the existence of the homogeneous concept of cultic *kipper* which probably consists of the two main elements, purification and bearing guilt.[52]

One may wonder why there are different sacrifices. This is a question with very wide ramifications which cannot be explored here. But as far as *kipper* is concerned, it may be pointed out that not all sacrifices are related to *kipper*, and that each animal sacrifice has its own emphasis on expiation; the *hattat* maximal, the שלמים minimal (see below).

C. *Lev 17.11*

Finally we come to discuss Lev 17.11 and the light it sheds on the concept of *kipper*.

כִּי נֶפֶשׁ הַבָּשָׂר בַּדָּם הִוא	v. 11aα
וַאֲנִי נְתַתִּיו לָכֶם עַל הַמִּזְבֵּחַ לְכַפֵּר עַל-נַפְשֹׁתֵיכֶם	v. 11aβγ
כִּי הַדָּם הוּא בַּנֶּפֶשׁ יְכַפֵּר	v. 11b

This passage has been traditionally regarded as the sole passage which provides the rationale of blood manipulation in all the animal sacrifices. If the passage may be applied so generally, it must also apply to the *hattat* blood. However, this traditional view has been recently challenged by J. Milgrom on contextual grounds (see below), and it needs to be reconsidered.

The passage also raises crucially important philological-theological issues; not only does it explicitly discuss the concept of *kipper*, which appears twice and is the focus of our interest at the moment, it also poses the question whether 'substitution' is implied in sacrificial ritual.

These issues will be discussed below under the headings (1) Context of Lev 17.11, (2) Exegesis of Lev 17.11, (3) The Etymology of *kipper*, (4) Substitution in Lev 17.11.

1. *Context of Lev 17.11*

The passage is a motive clause to v. 10, which prohibits the consumption of blood by the Israelites and the resident alien. As mentioned above, v. 11 has been traditionally taken as speaking of all the animal sacrifices. However, Milgrom[53] has levelled an incisive criticism by pointing out that v. 10 concerns only the danger of partaking of blood while eating meat, the possibility of which exists only in the case of the שלמים. But according to Milgrom the שלמים does not possess *kipper* function, whereas the phrase לכפר על-נפשתיכם (by analogy with Exod 30.12ff. and Num 31.49) implies a capital offence against God. To the question why 'the danger of death' is envisaged in v. 11 Milgrom finds a clue in vv. 3-4, which declare that 'animal slaughter constitutes murder except at the authorized altar',[54] and he links these verses with v. 11. Thus he concludes: 'the blood must be brought to the altar to expiate for the murder of the animal because "the life of the flesh is the blood ... for it is the blood, as life, that expiates"'.[55] As for the non-expiatory nature of the שלמים Milgrom suggests that 'Lev 17.11 may fit into an altogether different priestly theology'.[56]

Milgrom's argument from the context of Lev 17.11, however, seems unlikely, for the following reasons.[57]

a. Milgrom may be correct in arguing that v. 10 concerns the consumption of blood in connection with the שלמים. But this does not warrant the conclusion that the context of v. 11 should be related only to the שלמים; for v. 11, being a motive clause,[58] may well speak of a general principle underlying the prohibition of blood consumption. And indeed all three parts of v. 11 are couched in highly general language. It seems then that 'the blood' in v. 11 could apply to the blood of all sacrifices. Nevertheless it must be admitted that if this is so, even the blood of the שלמים possesses *kipper* function. But this faces the objection that as Milgrom argues,[59] the שלמים is unlikely to be associated with *kipper*, even in Ezek 45.15, 17.

b. It is arbitrary and forced to link vv. 3-4 with v. 11 in the way that Milgrom does. It is true that slaughtering the animal except at the altar is regarded as murder (v. 4). But the *karet*-penalty is meted out for it. Similarly the consumption of blood is also punished by the *karet*-penalty (v. 10). However, no remedy for these sins is mentioned in Lev 17; v. 11 simply gives the reason why blood should not be consumed. This highlights the fundamental problem with Milgrom's view: if the offerer brought a sacrificial animal to the sanctuary and slaughtered it, this act would constitute a totally *legitimate* act. It is

not a sin; he has not committed a murder. In other words, vv. 3-4 do
not imply any capital offence to be expiated, and there is no reason to
mention the fact that the blood may not be consumed. On the other
hand, if the offerer killed his animal outside the sanctuary this
passage offers no ritual remedy. In either case the comment in Lev
17.11 is irrelevant on Milgrom's interpretation.[60]

c. That לכפר על-נפשתיכם in v. 11aγ implies a capital offence is
deduced partly by the meaning of the independent word נפש and
partly by analogy with Exod 30.11-16 and Num 31.48ff. But it is
methodologically incorrect to infer from the identical phrase
כפר על-נפשתיכם that Lev 17.11 and Exod 30.11-16 both deal with
similar capital offences. It is one thing to argue that *kipper* has the
same sense in both sections, but quite another to argue that the
extra-linguistic situation of כפר על נפשתיכם is also alike or identical
in both sections.[61] As for the latter there is no support in the context
of Lev 17.

Thus, since Lev 17.11 does not refer to the expiation of a murder
but is a general statement, it seems reasonable to assume that it
speaks of the blood of all animal sacrifices; this is the traditional
understanding. The merit of Milgrom's criticism lies, however, in his
pointing out the apparently weak point in the traditional view, that
the שלמים has hardly any expiatory function, yet it seems to be
included in Lev 17.11.

Recently Rodriguez has criticized the alleged non-expiatory
character of the שלמים, adducing Ezek 45.15, 17, in which *kipper* can
comprehend the שלמים.[62] However, as Rodriguez himself admits,[63] it
is a fact that this sacrifice is least associated with *kipper*, and thus
with the notion of expiation. Nevertheless it must be argued that the
non-expiatory character of the שלמים does not necessarily lead to the
conclusion that the *blood* in it is also non-expiatory. It may well be
that since the *major* function of the שלמים does not lie in expiation,
the sacrifice is not normally linked with *kipper*; but it is an entirely
different matter to draw the conclusion from this fact that the blood
of the שלמים has no expiatory function, either. We therefore prefer the
view of Kurtz:

> If the sprinkling of blood in connection with the burnt-offering and
> trespass offering served as an atonement (לְכַפֵּר עָלָיו), the sprinkling
> of blood of the peace-offering, which was performed in precisely
> the same way, must necessarily have had the same significance.[64]

2. *Exegesis of Lev 17.11*

Having established that Lev 17.11 may be referring to the function of
blood manipulation in any sacrifice, we shall now seek by careful
exegesis to determine precisely what it says about the role of blood in
sacrifice.

The following discussion on this passage consists of (a) a
grammatical-syntactic overview of the passage and (b) defining the
meaning of ב in בנפש.

a. Grammatical-syntactic overview

The passage as a whole appears to consist of two motive clauses
introduced by כי. The first כי introduces the reason why the
consumption of blood is prohibited: because 'the life of flesh is in the
blood and it is I who have assigned it[65] to you upon the altar to make
atonement for your lives'. It appears that נפש הבשר בדם הוא presents
a theological postulate, and that the chief reason for the injunction in
v. 10 is in ואני ff.; because blood is the divinely appointed means of
atonement.[66]

As for v. 11b, it is clearly not a simple repetition of v. 11a, judging
from the change from לכפר עַל-נפשתיכם to בנפש יכפר.[67] Thus the
question arises: what in v. 11a does v. 11b explain? Ultimately this
question cannot be answered without determining the meaning of
בנפש in v. 11b. However there is one preliminary question to be
addressed before we answer the question. Who is the agent of לכפר in
the phrase לכפר על-נפשתיכם 'to make atonement for your lives'?[68]
There are four possibilities: (1) God, (2) blood, (3) the Israelites, (4)
'indefinite'.

(1) Since God is the one who assigned the blood upon the altar it is
conceivable that he is also the agent of לכפר. However, although this
is certainly true theologically, it is questionable whether it is correct
syntactically. For the emphasis of 'I'[69] appears to fall on נתתיו and
does not necessarily appear to govern לכפר. It therefore seems
unlikely that God is the subject of לכפר. (2) Could 'blood' be the
subject of לכפר?[70] Yes, it could. However this does create redundancy
between v. 11a and v. 11b, both of which emphasize then that the
blood יכפר. A different subject in לכפר could avoid such redundancy.
(3) 'The Israelites' could be the agent of לכפר, at least grammatically.
But theologically that is highly unlikely; for the idea that the
Israelites can atone for themselves contradicts not only priestly
theology in general but v. 11b. (4) The agent of לכפר could be
indefinite. And this possibility commends itself most. Firstly,

because v. 11aβγ is then naturally followed by v. 11b, which emphasizes the blood as the agent of לכפר[71] and secondly, because the blood manipulation is normally performed by priests. In other words, as observed above,[72] it is unnecessary to identify the agent of לכפר here, because the phrase simply serves to express the purpose.

Then what does v. 11b explain, v. 11aα or 11aβγ, or both? It seems to be related to both, in the light of the following two observations. Firstly, *kipper* appears both in v. 11aβγ (לכפר) and v. 11b (יכפר). As mentioned above, the relationship between v. 11aβγ and v. 11b can be taken in such a way that the indefinite subject of לכפר in v. 11aβγ is clarified by the emphatic יכפר . . . כי הדם הוא in v. 11b. Secondly, as Janowski has noted,[73] there is a chiasmus of נפש and דם between v. 11aα and v. 11b:

$$\text{v. 11aα} \qquad \text{כי נפש הבשר בדם הוא}$$
$$\text{v. 11b} \qquad \text{כי הדם הוא בנפש יכפר}$$

This chiasmus shows that though v. 11b explains v. 11aβγ, it is based on v. 11aα in some way. To be more specific about this, the phrase בנפש must be clarified.

b. בנפש

With regard to the meaning of ב, three kinds of interpretation have been proposed.

Firstly, ב can be a *beth instrumenti* in conformity with the phrase כפר ב in other contexts (e.g. Lev 5.16). According to this view the actual means of atonement is 'life' contained in the blood.[74]

Secondly, ב can be a *beth essentiae*: 'For it is the blood, as life, that expiates'.[75]

Thirdly, ב can be a *beth pretii* expressing the notion of 'price'. Some translate it 'for, at the cost of',[76] others 'in exchange of'.[77] In either case הנפש in בנפש is taken to refer to human life unlike the above two views, which suppose it refers to the animal's life.[78]

As Rodriguez and Janowski[79] have pointed out, the *beth essentiae* is most unlikely because v. 11b is not a simple repetition of v. 11aα. Either *beth instrumenti* or *beth pretii* would be appropriate. Yet the decision also depends on the question whether הנפש refers to animal life or human life; if it refers to human life, then ב would inevitably be a *beth pretii*.

Following Levine, Rodriguez,[80] who takes ב to be a *beth pretii* and הנפש to refer to human life, argues that if ב were a *beth instrumenti*, the text would have read בנפשו instead of בנפש. However, in view of

v. 11aα, which does not read נפש הבשר בְּדָמוֹ הוא (cp. v. 14) Rodriguez's argument seems to be inconclusive.

Brichto argues that חנפש cannot refer to human life, on the ground that the redemption of human life is already mentioned in לכפר על נפשתיכם (v. 11aγ), 'for/on behalf of your lives'.[81] This criticism, though pungent, overlooks three crucial points. First, the notion of 'for/on behalf of' is different from that of 'for/at (the cost of), in exchange of'. Second, as argued above, the agent of לכפר is not 'blood' but indefinite. Third, it is not explicitly stated in v. 11aβγ what actually takes place on the altar in order to make atonement for the Israelites, except that God assigned the animal blood on the altar. In other words, v. 11aβγ (ואני ff.) speaks generally of the God–blood–altar–Israelites relationship, whereas v. 11b specifies what takes place on the altar. In view of these considerations the *beth pretii* approach appears still possible.

However the *beth pretii* approach is unlikely for the following reason. As mentioned above there is a chiasmus of נפש and דם between v. 11aα and v. 11b, while it is natural to take the article in בנפש as referring to a thing already mentioned before. And this consideration seems to be conclusive as to בנפש. It then follows that בנפש refers to animal life mentioned in v. 11aα, and that the ב is a *beth instrumenti*.

Having excluded the *beth pretii* approach, however, we need to consider exactly how ב should be translated: 'by' or 'through'? As argued above, v. 11b emphasizes the subject of יכפר, the blood.[82] Then to translate ב with 'by' appears to conflict with the very intention of v. 11b since, according to this translation, the virtual means of atonement is 'life', not 'blood'. Since in v. 11aα 'life' is said to be indissolubly united with the 'blood', the translation 'through' seems better.

To sum up, the relationships between v. 11b and v. 11aα on the one hand, and between v. 11b and v. 11aβγ on the other are as follows: Assuming the statement in v. 11aα, v. 11b explains what takes place on the altar, which is unspecified in v. 11aβγ. This relationship between v. 11aβγ and v. 11b implies clearly the substitution of human נפש (v. 11aαγ) by animal נפש (v. 11b), whatever the exact meaning of *kipper* in this passage.

3. The Etymology of kipper
Confirmation of this interpretation of *kipper* is provided by the most likely etymology of the term.

That *kipper* is probably related to the *qal* noun כֹּפֶר has been well argued by Milgrom.[83] According to him, this applies to *kipper* in Lev 17.11 as well as 'the Kippûr function of the Levites (Num 8.19; 18.22ff.) and the kippûr death for homicide and idolatry (Num 35.33, 25.4, 11, 13)'.[84]

It seems that this כֹּפֶר-character matches our interpretation of Lev 17.11; animal blood serves as a כֹּפֶר of human life. Milgrom himself does not, however, apply this כֹּפֶר—*kipper* connection to other *kipper*-passages particularly in the *hattat* context. But if, as we have argued, Lev 17.11 has in mind all the blood sacrifices, this *kipper*-character may well be assumed in the *kipper* of normal sacrificial contexts. In fact we have argued independently of Lev 17.11 that *kipper* in the *hattat* context includes the concept of נשא עון. Since כֹּפֶר substitutes for the death penalty, it clearly has conceptual affinity with נשא עון (= bear guilt). However, one might argue that *kipper* or נשא עון in the contexts of Num 8.19; 18.22ff.; 25.13, 35.33 appears on a dimension different from that of sacrifice proper. This is true, but nevertheless, as we have argued in B above, the concept or the sense of *kipper*, and not its extra-linguistic situation, can be invariable, especially in view of the fact that *kipper* is related to נשא עון in some sacrifical contexts. Therefore it seems highly plausible to assume that *kipper* is related to נשא עון on a substitutionary level, and that *kipper* in sacrificial law has also כֹּפֶר-character.

4. *Substitution in Lev 17.11*

The above interpretation of v. 11 supports the view that the principle of substitution is at work on the altar: animal life takes the place of human life. However, this statement must face two other different approaches.

Firstly, based on contexts like Exod 21.23; Lev 24.18; Num 17.3; Deut 19.21 and Exod 30.12, 16 Milgrom has inferred that נפש in Lev 17.11 connotes a capital crime, thus 'life in jeopardy', and that the passage does not deal with the expiation of 'ordinary sin'.[85] It has been argued, however, that the passage does deal with the expiation of 'ordinary sin'. The question which this raises is whether it is right to assume that the sinner in Lev 4–5 is not in the state of 'life in jeopardy'. However it seems arbitrary to hold that the sin in Exod 30.12ff. puts a person's life in jeopardy whereas the sin in Lev 4–5 does not.

Secondly, those uncomfortable with the principle of substitution[86] have argued that the sacrificial system does not deal with 'the sin worthy of death'. In response to this, proponents of 'substitution' have emphasized the serious nature of what Milgrom calls 'ordinary sin'. Thus Rodriguez has pointed out that the sin related to the *hattat* is not limited to inadvertent sin,[87] while Kurtz assumed that even a trivial sin deserves the death penalty.[88]

However, apart from the question of 'substitution', the term 'the death penalty' seems to be misleading. For one thing, since the phrase מות יומת or the *karet*-penalty is not found in Lev 4–5 this suggests that these sins do not deserve the death *penalty*. For another, as Milgrom points out,[89] it is unintelligible to assume that the parturient deserves the death penalty. Thus it seems better to avoid using 'the death penalty' in discussing sacrificial expiation. We use the term 'death' instead.

Now in the above discussion about the 'substitution' there is erroneous reasoning shared by both proponents and opponents of 'substitution'. It is shown below along with what we think is the correct reasoning.

Sin/Uncleanness ⟶ Death   Sacrifice ⟶ Life

Sin/Uncleanness ⟶ Sacrifice   Death

The former envisages that the death of a sinner is the result of sin/uncleanness, but that the sacrifice reverses this situation. The latter assumes that the ultimate end of sin/uncleanness is indeed death (see Lev 15.31), but that the connection is dissolved by a sacrifice. Although both approaches assume the connection between sin/uncleanness and death, the latter picture seems to do more justice to the idea of expiation than the former. But this still allows for the idea of substitution, for the following reasons.

As has been shown in Chapter 2, uncleanness, which symbolizes death or the aura of death, is ascribed not only to corpses or carcasses but to things and persons which have contact with them. The same is true for an inadvertent sin. Though it does not deserve the death penalty, the sinner is regarded as being in the realm of death.

It would, however, be artificial to argue from this that the *hattat* deals with the *aura* of death and not death, because if nothing is done to uncleanness or sin that will lead to a person's death. So it could be posited that a sacrifice indeed saves the life of a sinner or an unclean person, and that the exchange of נפש in Lev 17.11b should be understood in this sense.

Lastly, though נפש in Lev 17.11aα, b means 'life-essence', it would be reasonable to assume that this 'life' actually means 'life given up in death'.[90] For one thing, it is easily conceivable because the animal is slaughtered in the sanctuary. For another, as has been argued, the term *kipper* itself connotes substitutionary death.

Since the blood symbolizes 'life', it may be assumed in connection with the *hattat* that the purifying process expressed by such terms as טִהַר and קָדֵשׁ are in fact 'life-giving' processes. Yet it must be borne in mind that the agent of purification or atonement in the *hattat* context is almost always the priest, and that the priest bears guilt when he purifies sancta. In view of this fact it could be posited that 'substitution' is envisaged on two levels, the blood and the priests.

Conclusions

The following conclusions can be drawn from the discussion of this Chapter.

1. The discussion on the three prepositions עַל, אֶת and בְּעַד after *kipper* has led to the inference that their use is differentiated by whether the beneficiary of the *kipper* act is sancta or persons; עַל can be follwed by both, whereas אֶת is followed exclusively by sancta and בְּעַד by persons.

2. The examination of various alleged synonyms of *kipper* such as טִהַר, קָדֵשׁ and חִטֵּא has shown that those terms should be called *hyponyms* of *kipper*. In the light of this conclusion another semantic component, נָשָׂא עָוֹן, could also be a *hyponym* of *kipper*. In terms of what is happening on the altar, all these terminological relations suggest that the priest cleanses the altar but simultaneously bears guilt. Since the cleansing act is the 'life-giving' process (Lev 17.11), it could be envisaged that the priest gives 'life' to the sancta (= purifies them) but simultaneously bears death on a substitutionary level. This means that comparing the *hattat* blood to a detergent is inadequate.

3. Lev 17.11 concerns all kinds of blood sacrifices. It involves two major theological postulates. First, animal blood substitutes for human life on the altar (v. 11aβγ-b). Second, that substitution was instituted by God himself (v. 11aβγ). It seems, then, that our vague observation, made in Chapters 1 and 2, that the *hattat* deals with both uncleanness and guilt is confirmed by the conclusion of our study of *kipper*, that when the priest purifies sancta he bears the guilt associated with uncleanness.

Chapter 5

SOME COMPONENTS OF THE *HATTAT* RITUAL

Introduction

In the previous Chapter we concluded that when the priest purifies sancta he bears the guilt associated with uncleanness, and that Lev 17.11 implies the principle of 'substitution'. With these conclusions we consider further some components of the *hattat* ritual. Although ideally the meaning of all the components of the *hattat* ritual should be discussed, that does not seem particularly constructive, for two reasons. First, it is likely to go beyond the scope of our investigation, because the ritual acts of slaughtering, burning of fat and so on are common to the עולה and שלמים offerings.[1] Second, the distinctive nature of the *hattat* ritual seems to lie in rites such as the blood manipulation and the burning (eating) of the *hattat* flesh. Therefore we shall concentrate our discussion on the three major ritual acts which seem to be directly relevant to the function of the *hattat*, or at least to which special attention has been paid in the study of the *hattat*. They are the imposition of hand(s), the blood manipulation and the disposal of the *hattat* flesh.

In the *hattat* ritual the imposition of hand(s) usually comes between the bringing of the *hattat* to the entrance of the Tent and the slaughtering of it. Although this rite is common to the עולה (Lev 1.4) and the שלמים (Lev 3.2, 8, 13), it needs to be discussed, not because we assume that it is related to the essential function of the *hattat*,[2] but mainly because there has been a debate whether the transference of sin (guilt) is envisaged in that act. This question is, as will be shown, central to the function of the *hattat* even apart from the meaning of the imposition of hand(s), though it will not be answered definitively until the disposal of the *hattat* is discussed. Thus the imposition of hand(s) is studied not so much to determine the meaning of the rite as to introduce some theological issues which have been raised in connection with the gesture.

The *hattat* ritual includes the distinctive blood manipulation, the daubing (נתן) and the sprinkling (הזה) of blood. Although these undoubtedly symbolize purification of sancta, they not only raise the question whether the distinction of the two rites is significant, but they are also related to the problem of the *hattat* symbolism; i.e. how the ritual in Lev 4.1-5.13 is related to the one in Lev 8-9.

Lastly, the *hattat* ritual ends with the disposal of the *hattat* flesh, either by a priest eating it in a holy place within the sanctuary or by burning it outside the camp. In pursuing the symbolic meaning of each act, the 'contagiousness of the *hattat* flesh' will be the focus of the discussion, i.e. whether the *hattat* flesh conveys uncleanness or holiness. So the problem of 'transference of sin' introduced in connection with the imposition of hand(s) will, it is hoped, be settled at this point.

A. *The Imposition of Hand(s)*

The idiomatic expression for the imposition of hand(s), ידים / יד + סמך + על, is attested in the following contexts.[3]

Sacrifices		
	עולה	Exod 29.15; Lev 1.4; 8.18
	שלמים	Lev 3.2, 8, 13
	חטאת	Exod 29.10; Lev 4.4, 15, 24, 29, 33; 8.14 (2 Chron 29.33)
	איל המלאים	Exod 29.19; Lev 8.22
	עולה + חטאת	Num 8.12
The Azazel rite		Lev 16.21
The case of blasphemy		Lev 24.14
Dedication of the Levites		Num 8.10
Appointment of Joshua		Num 27.18, 23; Deut 34.9

In sacrificial contexts, with which our chief concern lies,[4] the imposition of hand(s) is performed by the offerer or the beneficiary of atonement. Hence it appears natural to assume that the gesture expresses some relationship between the offerer and the sacrificial animal. However despite abundant works on this gesture,[5] there seems to be as yet no scholarly consensus over its symbolic meaning. The investigation seems to have been hampered by the fact that no sacrificial text provides the key to the symbolic meaning of the gesture except Lev 1.4 (the עולה) and the problematical Lev 16.21 (the Azazel-goat ritual). Moreover, while Lev 1.4 appears to allow several interpretations of the gesture, Lev 16.21, which apparently refers to the meaning of the rite, has often been held as irrelevant to the imposition of hand(s) in sacrificial contexts. Recently R. Péter has added another dimension to the issue by arguing that the imposition of *one* hand is limited to sacrificial contexts, expressing 'identification of the offerer with the animal', whereas the imposition of *both* hands appears in non-sacrificial contexts (Lev 16.21; 24.14; Num 8.10 (?); 27.18 (LXX), 23; Deut 34.9), expressing the notion of transference.[6]

In view of this situation we first respond to Péter's thesis and then turn to the central issues surrounding Lev 16.21 and Lev 1.4.

Péter's distinction between the imposition of one hand and that of both hands is possible and may be significant. But whether that distinction corresponds to a distinction in the symbolic meaning of the gesture is another question; the difference in form as such does not necessarily imply a difference in the meaning of the gesture. In fact, the imposition of both hands in Lev 16.21 may simply solemnize the rite.[7]

The whole issue centres, however, on the question whether the meaning of the imposition of hands on the Azazel goat in Lev 16.21 can be applied to usual sacrificial contexts, though it is unanimously agreed that the passage speaks of 'transference of guilt'.

For the ancient Jewish exegesis the meaning of the imposition of hands in Lev 16.21, i.e. transference of sin, was the model on which other cases of the rite in sacrificial contexts should be construed.[8] This view, that by laying on his hand the offerer transfers his sins to the animal, still finds its proponents today.[9] But the view has been rejected by the majority of modern exegetes on (a) contextual and (b) conceptual grounds.

a. For instance, Janowski argues that Lev 16.21 must be excluded from the consideration of the meaning of the laying on of one hand in sacrificial contexts because the three elements which characterize the Azazel rite, (1) imposition of *both* hands on the head of the goat (2) transference of *materia peccans* to the evil bearer (3) sending off of the goat to the wilderness, are missing in sacrificial contexts. Above all he emphasizes that the Azazel goat is not a sacrifice.[10]

It is questionable, however, whether these points constitute a reason why Lev 16.21 should be excluded from the consideration of the imposition of a hand in sacrificial contexts. Firstly, as argued above, the imposition of both hands in Lev 16.21, as opposed to that of one hand, does not itself seem to prove anything. Secondly, the meaning of the imposition of both hands in Lev 16.21, i.e. unloading the guilt, should not be combined with the other features of the Azazel rite, such as sending off the goat to the wilderness, so as to invalidate the possibility that the imposition of a hand in sacrificial contexts expresses 'transference of sin'. To stress the special nature of the rite as a whole is one thing, but it is quite another to argue from that that the symbolic meaning of the imposition of hands in Lev 16.21 has nothing to do with its meaning in sacrificial contexts. Thirdly, Janowski presumes that in sacrificial contexts there occurs no 'elimination of *materia peccans*'. This may be true. But the fact is simply that no explicit mention is made concerning the meaning of the imposition of a hand except in Lev 1.4b. It is fairer, then, to say that 'the elimination of *materia peccans*' may or may not be present in sacrificial contexts. Lastly, the ritual in Lev 16.21ff. is treated by Janowski[11] and others as an isolated ritual having no meaningful relationship with the surrounding text. This issue will be discussed in the next chapter and Janowski's assumption will be challenged.

In short, the reasons Janowski has given for isolating Lev 16.21 in the consideration of the imposition of hand(s) are not sufficient to invalidate the application of the meaning of the imposition of hands in Lev 16.21 to sacrificial contexts.

b. As the above arguments show, there have been two divergent approaches to the meaning of the imposition of hand(s). One stream of interpretation, relying heavily on Lev 16.21, holds that the sacrificial animal becomes sinful or unclean by the imposition of hands.[12] The other, rejecting Lev 16.21 and the idea of 'transference of sin', seeks in Lev 1.4 the meaning of the imposition of a hand in sacrificial contexts.[13] We shall examine the former standpoint first and then the latter.

The former approach, which assumes 'transference of sin', was criticized by J.C. Matthes who marshalled the following arguments:[14]

1. The *hattat* blood purifies; but that is unlikely if the animal is laden with sin and guilt.
2. In Lev 10.17 the *hattat* flesh is called קדש קדשים.
3. The fact that the burning of the *hattat* flesh is done in a clean place (Lev 4.12) also indicates that the *hattat* is pure.
4. The contagion of the *hattat* in Lev 6.20ff. and Lev 16.24, 28 is that of holiness and should be distinguished from the defilement of a man who sends off the Azazel goat (Lev 16.26).

As these arguments by Matthes show, the meaning of the imposition of a hand in the *hattat* context ultimately hinges on the status of the *hattat* from the stage of blood manipulation to that of the disposal of the *hattat* flesh. Later we shall discuss in detail the disposal of the *hattat* (the above points 3 and 4). At this stage we question whether reasoning 1 is appropriate.

The fundamental fact is that sacrificial death on the altar is not regarded as defiling (Lev 17.11); it is rather 'life' taking the place of the death of the sinner, though the death of an animal outside the sanctuary may defile (e.g. Lev 11.39ff.). Therefore it seems wrong to assume that the *hattat* becomes sinful or unclean in the wake of the imposition of a hand.[15]

However, Rodriguez has recently argued that it is logically one-sided to hold that because the sacrifice is called קדש קדשים the transference of sin could not possibly have taken place.[16] Pointing out that in Lev 10.17 the *hattat* flesh is assumed to have borne sin but simultaneously is termed קדש קדשים, Rodriguez concludes that 'the sin that was borne by the animal, and later by the priest, did not affect their holiness'.[17] This view could be characterized as one allowing for the coexistence in the *hattat* of holiness, the function of bearing guilt and the transference of sin.

In our opinion, this view is worthy of note, though it seems to involve some misleading assumptions.

The view is valuable in that it does not see a contradiction in the sacrifice's being holy and simultaneously related to sin/guilt. This is also true for Lev 4.1–5.13 in which the *hattat* has undoubtedly something to do with the sin.

However, Rodriguez's assumption that the *hattat* bears the sin is doubly problematical. First, although it may be naturally envisaged that the *hattat* has something to do with the guilt, it is the priests who bear it, and not the *hattat*. Second, what is borne by the priests is, on our interpretation of Lev 10.17 and Lev 4.1–5.13, 'guilt' and not 'sin'.[18] It may be pointed out that generally the confusion of terms such as 'sin', 'guilt' and 'uncleanness' has obscured the whole issue of 'transference of sin/guilt'.

Now we have already argued that in the context of Lev 4.1–5.13 the *hattat* deals with both the act of *sin* and its consequence.[19] If we are to follow the priestly terminology rigorously, we cannot apply directly the meaning of the imposition of hands in Lev 16.21 to the usual *hattat* context, because if the notion of 'transference' is assumed, what is transferred in Lev 16.21 (= MT עונת) is different from what the *hattat* deals with (= the act of sin and its consequence), as the following table shows.

Usual *hattat* ritual	The Azazel rite
The *hattat* animal has to do with the act of sin and its consequence (Purification of sancta follows)	(Purification of sancta is over)
The priest *bears the guilt*.	The Azazel goat *bears the guilt*.

It is striking that the priest's bearing the guilt corresponds to the Azazel-goat's, though it is not certain what the significance of the relationship is.[20] Thus it becomes doubtful whether the imposition of a hand in the usual *hattat* ritual symbolizes the unloading of sin, i.e. transference of sin. However, one way of preserving Lev 16.21 for the meaning of the imposition of a hand in sacrificial contexts would be to assume that, whatever is transferred, the rite expresses the idea of 'transference'.

Before deciding on this matter it seems necessary to examine more carefully the two crucial passages, Lev 1.4 and Lev 16.21. Lev 1.4 reads:

וסמך ידו על ראש העלה ונרצה לו לכפר עליו

Although it is generally agreed that v. 4b interprets the meaning of the imposition of a hand in some way, some philological comments are in order for both נרצה לו and for לכפר עליו.

The root רצה[21] appears in v. 3b (לרצנו) as well as in v. 4b (ונרצה). Since the noun רצון has been translated 'acceptance', 'pleasure', 'will', the phrase לרצנו in v. 3b has accordingly been translated 'of his own voluntary will',[22] '... ihm Wohlgefallen zuteil',[23] '... that he may be accepted'.[24] In the light of the phrase in other contexts which discuss whether sacrifices are acceptable or not, the rendering of רצון by 'will' seems most unlikely. Yet if רצון means either 'acceptance' or 'pleasure' and the pronominal suffix clearly refers to the offerer, it is still unclear what relationship exists between the sacrifice and the offerer. On the analogy, however, between לרצנכם in Lev 22.19 and לא לרצון יהיה לכם in Lev 22.20, it could be assumed that in Lev 1.3b too the relationship between רצון and its pronominal suffix is dative. Thus the meaning of לרצנו in v. 3b would be 'for acceptance on his behalf'.

As for נרצה in Lev 1.4b it has a parallel form in Lev 22.25. From the context of Lev 22.19-25 it would be possible to infer that the

meaning of לא ירצו לכם (v. 25) is the same as that of לא לרצון יהיה לכם
(v. 20), and that consequently the same meaning can be applied to
נרצה לו in Lev 1.4b. Thus the meaning of Lev 1.4bα is: 'it (sacrifice)
will be accepted on his behalf'. That the term רצון in the contexts
cited above connotes 'substitution' rather than 'representation'
seems to be implied in Lev 7.18 which reads, 'If any meat from a
peace offering is eaten on the third day, the man who offered it will
not be accepted (לא ירצה המקריב אתו)'. It could be inferred that here
the rejection of the sacrifice is identifcal with that of the offerer.

Then the fact that the imposition of a hand in Lev 1.4a is
mentioned between the bringing of the sacrifice (v. 3b) *for* acceptance
on behalf of the offerer and the declaration that the sacrifice will be
accepted on his behalf shows that the meaning of the imposition of a
hand is implied in נרצה לו 'it will be accepted on *his* behalf'.

The next phrase, לכפר עליו in Lev 1.4b, poses a more crucial
problem. Assuming that כפר על means 'make atonement for', how
should the *lamed* in לכפר be construed? Broadly two approaches have
been proposed.

1. 'and it shall be accepted on his behalf *by* making atonement
    for him' [25]
2. 'and it shall be accepted on his behalf *to* make atonement for
    him'[26]

Interpretation 1 raises the question whether atonement hinges on
the imposition of hand.[27] The question has been answered in the
negative by some.[28] But if so, the interpretation makes the significance
of the location of Lev 1.4b minimal for the meaning of the imposition
of a hand, because it assumes that the acceptance of the sacrifice
(נרצה לו) is dependent on the ritual as a whole rather than on the
imposition of a hand alone. Interpretation 2 is better in that it
presents no such problem. It assumes that the meaning of the
imposition of a hand is implied in נרצה לו alone,[29] and that the
atonement (לכפר עליו) is the purpose of the acceptance of the
sacrifice.[30]

We thus infer, in conclusion, that the imposition of a hand in Lev
1.4 simply expresses the idea of substitution.[31]

Can this meaning of the gesture be applied to other sacrifices such
as the שלמים and the *hattat*? Since the gesture is common in the
rituals of the עולה שלמים, and *hattat*, the meaning of it should not be
determined by overemphasizing any particular ritual: the symbolic
meaning of the gesture in different sacrificial contexts must be the

same. Now Janowski assumes that the gesture involves not only the identification of the offerer with the sacrificial animal but also substitutionary *death*.[32] This assumption appears natural in that all the sacrificial animals are slaughtered. However, the assumption seems slightly speculative and unlikely for two reasons. First, in Lev 1.4 the idea of 'substitution', which could be the symbolic meaning of the imposition of a hand, is unlikely to include that of 'atonement'. Second, נרצה לו in Lev 1.4bα is not directly related to the slaughtering (v. 5).[33] Thus Janowski's idea that the imposition of a hand also implies substitutionary *death* reads too much into this gesture, though this is not to say that such a concept may not be expressed by other parts of the sacrificial ritual. And we assume that the symbolic meaning of the imposition of a hand in Lev 1.4 can be applied to other sacrifices in this limited sense of 'substitution'. By placing one hand on the animal, the offerer is indicating that the animal is taking his place in the ritual.

We are now in a position to reassess the issue of 'transference of sin', based on our interpretation of Lev 1.4. For Gese and Janowski[34] the matter is clear: while the imposition of two hands in Lev 16.21 represents 'Objektabladung', the imposition of one hand in Lev 1.4 represents 'Subjektübertragung'.[35] Since we have established our standpoint with regard to the latter we address here the characterization of Lev 16.21 as 'Objektübertragung'. Two remarks are in order. Firstly, it is true that in Lev 16.21 the guilt (= עונות) is represented as if it were a substance. However, it seems debatable whether only the sinful substance is transferred to the Azazel goat in contrast to the transfer of a person which Janowski sees in Lev 1.4. For when Aaron handles כל עונת בני ישראל it seems possible to assume that he affects the fate of all the Israelites, since the guilt cannot be envisaged separately from the persons who produced it.[36] Secondly, as Aaron's imposition of hands is followed by his confession of sins rather than preceded by it, the imposition of hands by itself is unlikely to have involved an automatic transfer of sins.[37] Thus, although the *purpose* of the imposition of hands is certainly to transfer the guilt of the Israelites to the Azazel goat, the act *itself* does not necessarily symbolize the 'transference of guilt' mentioned in v.21bα. The meaning of the imposition of hands in Lev 16.21 does not seem to be 'transference of sin' as unambiguously as it has been assumed.

For these reasons it seems possible to argue that the imposition of hands in Lev 16.21 also symbolizes the idea of 'substitution' as in

Lev 1.4. However, since on this occasion Aaron lays his hands on the goat on behalf of the Israelites, the question remains in what sense the substitution is envisaged.[38]

To summarize: The imposition of a hand in sacrificial contexts may express simply the idea of substitution, as can be inferred from Lev 1.4. And this could also apply to the gesture in Lev 16.21. Since, however, the evidence for the meaning of the gesture is scanty, one should not read too much into it about the meaning of the sacrifice. More significant for the *hattat* is our assumption, inferred independently of the meaning of the imposition of hand(s), that if the sacrifice deals with sin/guilt, this does not affect the holy status of the sacrifice.

B. *Blood manipulation in the* hattat *ritual*

In contrast with other sacrifices the *hattat* ritual involves a distinctive manipulation of blood; the blood is sprinkled (*hizzāh*) towards/onto the *pārōket veil*, the *kappōret* and presumably the incense altar, and smeared (*nātan*) on the horns of the altar of burnt offering. The occurrences of the *hizzāh* and *nātan* rites in the context of the *hattat* can be shown diagrammatically in anticipation of the subsequent discussion (see overleaf).[39]

Although the contexts of the *hizzāh* and *nātan* rites clearly indicate that those rites symbolize 'purification', the existence of the two modes of blood manipulation raises the obvious question how and why they differ from each other, apart from the practical difference in blood application (sprinkling versus daubing). As will be clear in the course of discussion this question will lead to some typological aspects of the *hattat* ritual, which are also highly relevant to the meaning of the disposal of the *hattat*, to be discussed in the next section.

Traditionally it appears that the two acts (*hizzāh* and *nātan*) have not generally been differentiated and that more attention has been paid to the daubing (*nātan*) of blood.[40] Two general assumptions seem to explain this circumstance: one is that the altar represents the divinity and that the blood expiates sin; the other is that in Lev 4 the graver the sin, the further into the tabernacle is the blood brought.

With such situations in view Th. C. Vriezen devoted a comprehensive study to the *hizzāh* rite.[41] According to Vriezen the *hizzāh* rite concerns 'consecration of blood' in preparation for the main act of the *nātan* rite which constitutes the *kipper* act.[42] Though

הזה	הזה (the פרכת -veil)	נתן (the altar of burnt offering)
+	Lev 4.6-7, ↓ 17-18	Lev 16.18-19 ↓
נתן	נתן (the incense altar)	הזה

נתן	Exod 29.12 (the altar of burnt offering)	Ezek 43.20 (the altar of burnt offering)
	Lev 4.25, 30, 34 (")	Ezek 45.19 (the post of the
	Lev 8.15 (")	house, four corners of the
(alone)	Lev 9.9 (")	settle of the altar, posts of the gate of the inner court)

הזה	Lev 16.14-15 (the כפרת)	Lev 5.9 (the wall of the altar of burnt offering)
		Num 8.7 (the Levites)
(alone)	Lev 16.16b (the incense altar; implicit in ועשה)	Num 19.4 (towards the Tent) Num 19.18, 19, 21 (unclean persons)

the view has been accepted by some[43] it has been recently criticized by Janowski as follows: 1. No relevant text (Lev 4.6, 17; 5.9; 16.14 [bis], 15, 19; Num 19.4) implies that God has accepted the sprinkled blood. 2. The reverse sequence (the *nātan* rite → the *hizzāh* rite) is attested in Lev 16.18ff. (see the table above) 3. Any research into the *hizzāh* rite should not be done without referring to the question of the traditio-historical location of the relevant texts and of the cultic-historical problem reflected in them.[44]

It seems that Vriezen's view is disproved by points 1 and 2. However, it seems right to look at Janowski's view of the texts relevant to the two modes of blood manipulation before we inquire into the matter independently.

According to Janowski[45] the *hattat* rituals in Lev 4.1–5.13 are to be classified into two types of blood manipulation; the small blood-rite (Lev 4.25, 30, 34) which consists of daubing (נתן) the blood on the horns of the altar of burnt offering and pouring (שפך) the rest of the blood at the base of the altar, and the great blood-rite (Lev 4.5-7, 16-

18) which consists of sprinkling (הזה) blood towards the *pārōket* veil, daubing (נתן) the blood on the horns of the incense altar and pouring (שפך) the rest of the blood at the base of the altar of burnt offering. For the following three reasons the small blood-rite should be judged as more original than the great blood-rite from a traditio-historical point of view.[46]

1.   The literarily primary sections of Lev 4.1–5.13, i.e. Lev 4.22-26, 27-31, 32-35, know only the small blood-rite.
2.   The incense altar appeared only late in the official temple cult, which corresponds to the blood manipulation in Lev 4.6-7, 17-18.
3.   In Lev 8–10 (Pg), which is source-critically earlier than Lev 1–7, the *hattat* ritual (Lev 8.14-17 Pg[1]; Lev 9.8-11 Pg[2]) still takes place in connection with the altar of burnt offering, and does not know the *hizzāh* gesture towards the *pārōket* veil.

Janowski believes[47] that the original 'small blood rite' is also found in pre-priestly texts such as Ezek 43.20; 45.18b, 19, the tradition of which Lev 8.15aβ, bβ; Exod 29.36ff.; Lev 16.18 and Exod 30.10 also represent. Characteristic in these texts is the direct connection between the blood rite and the terms כִּפֶּר/חַטֵּא. According to Janowski the original function of the *hattat* is found in the above-cited Ezekiel tradition, in which atonement of the altar and the whole sanctuary is achieved by applying the *hattat* blood to the altar of burnt offering.

In addition to this Ezekiel tradition which was taken over by P, there existed in P a different tradition, according to which the *hattat* blood atones not for sancta but for Israel, its cultic representatives and individuals.

The historical relationship between the two traditions, i.e. the consecration of sancta on the one hand and the sacrificial atonement for persons (Israel, its cultic representatives and the individuals) on the other is as follows.[48] Originally the small blood-rite was associated exclusively with the consecration of sancta (Ezek 43.20; 45.19) and of Aaron and his sons (Lev 8.15aα), and then secondarily with the cultic atonement for persons (Lev 4.22ff., 27ff., 32ff.). However, the twofold character of the great blood rite (Lev 4.6-7, 17-18) for the atonement for the high priest and all Israel indicates a further development in cultic history. This is due to the influence of the *hizzāh* rite in Lev 16.14ff., by which Aaron makes atonement for himself, his house and all Israel. However because of the unique occasion of the day of Atonement and Aaron's privilege to enter the adytum that day, the author of Lev 4.6, 17 changed 'the adytum' into 'the *pārōket* before the adytum'. So the great blood-rite, which represents a later stage of development in cultic history, shows an intensification compared with the small blood-rite, because in the former the blood is brought as close to God in the adytum as possible.

However, noting that the two rites, the *hizzāh* and the *nātan* rites, which appear in atonement for persons, have always to do with sancta, Janowski concludes that conceptually the two traditions, *hattat* for atonement of sancta and *hattat* for atonement of persons, are not mutually exclusive.[49]

We have already considered, albeit partially, the above outline of the cultic history of blood manipulation. It has been noted that the assumption that the incense altar appeared only late in the official temple cult is unlikely.[50] Also it has been concluded that the reason why the *hattat* ritual in Lev 8–9 takes place in connection with the altar of burnt offering is that Aaron enters the tent of meeting for the first time in Lev 9.23 and not that Lev 8–9 did not know the incense altar or the *hizzāh* rite.[51]

Therefore it is dubious whether the *hattat* rituals in Lev 8–9 represent a tradition earlier than the tradition in Lev 4, especially in Lev 4.3-21. If the above basic suppositions of Janowski are excluded, the difference between the *hattat* ritual in Lev 4 and that in Lev 8–9 can be ascribed to the difference in occasion. Thus it may be argued that the *hattat* ritual in Lev 8–9 concerns the priests' installation, while the ritual in Lev 4, presupposing the priesthood, concerns the expiation of particular sins on regular occasions. Our argument is that though the *hattat* rituals in Lev 4 and Lev 8–9 may reflect some developments in cultic history, that history is different from Janowski's.

We thus turn to our independent inquiry into the differences between the two gestures (*hizzāh* and *nātan*) and the symbolic problems related to them.

First of all, some simple possible explanations of the two modes of blood manipulation should be presented. A ready explanation would be that the *nātan* gesture is general, because it appears frequently in connection with the altar of burnt offering, whereas the *hizzāh* gesture is specific or special because it is performed mostly in connection with the inner sancta and is therefore infrequent.

However, one cannot say how frequently the *hizzāh* gestures in Lev 4.16 and Num 19 were performed in ancient Israel. Or one may argue, that the *hizzāh* gesture takes place mostly in the Tent because inner sancta are so dangerously holy that even the high priest cannot have direct physical contact with them, as he does in the *nātan* gesture. However, this can apply to Lev 4 and Lev 16.14–16, but it is not convincing regarding Num 19 and Lev 16.18–19 where both gestures appear in succession.

Having set forth the above general observations we add the following:

1. The *hizzāh* gesture appears in connection with the Tent except in Lev 5.9[52] and Lev 16.19, where the blood is sprinkled to the outer altar, whereas the *nātan* gesture appears exclusively in connection with the altars.
2. Lev 16.19 is the only passage in which the blood is said to be sprinkled onto the altar of burnt offering.
3. The reverse sequence of *hizzāh–nātan* in Lev 4.6-7, 17-18 is found in Lev 16.18-19.[53]

These observations seem to call for a closer look at the rituals in Num 19.4; Lev 4.6-7 (17-18); 16.18-19, because what is unclear is the significance of the *hizzāh* gesture in its relation to the *nātan* gesture.

a. *Num 19.4*

We have agreed above with Janowski that Vriezen's theory should be rejected. However, when it comes to Num 19.4, scholars including Janowski seem almost unanimous in holding that the sprinkling of blood seven times towards the Tent symbolizes consecration of blood.[54] This view seems to rest on the fact that the blood does not have actual contact with sancta. But this observation does not necessarily imply that the rite symbolizes consecration of blood.[55] Moreover, why is there any necessity to consecrate the blood? Is the supervision of the priest (v. 3) not sufficient to give the heifer a sacred character? An alternative view that the rite has something to do with the purity of the Tent deserves consideration;[56] for if the object of the *hizzāh* gesture is purified (see vv. 18, 19), it appears reasonable to infer that in v. 4, too, the sprinkling of blood is somehow related to the purification of the Tent. Now the facts that the blood of the heifer is necessary for preparing the ashes, and that the ashes are destined for the purificaion water (vv. 17-18), suggest that the heifer is supposed to purify the Israelites from the contamination caused by death. According to vv. 13, 20 this death contamination affects the purity of the Tent when the purification rules are not observed. Indeed this implies that uncleanness from corpses does not itself affect the Tent as long as the purification rules are observed.[57] But if nothing is done, the defilement (vv. 13b, 20b) affects the Tent, so the purification from corpse contamination, which the red heifer accomplishes, can be viewed as an indirect way of purifying the Tent. Indeed sprinkling of blood *towards* the Tent suggests this is the nature of the purification effected.

b. *Lev 4.6-7, 17-18*[58]

Lev 4.6-7 prescribes that when the anointed priest sins he should first sprinkle the blood seven times before the Lord towards/onto the *pārōket* veil of the adytum and then daub the horns of the incense altar with some of the blood. The prescription itself suggests nothing about the significance of the two modes of blood manipulation. One wonders, however, why the blood should be sprinkled towards/onto the *pārōket* veil.

A common answer has been that the blood ought to be brought in to that point because of the seriousness of the sin of the anointed priest.[59] Though widespread, this view seems to require reconsideration. For in view of the similar formulation in Lev 4.2-3a, 13, 22, 27, theoretically even the *same* sin can be envisaged for all the cases. This means that the notion of 'degrees of sin' is not the leading factor determining the modes of rituals. It is rather the cultic status of sinners that determines the ritual mode. Even if one argues that the same sin can have graver *consequences* when the sinner is the anointed priest, the situation remains the same; it all hinges on the cultic status of a sinner. In other words, the common view has obscured what the determinant of the ritual in Lev 4 is. We thus argue that the sprinkling of blood towards/onto the *pārōket* veil is necessitated by the fact that the sinner is the anointed priest or the whole congregation, rather than just by the fact that the consequence of sin, i.e. uncleanness, reaches there.

But more importantly, according to Milgrom, who understands את פני פרכת הקדש as '*before* the *pārōket* veil', the *hizzāh* gesture here implies defilement of *the shrine*.[60] But this interpretation seems to be wrong for several reasons.

Firstly, the phrase את פני פרכת הקדש, particularly the term הקדש, appears to refer to the adytum. Indeed though the *hizzāh* rite is to be performed before the *pārōket* veil, the term הקרש appears to relate the rite to the adytum. That special emphasis is placed on the term הקרש is evident in view of the fact that in other mentions of the *pārōket* veil the term הקרש never appears (cf. Exod 26.31, 33, 35; 27.21; 30.6; 35.12; 36.35; 38.27; 40.3, 21, 22, 26; Lev 4.17; 16.12, 15; 21.23; 24.3; Num 4.5; 18.7) except in Lev 16.2, though the veil is self-evidently assumed to separate the shrine from the adytum.

Secondly, that the *pārōket* veil cannot be separated functionally from the *kappōret* is clear from the fact that it is patterned with the cherubim (Exod 26.31; 36.35). We agree with Haran that the veil 'serves as a kind of projection and "shadow" of the kapporet behind it'.[61]

Thirdly, the phrase את פני also deserves attention.[62] In connection with the *hizzāh* rite the phrase appears only in Lev 4.6, 17. Although it can mean 'before' in the light of Gen 19.13, 27; 33.18; 1 Sam 2.17, it may well have the specific connotation of '*vis-à-vis*', because the meaning 'before' can be conveyed by לפני, and there actually exists the phrase הזה לפני (Lev 14.16, 27; 16.14, 15). Whether the blood is actually to make contact with the *pārōket* veil is difficult to decide. But since הזה is frequently followed by על (Exod 29.21; Lev 8.11, 30; 14.7; 16.15, 19; 5.9; Num 8.7; 19.18, 19), אל (Lev 14.51) or על פני (Lev 16.14), and since apparently contact is assumed to be made, the rare phrase את פני may not imply contact but only the direction in which the blood ought to be sprinkled (cp. Num 19.4). At any rate it is undeniable that the phrase refers to the direction where the adytum is located.

On this passage Lev 4.6 Kurtz observed:

> The sprinkling seven times, whether against or in front of the curtain, had reference not to the curtain itself, which was not an instrument of expiation, but to the Capporet behind it, which was thus to be sprinkled not directly but indirectly.[63]

Indeed as Kurtz observed, what is really needed here is purification of the adytum such as is set forth in Lev 16.14ff. That the anointed priest cannot enter the adytum in Lev 4.6, 17 because the day of Atonement is the only occasion on which he can enter there, has been recognized also by scholars such as K. Koch and B. Janowski, who explain the relationship between Lev 4.3-21 and Lev 16.14ff. by assuming some editorial work or historical development.[64]

So if we are asking which part of the sanctuary is being cleansed from uncleanness, it follows that, contrary to Milgrom's assumption, it is the adytum, not the shrine, that is assumed to be defiled by the sin of the anointed priest or the whole congregation. Thus the circumstance that the adytum is defiled but not directly cleansed gives the impression that the two rituals in Lev 4.3-21 are somehow incomplete. However what does the 'incomplete' ritual mean?

In support of the incomplete character of the *hizzāh* gesture in Lev 4.6, 17 another fact can be adduced: that in the ritual for the sin of the anointed priest the stereotyped formula, נסלח-כפר, does not appear, whereas it does in the ritual for the sin of the congregation (Lev 4.20b). Indeed this negative evidence has been variously construed. Ramban inferred from this that the anointed priest was not forgiven.[65] If the omission of the formula is intentional, this view may well be correct.[66] But one would naturally ask what then the *hizzāh* and the *nātan* gestures are for. Contrary to Ramban, Abarbanel saw the formula for the anointed priest in v. 20.[67] But it is unnatural for him to include the anointed priest in להם and עליהם in v. 20b. The section of vv. 13ff., though it refers to vv. 3-12 from the viewpoint of ritual procedure (see v. 20a), deals with a different case and should not be confused with the section of vv. 3-12.

Recently M. Noth has commented:

> the complete dependence of the second section on the first suggests that the final sentence once stood at the end of the first section, and in the end disappeared from it only by mistake.[68]

However, two facts, the systematic appearance of the formula and the independence of the first section from the second, will justify the search for a reason why the formula is missing in the first section.

One of the clues to the question seems to lie in the phrase לאשמת העם in Lev 4.3, which could mean 'causing guilt to the people'.[69] Needless to say, by his sin both the anointed priest and the whole people become guilty, and not just the whole people. The phrase could indicate, therefore, that the anointed priest never commits a sin without making the people guilty.[70] Conversely this suggests that atonement for the anointed priest is never made without it being accompanied by the atonement of the people. This assumption is confirmed by Lev 9.7 and Lev 16.14-17, in which atonement is made for both Aaron and the whole people. But although the assumption is right in itself, it fails to explain the second case in Lev 4, in which נסלח-כפר appears.

In our view the rationale of the earlier omission of נסלח-כפר may be sought in the very concept of the term *kipper*, for as argued above, it includes both the bearing of guilt as well as the cleansing of sancta. Now although purification of sancta might have been done in the first (Lev 4.3-12) and second (Lev 4.13-21) sections, there may well be a difference between the two occasions as far as 'the bearing of guilt' is concerned, in that in the second the anointed priest can bear the guilt of the congregation, whereas in the first there is no agent who can bear substitutionarily the guilt of the anointed priest and the whole people, since the anointed priest himself is guilty.

However, it may be objected that Aaron makes atonement for himself in Lev 9.7 and Lev 16.6, 11, 17, and that therefore the principle that the guilty cannot bear his own guilt is not always valid. But this view is superficial.

Firstly, we have argued that the *hattat* ritual in Lev 9 is different in nature from that in Lev 4, because the former deals with general, and not particular, sinfulness in the context of dedication, whereas Lev 4 deals with the expiation of particular sins.[71] Rather Lev 4 is similar to Lev 10 in that both concern particular sins: the former the sin of the anointed priest, the latter the sin of Aaron's sons.[72] Furthermore it has been argued that in Lev 10 the situation envisaged is that Aaron cannot bear the guilt of his house because of the death of Nadab and Abihu. Thus it may be inferred that Aaron cannot bear the guilt of particular sins committed either by himself or by his family members.

Secondly, atonement is indeed made for Aaron and the whole people in Lev 16. But on this occasion there exists an agent for bearing the guilt, the Azazel goat. Certainly it is unclear at this stage how the atonement of sancta is related to the Azazel-goat ritual. However, if, as hinted in Chapter 3, it is possible to assume that the problem posed in Lev 10.16ff. (i.e. atonement of Aaron's family) is resolved in Lev 16, the principle that the guilty cannot bear his own guilt seems to be valid in Lev 10 and Lev 16. In other words, we are suggesting that both Lev 10 and Lev 4.3-12 assume—each in its own way—the Azazel-goat ritual, by which the guilt of all Israel is to be removed from the sanctuary.

What, then, does the blood manipulation in Lev 4.6-7 achieve? On the principle discussed above, the blood manipulation cannot remove the guilt imposed on the people as well as that of the anointed priest. Nevertheless, it could be assumed that the adytum and the incense altar are partially purified by the blood manipulation. That sancta are purified but people are not atoned for (*kipper*-ed) is not as strange an idea as it appears at first sight. Various rituals make it clear that

there is a stage between purification and atonement (Exod 29.4
versus v. 10; Lev 14.5-20, 49-53; Num 8.6-7 versus v. 12 and v. 21;
Num 31.19-24 versus vv. 49-50). The major difference between the
case of Lev 4.3-12 and the cases cited is that in the former the
purification-atonement spans two different occasions (Lev 4.3-12 +
Lev 16.14ff.), whereas in the latter it takes place on a single
occasion.

To recapitulate: The two rituals in Lev 4.6-7, 17-18 relate the
hizzāh gesture to the purification of the adytum, assuming the ritual
in Lev 16.14ff. The reason for the omission of *kipper* in Lev 4.3-12 is
that Aaron cannot bear his own guilt.

c. *Lev 16.18-19*

As noted above, along with Lev 5.9 this passage provides a rare case
in which the blood is sprinkled onto the outer altar.

Before considering the purification rite in this section, however, it
seems appropriate to address the question which altar is referred to
in v. 18. The implausibility of the view advocated by traditional
Jewish exegetes that המזבח in v. 18 refers to the incense altar[73] is
indicated by two points.[74] First, v. 20 (v. 33) shows that the
atonement has been made in three stages, that of the adytum, the
shrine and the altar. This means that the ritual envisaged in v. 16b
cannot be identified with the ritual in vv. 18-19. Second, v. 16b,
which reads "and *so* shall he do. . .", excludes the possibility of המזבח
in v. 18 being the incense altar. For, since sancta in the shrine
(אהל מועד) differ from those in the adytum, by וכן in v. 16b the author
must mean that the mode of blood manipulation is the same as that
in vv. 14-15, which is clearly different from the blood manipulation
in vv. 18b-19. Thus it is assumed in v. 16b that just as Aaron atones
for the entire room of the adytum by sanctifying the *kappōret*, he also
atones for the entire room of the shrine by sprinkling the blood once
onto the incense altar and seven times in front of it.[75]

The blood manipulation in vv. 18b-19 consists of the *nātan* gesture
(v. 18b) and then the *hizzāh* gesture, in contrast to the reversed
sequence of gestures in Lev 4.6-7, 17-18. Further the effect of the
blood manipulation is designated טהרו וקרשו. Yet it seems artificial to
construe טהר as referring to the *nātan* gesture and קרש as referring to
the *hizzāh* gesture. Equally artificial seems the proposal to make
מטמאת בני ישראל belong only to טהרו.[76] Both gestures together could
be taken to 'cleanse and sanctify' the altar. It should be noted that vv.
18bβ-19 show close linguistic affinity with Lev 8.15: 1. In both, the

phrase על קרנות המזבח סביב appears along with the verb נתן, but nowhere else in the whole cultic law, let alone in the *hattat* context. 2. The altar of burnt offering is said to become 'sanctified' (קרש) only in Lev 8.15 (Exod 29.37) and Lev 16.19. Given this literary relationship it may be inferred that the ritual in Lev 16.18-19 aims at rededicating the altar of burnt offering.

Another important aspect of the blood manipulation in vv. 18b-19 is given by the explicit instruction ולקח מדם הפר ומדם השעיר, viz. that the blood should come from that of the bull and the goat which has been already used in the purification of the adytum and the shrine. Thus it could be assumed in general that "using the blood of both animals symbolized the fact that the altar had to be cleansed from the defilement of priests and people".[77] The fact that the atonement of the outer altar follows that of the adytum and the shrine suggests strongly that the former is contingent upon the latter. More specifically, since the adytum is sanctified by the sprinkling of blood on and before the *kappōret*, the sanctification of the outer altar is even contingent upon that of the *kappōret*. In other words, the blood manipulation regarding the outer altar cannot be effective on this occasion, if it is not preceded by the sanctification of the *kappōret*. This rationale may explain the single occurrence of the *hizzāh* gesture in connection with the outer altar. The outer altar which has been defiled has to be restored to its original sanctity; however, that can be achieved only by the *hizzāh* gesture, which sanctified the *kappōret* and is never performed on other occasions.

With the above exposition of Lev 16.18-19 we seem to be in a better position to see the relationship between Lev 4.6-7, 17-18 and Lev 16.14ff. and to draw some inference with regard to the *hizzāh* and *nātan* gestures.

It has been argued that the sprinkling of blood towards the *pārōket* veil in Lev 4.6, 17 presupposes defilement of the adytum and not the shrine because את פני פרכת הקדש alludes to the adytum. However, is it adequate to characterize these rituals in Lev 4 as 'incomplete', as we have done? In view of our contention that the adytum is purified, though indirectly, by the *hizzāh* gesture in Lev 4, it would be inadequate to assume that the incomplete rituals in Lev 4.3-21 are completed or supplemented in Lev 16.14ff. The most plausible explanation of the relationship between the two sections is that the *hizzāh* gestures in Lev 4.6, 17 *foreshadow* the *hizzāh* gesture in Lev 16.14-15, expressing the need for the full rite there. Therefore the apparent incompleteness of the rituals in Lev 4.6-7, 17-18 should not be taken as if nothing substantial was achieved; the rituals are incomplete in the sense that they foreshadow fuller ones.

As regards the *hizzāh* and *nātan* gestures, we conclude that both symbolize purification of sancta. Yet we may point out two differences: 1. The *hizzāh* gesture is undoubtedly associated with the purification of the Tent (Num 19.4; Lev 4.6, 17; 16.14, 15, 16b), while the *nātan* gesture is associated with the altars. 2. The incense altar is purified by the *nātan* gesture in Lev 4.7(18), but by the *hizzāh* gesture in Lev 16.16b (assumed); while only in Lev 16.18b-19 is the purification of the outer altar associated with the *hizzāh* gesture. These data suggest that the *hizzāh* gesture is a form of blood manipulation, more potent than the *nātan* gesture.

C. *Disposal of the* hattat *flesh*

Having discussed the blood manipulation, we now examine another distinctive component of the *hattat* ritual.

The *hattat* ritual in various contexts is connected, explicitly or implicitly, with the two modes of the disposal of the *hattat* flesh, eating of it by priests and burning of it outside the camp. Directions to the priests concerning the disposal of the *hattat* flesh are given in Lev 6.17-23. As already noted, the fact that the burning of the *hattat* is always mentioned explicitly in the ceremony (Exod 29.14; Lev 4.11-12, 21; 8.17; 9.11; 16.27) but the priestly consumption of it is not (e.g. Lev 4.26, 31, 35), gives the impression that the burning of the *hattat* constitutes part of the *hattat* ritual, whereas the priestly consumption does not.[78] And again, as will become clear, Lev 10.16-20 presents an episode significant for the relationship between the two modes of the disposal of the *hattat*.

The two modes of the disposal of the *hattat* become, however, slightly complicated when they are seen in connection with their corresponding modes of blood manipulation. Seen from this angle three types of *hattat* ritual emerge:

A.   The application of blood to the outer altar + the burning of the flesh outside the camp (Exod 29.12, 14; Lev 8.15, 17; 9.9, 11)

B.   The application of blood to the outer altar + [priestly consumption of the flesh] (Lev 4.25, 30, 34 etc.; Lev 6.17-22)

C.   The bringing of blood into the inner sancta + the burning of the flesh outside the camp (Lev 4.5-12, 16-21; 16.14ff., 27; Lev 6.23)

As this classification shows, the directions in Lev 6.17-23 correspond to types B and C but do not match type A, presumably because they assume the completion of the installation of priests, hence regular occasions.

In the following discussion we shall address three major questions: 1. How are the above three types of ritual related to each other? 2. What does 'burning the *hattat*' symbolize? 3. Is the *hattat* flesh unclean? These questions will be discussed under the following heads: a. Two approaches to the symbolism of the *hattat* flesh. b. Symbolic meaning of the disposal of the *hattat* flesh. c. Contagiousness of the *hattat*.

a. *Two approaches to the symbolism of the* hattat *flesh*
The approaches of Janowski and Milgrom are quite different. B. Janowski adopts the traditio-historical method based on a particular literary analysis, while J. Milgrom, assuming by and large the homogeneity of the relevant texts, has recourse to the notion of uncleanness. We shall delineate each standpoint below with a view to focusing on crucial problems.

Drawing heavily on the literary analysis of Elliger, Janowski[79] starts, as in the case of blood manipulation, from the assumption that the rituals in Lev 4.5-7, 16-18 are secondary to those in Lev 4.22ff. He contends that the rite of burning the *hattat* in Lev 4 is not original on the ground that in all the texts except Lev 4.3-12, 13-21 the rite belongs to the ritual associated with the altar of burnt offering (Ezek 43.19-21; Lev 8.14-17; 9.8-11), which is more original. Further, assuming that in the ceremonies in Lev 4.22ff. the *burning* of the *hattat*-flesh is missing, Janowski asserts that the rule in Lev 6.17-23 about the disposal of the *hattat* flesh emerged only after the development of the tradition concerning the remaining part of other sacrifices, particularly the אשם. As for Lev 10.16-20, Janowski accepts Elliger's view that the section, presupposing Lev 6.17-23 and Lev 4.3ff., attempts to adjust the differences in the disposal of the *hattat* flesh between Lev 6.17ff. and Lev 9.15.

What has been pointed out above regarding Janowski's view of the blood manipulation applies to his view of the disposal of the *hattat* flesh.[80] It is unwarranted to assume that the rituals in Lev 4.3-21 are secondary to those in Lev 4.22ff. Here two additional counterarguments may be added: 1. The assumption that in Lev 4.22ff. the burning of the *hattat* flesh is missing is one-sided and unnecessary. The omission of directions regarding the disposal of *hattat* flesh can be explained partly by our postulate that the priestly consumption of the *hattat* is not part of the ritual, and partly by Lev 6.17-23 itself. 2. As will be shown below, it is true that Lev 10.16-20 presupposes Lev 6.17-23 and even Lev 4.3ff. However, it is unnecessary to assume differences in ritual procedure between Lev 6.17ff. and Lev 9.15. The latter text refers to the blood manipulation alone and does not say that the congregation's *hattat* should also be burned outside the camp.[81]

Thus we cannot support Janowski's reconstruction of the cultic history. Moreover, in that delineation of the cultic history little attention seems to be paid to the symbolic meaning of the two modes of the disposal of the *hattat*, on which Milgrom has much to say.

For Milgrom,[82] the *hattat* to be eaten is 'the largess granted the priest for assuming the burden . . . of purging the sanctuary'.[83] By contrast, he argues, the burnt *hattat* represents degrees of uncleanness higher than the eaten *hattat*, which explains the contagiousness of the former (e.g. Lev 16.23-24, 27-28).[84]

Milgrom thus wrote:

> The eaten *ḥaṭṭā't* purges the outer altar . . . At this lowest level, the impurity is not transferrable to the *ḥaṭṭā't*, and hence, it is eaten by the priests for their services. The burnt *ḥaṭṭā't*, however, represents higher degrees of impurity caused by inadvertences of the high priest and community, and at its worst, by presumptuous sins. The impurity is powerful enough to penetrate into the shrine and adytum and is dangerously contagious.[85]

Therefore the *hattat* is burned in the latter case. However, the theory, particularly the idea of 'degrees of uncleanness', hardly suits the burnt *hattat* in Lev 8-9, where no particular or serious sin is envisaged. In other words, Milgrom's theory fails to do justice to the *hattat* of ritual type A.

Thus the relationship of the three ritual types A, B and C does not seem to have been explained satisfactorily either by Janowski or by Milgrom. Nor does Milgrom offer a convincing rationale of the disposal of the *hattat*. It is unlikely that the two modes of disposal of the *hattat* are conditioned by degrees of uncleanness that the *hattat* deals with.

Now it may be observed that whether the blood is brought into the inner sancta (the shrine or the adytum) or not, is conditioned by the nature of the occasion: when atonement is made for priests, the blood is brought into the adytum, in the day of Atonement ceremony (Lev 16.14) but not in the eighth-day service(Lev 9.8ff.) The same holds true for the congregation (cp. Lev 16.15 with Lev 9.7). Can the same apply to the disposal of the *hattat* flesh? The disposal of *hattat* flesh appears to show a rationale different from that of blood manipulation; for instance, both in Lev 9.11 and Lev 16.27 the *hattat* ritual includes the burning of the *hattat*, and both in Lev 4.22ff. (assumed) and Lev 9.15 (10.16ff.) the priests are to eat the *hattat* flesh. Thus some rationale, which is independent of the nature of the occasion, seems to be at work. So we shall attempt below to determine the symbolic meanings of the eating and burning of the *hattat* and their rationale.

b. *Symbolic meaning of the disposal of the* hattat *flesh*
Of the two modes of disposal of *hattat* flesh, the symbolic meaning of the priestly consumption of the *hattat* flesh has been discussed in connection with Lev 10.17.[86] It has been argued that it is the privilege and duty of the priests to eat it, but that eating does not belong to the atoning process. The section Lev 10.16-20 also seems to assume that the eaten *hattat* is offered with the burnt *hattat* (see vv. 17-18).[87] Thus it seems possible to approach synchronically the symbolic meanings of eating and burning the *hattat*.

As for the burning of the *hattat*, there are two major questions to be addressed here, which may be essentially one: the symbolic meaning of the act, and its rationale.

It is certainly difficult to determine the meaning of the act because no cultic text explicitly explains it. Some suggestions have been made, however.[88] First, burning can be taken as the means of preventing profanation of the *hattat* flesh.[89] The difficulty with this view arises from the consideration that if that were the case, profanation could have been prevented by eating the *hattat*. Second, for the same reason it seems inadequate to regard the *hattat* flesh as a useless part of a sacrificial animal, if it is holy or sacred.[90] Third, as the *hattat* is purificatory, it can be assumed that its flesh, which becomes unclean, must be eliminated by burning.[91] However, though it may be true that the *hattat* flesh is the source of defilement outside the camp, it is debatable whether it becomes unclean with the commencement of blood manipulation.[92] In our opinion, each of the above three explanations is possible in itself, but none of them

can explain why burning is required instead of eating. Thus it seems
necessary to consider this question before discussing the symbolic
meaning of the burning of the *hattat*. We again take Lev 10.17 as a
starting point.

First of all, as argued above, Lev 10.17 gives the theological
explanation of the people's *hattat*; for v. 17b means, "and it (the
hattat) was assigned to you to bear the guilt of the congregation, thus
making atonement for them before the Lord'. However, it would be
unnatural to assume that only in the case of the eaten *hattat* do the
priests bear the guilt of the congregation, whereas the idea of bearing
guilt is extraneous to the burnt *hattat*. Rather it is reasonable to
assume that as long as the eaten and the burnt *hattat* concern
expiation of sin (sinfulness), both of them are equally related to
uncleanness and guilt.[93] In the case of the eaten *hattat* it is priests
who bear the guilt. The question is: who or what bears the guilt in
the case of the burnt *hattat*? There are two possibilities: either
Aaron, who is the agent of atonement (e.g. Lev 9.7), or the *hattat*
flesh itself. Since in Lev 9.7 Aaron is the agent of atonement for
himself as well as for the people, there is no reason to deny that
Aaron bears the guilt in the case of the burnt *hattat* as well. This is
also the corollary of our thesis that *kipper* includes in it the concept
of 'bearing guilt'. But why, then, does Aaron burn the *hattat* in Lev
9.11 instead of eating it? The reason can be sought in the
circumstance that the bearing of guilt is a substitutionary or
mediatory act in the eaten and the burnt *hattat*. So in the case of the
eaten *hattat*, priests are entitled to eat because they are the agent,
and not the beneficiary, of atonement. But when Aaron himself is
both the agent and the beneficiary of the atonement, there is some
element of self-contradiction, or imperfection, in the fact that Aaron
bears the guilt of his own (including the guilt in his capacity as the
high priest). There must be some agent for disposing of the guilt
Aaron bears, other than Aaron himself. Since there is no cultic
representative higher than Aaron, it may be inferred that the burning
of the *hattat* is related to the notion of 'removal of guilt'.

Lev 16.26-28 provides a significant datum for the symbolic
meaning of the burning of the *hattat*. It is remarkable that in vv. 28
and 26 the person who burned the *hattat* flesh outside the camp and
the one who handled the Azazel goat are assumed to be unclean, and
that the injunction to undergo purificatory rites is formulated in both
verses in exactly the same words:[94]

יכבס בגדיו ורחץ בשרו במים ואחרי כן יבא אל המחנה

This latter fact appears to suggest that the author intended to bring the symbolic meaning of the burning of the *hattat* to bear on what the Azazel goat does, i.e. bearing and removing the guilt.[95] Then it is highly likely that the burning of *hattat* symbolizes the removal of guilt, as suggested above.

We now conclude provisionally: The priestly consumption of the *hattat* signifies that priests have substitutionarily borne the guilt of the people, though the act of eating does not form part of the atoning process. The burning of the *hattat* outside the camp probably symbolizes 'removal of guilt'. Thus in the light of our proposal in Chapter 4 that *kipper* includes 'bearing guilt' as its semantic component, this rite may have some bearing on the atoning process. The rite is grounded upon the rationale that Aaron (or the high priest) cannot bear his own guilt substitutionarily.

c. *Contagiousness of the* hattat

Our suggestions about the rationale for eating and burning receive further support from a consideration of the contagiousness of the *hattat*.

Whether sin/uncleanness is transferred to the sacrifice has already been partially discussed in connection with the imposition of hand(s).[96] Although it was argued that in sacrificial contexts the idea of 'transference of sin/uncleanness' is dispensable, there are some problems which remain to be resolved. As noted above, Lev 16.28 prescribes washing of clothes and ablution of the person who burns the *hattat* flesh outside the camp. Moreover the ashes of the red heifer, which constitute a *hattat* (Num 19.9), also defile outside the camp those persons who have contact with the *hattat*. Can these instances justify the supposition that the *hattat* flesh is unclean? It thus seems necessary to inquire exegetically into the 'contagiousness' of the *hattat* flesh, which is discussed in Lev 6.17-23; 16.21-22, 23-24, 28; Num 19.

1. *Lev 6.17-23*

The section as a whole deals with the priestly dues regarding the *hattat* flesh and in vv. 20-21 makes some reference to the contagiousness of the *hattat* flesh and blood.

Some commentators[97] have taken these verses as a whole to refer to *holiness* contagion, though apparently without being much aware of the opposite view. This view seems to be clearly supported by two points: that the *hattat* flesh is stated to convey *holiness* (v. 20a), and that the splashed blood ought to be washed off in a *holy* place (v. 20b).

On the assumption, however, that the *hattat* blood absorbs uncleanness, Milgrom assumes that though v. 20a refers to *holiness* contagion, vv. 20b and 21 refer to *uncleanness* contagion.[98] This view seems to present a grave difficulty, because it assumes the coexistence of holiness and uncleanness in the same *hattat*, which is termed קדש קדשים. Furthermore, the mention of 'a holy place' in v. 20b suggests that the blood is nothing but holy.

Hoffmann, however, takes the two verses differently from the above two views. According to him,[99] v. 20a indeed refers to *holiness* contagion but v. 20b refers to *uncleanness* contagion, whereas v. 21 is the continuation of v. 20a, dealing with the *hattat* flesh (note the root בשל). Hoffmann gives two reasons for taking v. 20b as referring to *uncleanness* contagion: 1. Between v. 20a and v. 20b there exist such contrasts as יזה/יגע and מרמה/בבשרה. 2. The term תכבס suggests that cleansing from uncleanness is referred to. But these reasons are not compelling. It is true that the topic dealt with in each half verse differs: v. 20a the flesh and v. 20b the blood. But different topics do not necessarily mean different rules. It is also true that כבם appears in the context of purification from uncleanness (see e.g. Lev 11.35). However, the prescription that only the splashed part of the clothes must be washed (אשר יזה עליה) suggests that what is washed off is not uncleanness but holiness. For if it were uncleanness, this law might well have prescribed that all the clothes should be washed.[100]

Therefore we infer that the eaten *hattat*, both its flesh and blood, is קדש קדשים and conveys *holiness*, probably only to inanimate objects[101] within the sanctuary.

2. *Lev 16.21ff.*

Questions of uncleanness contagion are also raised by the Azazel-goat ritual.

It has been commonly assumed that by Aaron's imposition of hands the sins of the people materially transfer to the Azazel-goat, that the Azazel-goat becomes unclean accordingly, and that the person who sends out the Azazel-goat also becomes unclean.[102] The last two assumptions are problematic.

The fact that Aaron performs ablution and changes his garments (v. 24) does not seem to indicate that he becomes unclean.[103] The rite corresponds to the one in v. 4 and expresses the idea that even Aaron is unworthy to enter the holy of holies. That this change of clothing is not a mere formality is known from Exod 30.17-21, which says that the failure to wash hands and feet may lead to death. Yet as far as Lev 16.24 is concerned, it appears to express something more than Aaron's unworthiness in front of the holy of holies. Verse 24 specifies that Aaron must wash his body in a holy place (במקום קדוש). Along with Aaron's leaving his garments in the shrine (v. 23) this ablution does seem to express the idea that he washes off the high degree of holiness that has been contracted in the holy of holies (cf. Exod 29.37; 30.29).[104] At any rate it is unlikely that the rites in vv. 23-24 are required of Aaron because of uncleanness caused by handling the Azazel goat.

Despite the above arguments, the fact that the handlers of the Azazel-goat and the *hattat* flesh need to wash their clothes and undergo ablution (vv. 26, 28) appears to disprove the assumption that the Azazel-goat and the *hattat* flesh are not unclean. What is clear is that the handlers of the Azazel goat and the *hattat* flesh become unclean. But it is not clear why or how they do so.

3. *Numbers 19*

The idea that the instrument of purification defiles those who have contact with it finds a close parallel in Num 19, where all those concerned in preparing and employing the purification water become unclean. Most significantly this ritual too takes place outside the camp, as in Lev 16.26, 28.

The chapter deals with various rites concerning purification water (מי נדה) designed to purify persons and things defiled by corpses.[105] The peculiarity of the ritual lies in the fact that though the term *hattat* appears (vv. 9, 17), the whole ritual differs radically from that of the usual *hattat* ritual. A red heifer, instead of being slaughtered on the altar, is slaughtered outside the camp. And though the sprinkling of blood towards the shrine is prescribed, the whole heifer along with its remaining blood is burnt up. Furthermore, it is the ashes of the red heifer that are needed for making the purification water.

The most difficult question to answer is why all those involved in preparing the ashes and sprinkling the purification water become unclean, whereas they need to be clean before those acts. Various suggestions have been offered to solve this paradox of the red heifer, though some of them have already been presented above in connection with the usual burnt-*hattat*.

Firstly, there is a simple assumption that since the animal is unclean, it contaminates everything it has contact with.[106] However, this explanation, if not unlikely, does not appear to be consonant with the 'unblemishedness' of the heifer (v. 2), and the ashes being collected in a clean place (v. 9a) by a clean person (v. 9a) and being handled by clean persons (vv. 18, 19). A similar line of explanation can be found in the attempt to compare the slain red heifer to a carcass (נבלה, cf. Lev 11.39ff.). It too fails to explain the above facts, but anyway it is unlikely that a simple carcass is analogous to the red heifer, which is a purification agent.

The second approach is to assume that the defilement is caused not by the purification agent but by the uncleanness which it removes.[107] This explanation is distinguished from the first approach in that it assumes the animal to be holy. However, v.21bβ clearly implies that the ashes are the source of defilement.

The third approach is provided by a tannaitic saying 'Holy writ defiles the hand'.[108] The assumption that the red heifer and its ashes are holy appears to explain the paradox adequately. Since the clash between holiness and uncleanness must be avoided, it is only clean persons who can handle holiness, though that causes light defilement. But in one point this approach is unconvincing; if the red heifer cannot be unclean, it is never termed 'holy', at least in this context. But this fact may be in keeping with other purification agents such as 'running water', 'hyssop' and 'scarlet stuff' (vv. 6, 17-18) which are not termed 'holy' either.

The examination of the above three approaches seems to raise the following points: 1. The ashes are not called 'unclean' but defile. 2. The source of defilement is in the ashes and the purification water (v. 21bβ). 3. It seems problematic to consider the paradox of the red heifer in terms of 'holiness' and 'uncleanness' because neither of the terms explicitly qualifies the red heifer, the ashes and the purification water.

It may be suggested, then, that the concept 'death' is more appropriate to the nature of the ritual than 'uncleanness'. For it is highly likely that the person who burned the heifer became unclean because he had had contact with the symbolic death of the red heifer.[109] Hence we infer that defilement is caused by the ashes or the purification water because the latter symbolizes the death of the red heifer. However, though this 'death' is similar to the death of a human corpse (vv. 14ff.) in that both defile, there is a crucial difference. As the qualification of the heifer, i.e. fullness of life (v.2), and throwing of purifying agents (v.6) show, the ashes are regarded as the extract of the purifying agents. Therefore the ashes have an ambivalent character, in that they symbolize death, yet simultaneously are designed to counteract, as an antidote, the power of death caused by human corpses.

Further, it seems possible to point out an aspect of this antidote by comparing the defilement caused by burning of the heifer with the defilement caused by preparation of the purification water. In the former the purification agents are reduced to ashes, which symbolize death though they have the potential power of purification, whereas in the latter they are added to water. In other words, in the preparation of the purification water the death which the ashes symbolize is, as it were, diluted by 'running water' and 'hyssop', which symbolize life. And perhaps this situation may be reflected in different degrees of defilement which the purification agents (the ashes and the purification water) cause to their handlers, as the following comparison shows.

v. 7   הכהן--וכבס בגדיו הכהן ורחץ בשרו במים
ואחר יבא אל־המחנה וטמא הכהן עד־הערב

v. 8   השורף--יכבס בגדיו במים ורחץ בשרו במים
וטמא עד־הערב

v. 10   האוסף--וכבס האסף את־אפר הפרה את־בגדיו
וטמא עד־הערב

v. 21   ומזה מי־הנדה יכבס בגדיו
והנגע במי הנדה יטמא עד־הערב

One might argue that יכבס בגדיו or יטמא עד־הערב in v. 21 is an abbreviated form. But that these prescriptions should be taken literally is indicated by the fact that within vv. 7-10 וטמא עד־הערב is never abbreviated.[110] Moreover, in vv. 7-10 other purification rites appear to be graded subtly by the amount of uncleanness. Thus the priest (v. 7) and the person who burns the red heifer (v. 8) are required to undergo 'ablution', but the person who gathers the ashes is not. The reason for the difference may be that the former two actually had contact with the burning of blood whereas the latter did not. A further difference between v. 7 and v. 8, viz. the mention in v. 7 of ואחר יבא אל־המחנה, might be caused by the fact that v. 7 speaks of the priest while v. 8 speaks of a lay individual.[111]

To summarize: The red heifer represents purificatory death, an antidote to the death of human corpses. Because of the symbolic death it embodies, the handlers of the ashes and the purification water become unclean. However, thanks to the far lesser degree of defilement the red heifer causes, it can purify the seven-day corpse contamination.

Having surveyed the relevant sections of the *hattat* contagion, we attempt below to draw some conclusions as to whether the *hattat* becomes unclean or not.

Our examination of Lev 6.17-23; 16.21ff.; Num 19 leads to the conclusion that the *hattat* sacrifice conveys holiness within the sanctuary but that it defiles outside the camp. This implies that the contagiousness of the *hattat* derives from the sacrifice itself, but that the mode of its manifestation is dependent on the topographical distinction, whether the sacrifice is in the sanctuary or outside the camp.

However, it seems that the whole issue whether the *hattat* becomes unclean or not has been inadequately discussed, because the very terms used in the discussion, namely 'uncleanness', 'guilt' and 'holiness', have not been reconsidered.

First of all, it seems appropriate to make a distinction between 'uncleanness' produced by natural causes or sins, and 'uncleanness' envisaged in sancta. For sancta (including sacrifices) are never said to be 'unclean' (טמא), though they can be so envisaged (e.g. Lev 15.31; 16.16). Moreover, the distinction seems necessary to avoid the contradiction that sancta are simultaneously holy and unclean. This also applies to the red heifer, which, though defiling, is never called unclean.

Secondly, and a step further, the term 'uncleanness' or 'guilt' may not be adequate for characterizing the contagion in Lev 16.21ff. In view of the fact that עון and טומאה are both associated with 'death', it may be better to assume that the handlers of the Azazel goat and the *hattat* flesh are both defiled because they have had contact with death. And this 'death' motif indeed seems to characterize better the nature of contagion in Num 19, as well.

Thirdly, this 'death' motif also seems present in Lev 6.20-21. For it is striking that this section shows close linguistic affinity with Lev 11.33, 35; 15.12 which stipulate how the contaminated things should be disposed of.[112] It seems plausible, then, that by adopting the similar expressions Lev 6.20bff. hints that the eaten *hattat* appears to be holy but simultaneously and essentially symbolizes death.

It goes without saying that even when the term 'death' is adopted instead of 'uncleanness' for the description of the contagion of the *hattat*, it is still necessary to make a distinction between the actual death and the substitutionary (or antidotal) death.

Conclusions

The following conclusions may be drawn from the above discussion of 'the imposition of hand(s)', 'the blood manipulation' and 'the disposal of the *hattat*'.

In the light of Lev 1.4 the imposition of a hand in sacrificial contexts could symbolize 'substitution', and the same may apply to Lev 16.21. Though it has been almost unanimously agreed that the imposition of both hands in Lev 16.21 symbolizes 'transference of sin/guilt', this may not be the meaning of the act itself.

The symbolism of the *hattat* ritual should not be pursued only from the viewpoint of the mode of blood manipulation, the *hizzāh* and *nātan* gestures. For the varieties of the ritual are essentially motivated by their occasions. From this viewpoint there are essentially two types of ritual, both of which point to the ritual on the day of Atonement. One is the *hattat* ritual designed to expiate the sin (sinfulness) of the priestly house (Exod 29.10-14; Lev 8.14-17; 9.8-14, atonement of the whole people included in that of Aaron). It is performed on the occasion of priestly installation. But as argued above, the Nadab and Abihu incident shows the inadequacy of the ritual, and points to the all-sufficient ritual on the day of Atonement. The other is the *hattat* ritual which expiates the sin, or purifies the uncleanness, of the people (Lev 4.1ff.) on regular occasions. In this present Chapter it has been shown that the rituals in Lev 4.3-21 foreshadow the ritual on the day of Atonement (Lev 16.14ff.), indicating incompleteness in the blood manipulation. Milgrom's thesis that the determining factor of the four (five) rituals in Lev 4 is the amount of uncleanness seems unnecessary.

Both the *hizzāh* and *nātan* gestures symbolize purification of sancta. Yet the *hizzāh* gesture, being mostly associated with the Tent, may be more potent than the *nātan* gesture, which by contrast is mostly associated with the outer altar.

Eating the *hattat* is a priestly privilege and duty. It does not form part of the atoning process, nor is it likely to have been regarded as part of the *hattat* ceremony. In contrast, the burning of the *hattat* outside the camp appears to be part of the ceremony and may symbolize 'removal of guilt'. The rationale of burning the *hattat* is that when expiation involves the sin(-fulness) of Aaron (not only as an individual but also in his capacity as the high priest) the *hattat* must be burned outside the camp to remove his guilt.

The *hattat*, whether it is the eaten or the burnt one, is contagious. Yet the two kinds of *hattat* appear to show disparity in their contagiousness. The eaten *hattat* conveys holiness within the sanctuary, whereas the burnt *hattat* probably conveys holiness within the sanctuary but defiles, like the Azazel goat, its handler outside the camp. In a deeper dimension it is the death which the sacrificial animal symbolizes that causes both the holiness and uncleanness contagions.

Chapter 6

THE *HATTAT* OFFERING IN LEV 16

As has already been mentioned in passing, the *hattat* offering plays a central role in the atonement ceremony on the day of Atonement (Lev 16.3-28).[1] In this final Chapter we propose to discuss the ceremonies of this day more fully because they shed much light on the priestly theology of atonement and on the function of the *hattat* in particular.

According to Lev 16, Aaron is required to prepare five sacrificial animals, one *hattat* bull and one עולה ram for the atonement of Aaron and his house, and two *hattat* goats and one עולה for the atonement of all the Israelites.

We have, however, already discussed, albeit partially, various aspects of Lev 16 in the previous chapters (esp. chs. 3, 4, 5) and it only remains to clarify the function of those *hattat* and the nature of the whole ceremony, based on the conclusions reached in the previous discussion.

As already mentioned,[2] it has been widely held by modern critics that Lev 16 is literarily composite. How one should explain this compositeness is not the question we shall attempt to answer in this Chapter. Yet, though we do not deny the compositeness, it is the conviction of the present author that the atonement theology expressed through the ritual in Lev 16 is far more coherent than has hitherto been thought.

The central question raised by the *hattat* in Lev 16 concerns the function of the Azazel-goat ritual (vv. 5, 8-10, 21-22, 26); why are two goats required (v. 5)? And why is the Azazel-goat ritual necessary?

In an attempt to answer these questions we shall first offer an exegesis of passages relevant to the Azazel-goat ritual, especially vv. 5, 10 and 16/21 (A). Then (B) we shall try to explain how the atonement ceremony on the day of Atonement is related to the other ceremonies, and propose a possible interpretation of these rituals.

A. *The Relationship of the Rites of Blood Sprinkling and the Azazel Goat*

Presentation of the problem

By the two rites we mean the atonement ceremony performed for the purification of sancta (vv. 9, 11b-19) and the Azazel-goat ceremony (vv. 5, 10, 21-22). It is clear that these two rites are distinct from each other.[3] But the existence of the two rites poses the obvious question how they are related to each other. The relationship between the two rites, however, goes back to the relationship between the two *hattat* offerings taken from the congregation of the Israelites (v. 5), since the Azazel goat is one of the two goats assigned to make atonement for the Israelites. Basically the question resolves into one simple but fundamental one: Why is the Azazel goat necessary; or to put it another way, why is removal of guilt required on this particular occasion?

It appears that modern critics have tended to ignore this question for two major reasons. First, it has often been presumed that Lev 16 is composite, made up of various sources or literary strata, so that any attempt to view the atonement ceremony as a whole has tended to be seen as extraneous to the nature of the text.[4] Second, various ideas expressed by the Azazel-goat ritual have tended to be seen as so exceptional as not to allow a contextual reading of the text related to the ritual. This tendency is well reflected in Elliger's following comment:

> Das letzte Hauptstück des Sühnerituals in seiner jetzigen Form ist die feierliche Entlassung des Sündenbockes. Es ist, wie oben zu 8-10 schon betont, offensichtlich das älteste und war einmal vermutlich das einzige des Versöhnungstages. Denn der Brauch, ein Tier mit der menschlichen Schuld, dieser aus sich heraus weiter Verderben wirkenden Macht, zu beladen und es dann vom Aufenthaltsplatz der Menschen weit entfernt in der Einöde auszusetzen, so daß für die Urheber keine Gefahr mehr besteht, ist eine in sich völlig geschlossene Sache und bedarf keiner Ergänzung, geschweige denn einer Parallele.[5]

Indeed as regards the Azazel-goat ritual, scholars have paid attention almost exclusively to the non-sacrificial character of the goat and the enigmatic name Azazel.[6] However, although any investigation into the origin of the Azazel-goat ritual is justified and necessary, it is equally important to inquire into the meaning of the ritual in its present context, viz. what the supposed editor intended by incorporating this ritual into the present context. In the following section we shall attempt to answer this question by interacting with various commentators.

a. *Various approaches to the two rites*
In the history of the interpretation of Lev 16 there are some exegetes who have attempted to resolve the problem, assuming the present text describing the two rites. There seem to be three possible approaches to the relationship of the two rites, assuming that the two rites are distinct: 1. The two rites deal with two kinds of sin entirely different from each other. 2. The two rites are functionally continuous in some sense. 3. The Azazel-goat ritual expresses, in a different form, the meaning of the purification rite in the sancta, which has already been completed, without adding anything essentially new.

We shall critically examine below these approaches to the relationship of the two rites. As will be shown, approaches 1 and 3 have some reference to one of the following passages: vv. 5, 10, 16a/21a. These important passages will, however, be discussed separately.

1. Recently, drawing on Jewish tradition[7] Milgrom has maintained that 'the slain bull and goat purge the shrine of the (physical) pollution, טמאת, of the Israelites and their brazen sins, פשעים (Lev 16.16; cf. 16.19), and the scapegoat carries off their iniquities, עונת (16.20)'.[8] This view appears to be based on what the text says. However, both Milgrom and the rabbinic tradition assume that the source of sancta pollution is different from that of 'iniquities'. Furthermore, it is inferred that the function of the *hattat* on the day of Atonement includes purging 'rebellious sins' (פשעים).[9] Apart from the question how פשע should be translated, the inadequacy of this classification of 'uncleanness' and 'sins' seems to be indicated by the phrase פשעיהם לכל חמאתם, repeated in v. 16a and v. 21a; for this fact appears to indicate that the two rites deal with two aspects of the same sins. Moreover, we have argued in connection with Lev 10.17, firstly that it is inadequate to see עון as a concept extraneous to טמאה, and secondly that when the priests perform purification rites, they bear the guilt of the congregation.[10] Thus it seems unlikely that the purification of sancta is unrelated to the Azazel-goat ritual in the handling of the sins. Nevertheless this view deserves note for calling attention to the sin terminology in vv. 16a, 21a.

2. The majority of scholars have, however, made general comments on the relationship of the two rites, as follows:

Durch die Sündopfer und besonders das Blutsprengen ist für die begangenen Sünden Begnadigung und Straflosigkeit erwirkt. . . . Das gesühnte Volk ist seiner Sünden ledig und schickt sie nun, durch den HP. dem Bock aufgeladen, auf und mit diesem von sich weg. . .[11]

. . . through the ritual performed by the High Priest in the Tent, sin is removed from the sanctuary and through the laying on of hands, transferred to the goat.[12]

These explanations see the relationship of the two rites as one of *continuation*, or rather they dimly assume that Aaron's work in the sancta is completed by the Azazel goat. The idea itself is possible, but must face Kurtz's criticisms: 1. On this view, the confession of sins should precede the sprinkling of blood which re-established the God-man relationship, and not vice-versa. 2. If the sin were removed by the sprinkling of blood, the Azazel-goat ritual would have been unnecessary. If, conversely, the Azazel-goat ritual is required for the total annihilation of the sin, why is that sort of ritual not required in the ordinary *hattat* ritual (e.g. Lev 4)?[13] Underlying these criticisms is Kurtz's conviction that through the sprinkling of blood atonement of sancta is entirely completed, with which we agree. Then why is the Azazel-goat ritual required? In our opinion this stalemate stems from the circumstance that the concept of 'atonement' has not been clarified.

3. Referring to v. 5, some scholars have argued that the two rites form one symbolic whole. Thus S. Landersdorfer writes:

Die tatsächlich Entsühnung erfolgt durch die Darbringung des ersten Bockes und durch die Sprengung des Blutes im Heiligtum. Der Ritus mit dem zweiten Bock soll die bereits erfolgte Entsühnung nur symbolisieren, in anschaulicher, dem gemeinen Mann fasslicher Weise zur Darstellung bringen. . . . Es sollen eben eigentlich an dem einen Opfertier zwei verschiedene Zeremonien vorgenommen werden, die des Opferns zur Bewirkung der Sühne und die der Entsendung in die Wüste zur Symbolisierung der Sühnewirkung. Da sich beide Handlungen an ein und demselben Individuum nicht vollziehen lassen, werden sie auf zwei Tiere verteilt, die aber der Idee nach ein einziges Opfertier darstellen.[14]

It was Kurtz, however, who underlined the importance of our problem and reached the above standpoint after detailed argument.[15] For Kurtz,[16] who starts from the assumption that atonement of sancta has been completed without the Azazel-goat ritual, the

greatest problem is the phrase לכפר עליו in v. 10, to which he gives
the translation 'to perform an act of expiation *over* it'. Although
Kurtz does not think that the imposition of hands on the Azazel goat
is an act of atonement, he nevertheless includes the act of imposition
of hands in the concept of atonement by assuming 'the ideal unity of
the two goats' (v. 5). Thus he concludes that 'the act of laying the
sins upon the head of the goat had regard to the sins *already expiated*,
and that they were sent into the desert to Azazel not as still
unexpiated, and deserving the wrath and punishment of God but as
expiated, covered, and deprived of all their power'.[17] The corollary of
this inference is that the unloading and removal of guilt performed
by Aaron on this occasion is *implicitly* assumed even in ordinary
hattat ritual.[18]

Apart from Kurtz's interpretation of vv. 5, 10 his view of the two
rites must face the following criticisms. Firstly, not only is there no
Azazel-goat ritual in the ordinary *hattat* ritual but, as shown in the
previous Chapter,[19] it is unlikely that the imposition of a hand in the
ordinary *hattat* ritual symbolizes the transference of guilt. Secondly,
it is not clear what Kurtz means by 'the sin already expiated'.
Modern terms like 'sin' and 'expiation' must first be defined. At any
rate, if the sins are already disposed of in the purification of the
sancta, the Azazel-goat ritual appears to be unnecessary, as Kurtz
himself realizes.[20] Thirdly, not only does the rite in vv. 21-22 give the
impression that the guilt is unexpiated, being actualized by Aaron's
confession, but the fact that the handler of the Azazel goat becomes
unclean outside the camp indicates that the guilt loaded on the goat
is not expiated, covered, and deprived of all its power. This last point
must be stressed against any attempt to see the Azazel-goat ritual as
a mere symbolic act *emphasizing the completeness of the atonement
for the sancta.*

From the criticisms of the above three approaches we set out the
following assumptions as the starting point of our independent
inquiry.

1. While atonement (purification) of sancta is over, the
   removal of guilt is not over. This means that unlike Kurtz's
   view the relationship of the two rites must be one of
   continuation in some sense (cp. section 2 above).
2. It is likely that the sin terminology in vv. 16a, 21a refers to
   two aspects of the same sins.

In view of these points we suggest here the following hypothesis on

the relationship of the two rites. The clue to the relationship, we
argue, lies in the fact that the concept of *kipper* includes both
'purification' and 'bearing guilt', as has been argued in Chapter 4.[21]
When this fact is applied to the atonement ceremony in Lev 16.14ff.,
the connection between the two rites becomes immediately clear. By
purifying sancta from uncleanness Aaron bears the guilt of the
Israelites. Then the guilt he has borne is devolved upon the Azazel
goat when Aaron lays his hands on it and confesses the sins. To
substantiate this hypothesis we shall turn to the examination of vv. 5,
10, 16a/21a.

b. *Verse 5*
The passage reads:

ומאת עדת בני ישראל יקח שני-שעירי עזים לחטאת ואיל אחד לעלה

How should the phrase לחטאת be construed? The most natural
translation would be 'for the *hattat* offering'. This phrase has,
however, created an exegetical tension, because after Aaron casts
lots, one of the two goats is explicitly called חטאת (v. 9b) whereas the
other is not, though this fact may not imply that the Azazel goat is
not a *hattat*.[22] To avoid this apparent incongruity Dillmann proposed
to translate the phrase לחטאת 'für die Beseitigung der Sünde'.[23]
However, this is unlikely in the light of the other occurrences of the
phrase (e.g. Lev 4.3) and particularly of the following ואיל אחד לעלה;
the חטאת must be the name of the sacrifice.[24] As already mentioned,
some scholars have tried to explain the relationship of the two
ceremonies by drawing upon v. 5, which explicitly says the two goats
are one *hattat*. Against this approach Rodriguez has recently
maintained that 'since the goat for the *ḥṭṭ't* has not been chosen yet
(v. 5), potentially either one of them was a *ḥṭṭ't*'.[25] Clearly Rodriguez
assumes that the Azazel goat is not a *hattat*. However, though this
assumption appears natural, it seems to go slightly beyond the
evidence since, as mentioned above, that is simply not explicitly
stated in the text. Does ועשהו חטאת in v. 9b necessarily imply that the
other goat is not a *hattat*? Moreover it seems difficult to assume that
after two goats are destined for the *hattat*, one of them ceases to be a
hattat, even if the casting of lots is taken into account. Strictly
speaking, by Aaron's casting lots one goat is chosen for 'the Lord' as
opposed to being chosen for 'the *hattat*'.
    In the following we shall argue that the most likely view is that the
two goats form one *hattat*. We shall do this by considering the

disposal of the *hattat*, which has been overlooked in connection with the interpretation of v. 5. In Chapter 5 we argued that the symbolic meaning of the burning of the *hattat* was deliberately identified with that of the sending off of the Azazel goat; in both cases guilt is removed. In the light of this it may be further argued that the Azazel-goat ritual is a special form of the burning of the *hattat*. In other words, on other regular occasions 'the removal of guilt' is symbolized by the burning of the *hattat* outside the camp, whereas only on the day of Atonement is that element of the *hattat* ceremony solemnly expressed by the special form of eliminating the guilt. Since the *hattat* flesh is also part of the *hattat*, it is not implausible to infer that the Azazel-goat ritual is also regarded as functioning as the burning of the *hattat* flesh.

However, though we agree that the two goats form the *hattat* offering, our standpoint should not be confused with those who have attempted to explain the two rites by saying that the Azazel-goat ritual symbolizes the atonement that has taken place in the sancta. Rather, we infer that the two rites are continuous in terms of symbolism and that the Azazel goat is viewed as a special form of the *hattat*.[26]

c. *Verse 10*

The next crucial passage is v. 10, because it appears to refer to the Azazel-goat ritual in vv. 21-22. It reads:

v. 10   וחשעיר אשר עלה עליו הגורל לעזאזל יעמד חי
לפני ה' לכפר עליו לשלח אתו לעזאזל המדברה

The phrase לְכַפֵּר עָלָיו in this passage has caused much difficulty in understanding the passage as a whole. Yet, as we shall argue, this phrase constitutes a clue to the relationship of the two rites. Five interpretations have been proposed concerning the meaning of this phrase.

Firstly, Levine holds that 'the rites prescribed in verse 10 do not pertain directly to the scapegoat. They have as their referent the bull and the other goat, slaughtered as *ḥaṭṭā't* sacrifices'.[27] Since Levine believes that על + כפר means 'to perform rites of expiation in proximity to',[28] he understands that 'the scapegoat was merely stationed near the altar while the priest took some of the sacrificial blood for use in the expiatory rites'.[29] This interpretation is, however, totally unlikely, in that v.10 speaks only about the rite of the Azazel goat. Moreover, it is doubtful whether כפר על can mean 'to perform rites of expiation in proximity to'.[30]

As is clear from Levine's interpretation, the problem of the phrase centres on the questions what עליו refers to, and what or who the agent of לכפר is, rather than on the meaning of כפר.

The second possibility is to take it to mean 'to atone, or expiate for it (sc. the Azazel goat)'. Thus Keil construes it as meaning 'to expiate, i.e. to make it the object of expiation'.[31] This interpretation appears meaningless, however, since the animal is normally an instrument of expiation and not the object of it. For this reason most modern exegetes regard the phrase as a scribal error or an interpolation. This is the third option.[32]

The fourth approach (Dillmann) is to construe the phrase as 'the consecration of the scapegoat' for the rite in v. 21.[33] But as Dillmann admits, it is not clear why it is necessary to atone for the Azazel goat.

The fifth exegetical possibility is the view represented by traditional Jewish exegetes and some modern scholars that the phrase means 'to atone over it (sc. the Azazel goat)'.[34] However it should be noted that the interpretation is offered by scholars for different reasons. Milgrom, for instance, translates it this way on the basis of his assumption that when the reference is made to a non-human being כפר על must be taken literally. Others, like Kurtz, regard the phrase in v. 10 as exceptional. We have argued, however, that the distinction between human and non-human objects regarding כפר is arbitrary.[35] If כפר על in v. 10 means 'to make purification rites *over*', this usage must be regarded as exceptional.

Now it is a fact that in vv. 21-22 the preposition על serves four times to indicate the place, i.e. the head of the Azazel goat, where the imposition of hands (על ראש השעיר), the confession of sins (התודה עליו), the transfer of guilt (נתן על ראש השעיר) and the removal of it (נשא השעיר עליו) occur. Does this fact support the view that כפר על in v. 10 means 'to atone *over*'? Against the temptation to identify the fourfold על with על followed by כפר, it must be borne in mind that a similar relation exists between כפר על and נתן דם על, הזה דם על (see vv. 18-19) whereas כפר על is unlikely to mean 'to make atonement upon', as already argued. Moreover, it is doubtful whether Aaron's rites over the head of the goat constitute an act of atonement.

It seems that each proposal presented above has some forced element. But the exegetical possibilities are not exhausted. It is proposed here that the third-person pronominal suffix in כפר עליו

refers to Aaron, and that the agent of לכפר is the Azazel goat.[36] That this is the most natural (though theologically challenging) interpretation of the phrase is indicated by the following circumstances.

1. Verse 10 stands alone from the preceding and the following passages in that the whole sentence is constructed in the passive. The subject is השעיר and followed by יָעֳמַד, passive form of הֶעֱמִיד. In spite of Ehrlich's proposal that יָעֳמַד should be read יַעֲמִיד as in Sam,[37] the passive construction as it now stands makes perfect sense. Moreover though the proposal may stem from the existence of העמיד in v. 7, it must be noted that vv. 7 and 10 speak of two different stages of the ritual; v. 7 speaks of Aaron's stationing of the two goats before casting lots, whereas v. 10 refers to the period of time before the purification of sancta is completed (v. 20).

Now it is conspicuous that in vv. 7-9 Aaron has been dealing with the two goats equally, but in v. 10 the subject suddenly shifts to the live goat. More specifically it should be observed that in v. 9 the slain goat is the object of Aaron's handling, whereas in v. 10 the live goat is the subject of the sentence. It could be assumed that the shift of subject has something to do with the casting of lots, since before the casting of lots it is Aaron who handles the two goats. In view of this observation the passive structure of v. 10 could be deliberate, suggesting the reversal of the subject-object relationship in v. 7.

If v. 10 as a whole were read with an awareness of the subject-object relationship in vv. 7-9, it would not be strange that in v. 10 the pronominal suffix in עליו refers to Aaron, and that the agent of לכפר is the Azazel goat. According to this reading, the phrase לשלח etc. can be translated impersonally: 'by sending it'. The whole sentence would thus mean: 'But the goat on which Azazel's lot comes up must be stood alive before the Lord to make atonement for him (Aaron) by sending it to Azazel to the Wilderness'.

2. In the light of the above proposal the relationship between v. 10 and vv. 21b-22 can be clarified more clearly than it has been. The text runs as follows:

v. 10　והשעיר אשר עלה עליו הגורל לעזאזל יעמד חי
לפני ה' לכפר עליו לשלח אתו לעזאזל המדברה
　　B　　　　A

v. 21b　ונתן אתם על ראש השעיר ושלח ביד איש עתי המדברה
　　　B'

v. 22　ונשא השעיר עליו את כל עונתם אל ארץ גזרה
　　　A'

ושלח את השעיר במדבר
　B''

In Chapter 4 it has been argued that the concept of כפר includes that of נשא עון.[38] So A' can be the *kipper* act.[39] Then the change of subject in A and B is clearly reflected in A' and B', B''. Firstly, the fact that the agent of לכפר in A is the Azazel goat matches A' where the Azazel goat is the subject of the sentence. Secondly, as proposed above the agent of לשלח in B is impersonal. And this interpretation seems appropriate in that the subject of ושלח in B' is Aaron, whereas that of ושלח in B'' is probably איש עתי (= a man appointed for the job);[40] in either case the subject is not the Azazel goat. It should be added that A' is the only section in vv. 21-22 where the Azazel goat is the subject, a feature similar to v. 10. These observations thus seem to warrant the assumption that A corresponds to A'.

3. At this point we adduce Lev 1.4, which seems to support our interpretation of Lev 16.10, 21-22 thematically and syntactically.

Lev 1.4 reads:

וסמך ידו על ראש העלה ונרצה לו לכפר עליו

Here the offerer who lays his hand on the sacrifice (v.4a) becomes the beneficiary of the atonement made by the sacrifice (v. 4b).[41] This relationship in the imposition of a hand between the offerer and the sacrifice perfectly suits Lev 16.10, 21-22, where, we argue, the Azazel goat makes atonement for Aaron. Also Lev 1.4b provides a fitting example in which לכפר (the *lamed* expressing purpose) is preceded by a passive verb, i.e. נרצה. This syntactical feature is common to Lev 16.10, where לכפר is preceded by the passive יעמד. In the light of this parallel construction it may be inferred that, just as in Lev 1.4b the agent of לכפר is the sacrifice, in Lev 16.10 the agent of לכפר is the Azazel goat.

As already stated, it can be assumed that Aaron bears the guilt of the Israelites when he makes atonement for sancta (vv. 14-19), and that since he bears their guilt, he confesses it in v. 21 (cp. Lev 5.5); the guilt is then devolved on the Azazel goat and the latter carries it off into the wilderness. This possibility seems to be strengthened by our interpretation of v. 10 and its relationship with vv. 20-21.

Now it goes without saying that Aaron lays his hands on the Azazel goat on behalf of the whole people. However, unlike earlier interpretations of the two ceremonies in Lev 16, this view strongly emphasizes the substitutionary aspect of the rite, that Aaron is not simply a representative of the people, but he himself is envisaged as bearing their guilt. In other words, the idea behind vv. 21-22 is not that Aaron lays his hands on the goat instead of the Israelites, but that he himself is guilty in a substitutionary capacity. And it is probably in this sense that v. 10 refers to Aaron in עליו.

Though we think that the above interpretation is what v. 10 says, the last point, that the Azazel goat makes atonement for Aaron, will become more understandable in the light of the following two points. One of these has already been made, and the other concerns a common misunderstanding of the text.

Firstly, it should be recalled that in Lev 9.7 and Lev 10.17 Aaron is to bear the guilt of the priests as a whole and the guilt of the people. Although the intention of the atonement ceremony in Lev 9 is different from that of Lev 16, the basic principle seems to be reflected in Lev 16 as well. Therefore it would not be strange that Aaron is envisaged to be bearing guilt by purifying sancta, and that, more significantly, he bears the guilt of both priests and the people (see below).

Secondly, the purification of sancta and removal of guilt both concern the sins of בני ישראל (vv. 16, 21). But does this appellation include Aaron and his house? The obvious clue lies in vv. 18-19, where the blood is said to come from that of the bull (פר) and the goat (שעיר), used in the purification of sancta (vv. 14-15), i.e. from both the priests' and the people's offerings.[42] Therefore בני ישראל in v. 19 includes Aaron and his house. Consequently it is probable that v. 16 is a theological explanation not only of v. 15 but also of v. 14. This means that העם in v. 15[43] excludes Aaron and his house whereas בני ישראל in v. 16 includes them. This inference is confirmed by Lev 4.2-3; 9.7, 15, 18, 22, 23, 24; 10.3; 16.24.[44] Thus it should be concluded that בני ישראל in Lev 16.21 includes Aaron and his house as well as the people.[45] Thus, at least it is unlikely that Aaron, being *innocent*, lays his hands on the Azazel goat *instead of* the whole people. Rather, Aaron is regarded as guilty on a substitutionary level when he lays his hands on the Azazel goat.

More aspects of the relationship between the two rites will be discussed below. For if our interpretation is right, we must discuss one remaining obstacle. Does the text suggest that the sins and uncleanness atoned for on this day are different in kind from those usually dealt with by the *hattat*?

d. *Verses 16.21*

When the terms for sin in v. 16a are compared with those in v.21a, it is striking that מפשעיהם לכל חטאתם in v. 16a is repeated in v. 21a.[46] As mentioned above, this fact seems to indicate that the editor intended the two rites to have a common purpose, namely the removal of חטאת (sin).[47]

However, the difference between the two passages is equally significant: in v. 21a עונת appears instead of טמאת in v. 16a. As has been argued in Chapter 2, to construe עון as 'moral sin' is inadequate. Rather, it denotes the necessary relationship between sin/uncleanness and its consequence, death. In this context too the term could be rendered 'guilt'.

Then the question arises how טמאת in v. 16a is related to עונת in v. 21a. Before answering this question it needs to be asked how לכל חטאתם in v. 16a is related to the preceding.[48] Does it modify only פשעיהם or טמאת בני ישראל as well? We translate חטאת 'sin' and פשע 'transgression' for convenience's sake.[49] Then, since פשעיהם is clearly modified by לכל חטאתם (= with respect to all their sins),[50] the question is whether the latter can govern טמאת בני ישראל.

The importance of this question should be underlined. If it can,[51] it follows that the 'uncleanness' refers, at least, to a kind of uncleanness which is produced or envisaged in sancta when purification rites are not observed (Lev 15.31, see below), and not to simple physical uncleanness (e.g. Lev 11.24ff.). If, however, לכל חטאתם does not modify טמאת בני ישראל,[52] the latter could refer to all kinds of uncleanness.

Since this question is unlikely to be resolved by observing the immediate context of Lev 16.16, another passage Lev 15.31 must be brought into the discussion in order to decide on this question.

Lev 15.31 appears to allude to the ritual on the day of Atonement, especially to Lev 16.16b. There is an unmistakable linguistic affinity between the two passages:

15.31b   ולא ימתו בטמאתם בטמאם את משכני אשר בתוכם
16.16b   לאהל מועד השכן אתם בתוך טמאתם

Furthermore Lev 16.16b appears to presume Lev 15.31 in that the latter refers to the possibility of defiling the tabernacle while the former presumes the defiled sancta.

According to Elliger[53] Lev 15.31 is alien to the context of the cleanness/uncleanness laws in Lev 15 for the following reasons. First, Moses and Aaron are abruptly spoken to in this passage, which stands before the colophon vv. 32-33. Second, the idea that God's dwelling is defiled is entirely new in Lev 11-15. But since the idea is found in Lev 16.16 and also the motif of ולא ימות (Lev 16.2, 3) has a special role in Lev 8.35; 10.6, 7, 9 Elliger prefers to identify the author of Lev 15.31 with the redactor who inserted Lev 11-15 between Lev 10 and Lev 16.

It is beyond the scope of the present Chapter to discuss the literary strata of Lev 15 or Lev 11-15. But as for Lev 15 the recognition that in Lev 15.31 Moses and Aaron are spoken to depends on v. 1. However, it seems unnecessary to assume that the introductory formula represents a literary stratum different from that of the laws themselves. Rather stylistic features common to Lev 11 and Lev 15 should be noted at this point; Lev 15.1-2a closely resembles Lev 11.1-2a. The theological motivation (Lev 11.44-45; 15.31) comes just before the colophons (Lev 11.46-47; 15.32-33). In view of these features Elliger's proposal to separate Lev 15.31 from the surrounding text seems unnecessary. Except for this point, however, his observation that Lev 15.31 was inserted by the redactor of Lev 11-15 seems likely in the light of its relationship with Lev 16.16b mentioned above. In this case it follows that, though the idea of God's dwelling place being defiled is explicitly mentioned only here within Lev 11-15, the redactor intended to bring all the cleanness-uncleanness laws in Lev 11-15 under this theological principle.

What about the exact meaning of Lev 15.31? As it has been translated[54] it would mean 'You shall warn the Israelites against uncleanness, that they die not in their uncleanness when they defile my tabernacle that is in the midst of them'. The passage appears to envisage a failure to observe purification rules, which could lead to death. The cause of death in the event of the failure is twofold; uncleanness itself and the offence of defiling the tabernacle. Thus this passage appears to assume that the physical uncleanness set out in Lev 11-15 does not itself defile God's dwelling place as long as the purification rules are observed.

Now it must be stressed that משכני (= 'my tabernacle') in Lev 15.31 refers to the complex consisting of the adytum and the shrine, whereas the term אהל מועד in Lev 16.16b, which is interchangeable with משכן in other contexts,[55] is used in Lev 16 to designate only the shrine (see vv. 17, 20, 23, 33).[56] This means that the defilement of the adytum (טמאת בני ישראל, v. 16a) as well as that of the shrine (v. 16b) is caused, by the failure to observe the purification rules and not by simple physical uncleanness. Therefore we conclude that in v. 16a טמאת בני ישראל modifies לכל חמאתם. In other words, since both טמאת and פשעים are modified by חמאת, the purification of sancta deals with the uncleanness produced by sins. Furthermore, since the syntactical construction in v. 16a regarding לכל חמאתם is the same as that in

v. 21a, it seems probable that עונת in v. 21a expresses the other side of the same חטאת. This confirms the inference drawn in Chapter 2 that חטאת (sin) consists of 'uncleanness' and 'guilt'.[57]

To recapitulate: The above examination of vv. 5, 10, 16a/21a has led to the following conclusions.

1. The Azazel-goat ritual has tended to be isolated from its context. But it can be shown from our interpretation of v. 5 that it is a special form of the burning of the *hattat*.
2. According to our new interpretation of v. 10 the guilt that Aaron has borne in purifying the defiled sancta is devolved upon the Azazel goat. Thus the relationship of the two rites is a continuous one.
3. This relationship is also confirmed by the fact that 'uncleanness' in v. 16a corresponds to 'guilt' in v. 21a, both of which constitute important aspects of חטאת.

B. *Relationship with other Atonement Ceremonies*

According to our interpretation of vv. 16 and 21 it follows that the adytum, the shrine and the outer altar are assumed to have been defiled by the sins of the Israelites. This is a strong piece of evidence for supporting 'sancta pollution'. Yet the fact that on the day of Atonement all the sins of the Israelites are to be purified creates apparent redundancy, since expiation has been made for the same sins on regular occasions (Lev 4.1–5.13). Thus this circumstance calls for an explanation of the relationship between this atonement ceremony and other ones on regular occasions. Are the latter to be regarded as insufficient?

We have already suggested that the rituals in Lev 4.3-21 and Lev 9 are insufficient because the day of Atonement rituals in some way cover the same ground.[58]

However, it is problematic to regard the rituals in Lev 4 themselves as insufficient. For except in the first case, forgiveness, the purpose of atonement, is granted after the priest makes atonement for the sinner.

Thus the total overlapping of atonement, that the sins which were once expiated are once again in view on the day of Atonement, should caution modern writers against over-precise reasoning. At this point the view advanced in Chapter 2[59] concerning the repetitiveness of the ritual should be recalled in an attempt to explain this relationship between the atonement ceremony on the day of Atonement and those on regular occasions.

Two things were inferred on the basis of the ritual for the purification of the leper. 1. The leper is clean enough at each stage of the ritual, so that it is inadequate to compare one stage of the ritual with another in terms of the degree of cleanness. 2. At the final stage of the ritual the leper is assumed to be standing before the Lord as a person who needs purification. We shall propose here that these two aspects can be applied most reasonably in another sphere, the relationship between the ceremony on the day of Atonement and other ceremonies.

First, as sins are supposed to be cleansed on regular occasions, it seems inadequate to see the atonement on regular occasions to be insufficient. Rather it seems better to look at the ceremony on the day of Atonement in isolation without comparing it with other atonement ceremonies as far as their validity as means of atonement is concerned. Secondly, and conformably, on the day of Atonement it is assumed that all the Israelites need atonement; all the people stand before the Lord as guilty. Thus if the sancta are purified then, this should not be regarded as separate from the cultic status of the people; when the sancta are purified the people are also purified (cf. v. 30). It thus appears that the term 'accumulation' of sins suggests the atonement ceremony on the day of Atonement is impersonal in character.

Based on these postulates we shall look more closely at atonement ceremonies on other occasions, focusing on Lev 4.1–5.13 and on the *hattat* rituals in Lev 8–9 and 12–15.

As already argued in Chapter 5,[60] the first two rituals in Lev 4 (for the anointed priest and the whole congregation) foreshadow the ritual in Lev 16.14–15 in that in Lev 4.6(17) defilement of the adytum appears to be assumed, whereas the actual sprinkling of blood in the adytum takes place only in Lev 16.14–15. This foreshadowing seems to be caused by the fact that the occasion in view in Lev 4 is not the day of Atonement. However, it is also clear that the first two rituals in Lev 4 foreshadow the day of Atonement because these rituals refer to the adytum when it comes to the atonement of the anointed priest and that of the whole people. Thus apart from the nature of the occasion there seems to be a specific assumption in both Lev 4 and 16, that atonement of Aaron and of the whole people is to be made in the adytum.

By contrast, the comparison of the second (Lev 4.13-21) with the third and fourth (vv. 22-35) cases gives the impression that the two kinds of ritual are distinguished according to the criterion whether the sinner is individual or collective. In the third case it could be observed that the cultic status of נשׂיא is reflected in the sacrifice he must bring, which is slightly different from the lay individual's. Moreover, not only in Lev 4.22ff., but also in all the other cases of atonement for individuals, the rituals are performed in connection with the outer altar (see Lev 12.6; 14.11, 19; 15.14-15, 29-30; Num 6.10-11, 13, 16). In other words, the purification ritual is always performed in connection with the outer altar as long as the sinner or unclean person is a lay individual.

Does this mean that the sins of the lay individual defile only the outer altar and no further? The very fact that the whole people is constituted of individuals suggests that the sins of individuals are in some way related to the sins of the whole people, thus to the adytum. That this inference is not far-fetched is clearly shown in Lev 16.16a, where the adytum is assumed to be defiled by the sins of the Israelites.

Now it is striking that the atonement ceremony for the lay individual does not allude to the ceremony on the day of Atonement, unlike the ones for the anointed priest and the whole congregation in Lev 4.1-21.

This dichotomy between the two types of ceremony in Lev 4 can be explained first by assuming that the *hattat* rituals in Lev 4.22ff. are regular ones based on the *hattat* ritual in Lev 9. There the priests (Aaron) make atonement for the congregation in connection with the outer altar; for Lev 4.22ff. presupposes priests are already functioning because atonement is said to be made by the priest.

Second, the *hattat* rituals in Lev 12-15 are also regular ones in that they too presume the priesthood and particularly the ritual procedures in Lev 5.7-9; 4.32-35.[61] Yet at two points the *hattat* rituals in Lev 12-15 show more similarity to the ritual in Lev 9 than to those in Lev 4.22ff. 1. In the *hattat* ritual in Lev 12-15 the physical uncleanness, if it is severe, is not assumed to defile the tabernacle as long as the rules are observed (Lev 15.31), whereas in Lev 4.22ff. any sin defiles the tabernacle (Lev 16.16). 2. The *hattat* rituals in Lev 12-15 follow the same calendrical pattern, 7 days/8th day, as in Lev 8-9.

At any rate we infer that the atonement ceremonies in Lev 4.22ff. and Lev 12-15 do not allude to the one on the day of Atonement because they are based on the atonement ceremony described in Lev 9.

In fact the above twofold atonement structure could be reduced to the relationship between the ceremony in Lev 9 and that in Lev 16. This assessment of the nature of the two ceremonies has been arrived (see Chapter 3) through an analysis of the two incidents in Lev 10: the Nadab and Abihu incident and the *hattat* flesh incident. These incidents show the inadequacy of the atonement ceremony in Lev 9 to deal with the sin of Nadab and Abihu, i.e. a sin of the priestly family, though that is not to say that the atonement itself was invalidated. The eighth-day service is designed to enable the priests to enter the shrine, thus to introduce the regular priestly work (Lev 9.23; 10.9). That the atonement ceremony on that day was insufficient to cope with priestly sins may well imply the inadequacy of the regular priestly work in the shrine and the forecourt as a whole.

In the light of the above we conclude our discussion of the nature of the ritual on the day of Atonement as follows. Although the idea of sin defiling the sancta exists, this should not lead us to look at the sins in Lev 16 mathematically, i.e. in terms of 'accumulation' or 'amount', but in terms of the nature of the occasion, particularly of the atonement ceremony. In other words, all the sins over a certain period of time are envisaged as being atoned for again on the day of Atonement by the most potent blood manipulation. Conformably, the guilt related to the sins is to be removed, not by the burning of the *hattat* flesh, but uniquely by the Azazel goat which makes atonement for Aaron, thereby for all Israel.

CONCLUSIONS

In a sense most of the conclusions of our study of the *hattat* are incorporated in our interpretation of the day of Atonement ceremony in the previous Chapter. So here we shall outline those conclusions more systematically in accordance with the problems posed at the beginning of the study, which can be classified largely into two areas: 1. the basic function of the *hattat*; 2. the rationale of the variety of ritual types.

1. חטאת should be translated, as Barr and Milgrom suggest, 'purification offering' or 'purgation offering' rather than the conventional 'sin offering'. This is because the former translation conveys more comprehensively to the modern mind the basic function of the *hattat* than the latter, and not because the *hattat* does not deal with sin. The *hattat* indeed deals with חטאת (sin) (Lev 4.1–5.13) as well as with uncleanness (the *hattat* rituals in Lev 12-15), contrary to Milgrom's thesis that it only has to do with uncleanness. The problem of terminology arises from the fact that the cultic law distinguishes between physical uncleanness and חטאת (sin), whereas חטאת (sin) itself can be an intense form of uncleanness. This must be borne in mind when the *hattat* is translated 'the purification offering'.

Uncleanness, whether specific or general, is envisaged to be present in the sancta when the offerer stands before God, and not as Milgrom assumes, when a person commits an inadvertent sin or becomes unclean. And this assumption appears to do more justice to the *hattat* in contexts where no specific cause of uncleanness is assumed, such as consecration and dedication. Thus the priest purifies sancta such as the altar of burnt offering (see below), but in so doing he also purifies the offerer. Lev 17.11, which can be applied to all the animal sacrifices, is the key to a deeper dimension of this parallel between purification of the offerer and what takes place on the altar.

Firstly, Lev 17.11 confirms the above assumption because it assumes that the offerer is personally involved in the blood manipulation. Perhaps behind this relationship between the offerer and the sancta there lies an idea that the sancta invariably represent the people.

Secondly, the passage declares that blood contains life-essence. However, that purification should not be pictured as neutralizing death by life is indicated by the fact that the *hattat* blood itself can symbolize death in a substitutionary sense. In other words, the death caused by sin and uncleanness is annulled by substitutionary death. The alternative view that the *hattat* blood absorbs sin and uncleanness and becomes unclean is inadequate mainly because of its failure to distinguish between uncleanness in the camp (טמא) and uncleanness envisaged in the sancta.

The function of the *hattat* is inseparably connected with that of the priests, because it is they who manipulate the *hattat* blood to purify sancta, thus making atonement (*kipper*) for the people. From the investigation of the concept of *kipper* we have inferred that by purifying sancta the priest bears the guilt associated with uncleanness. In this context the phrase נשא עון should be construed in a substitutionary sense. Thus apart from the principle that the sacrificial blood substitutes for the offerer on the altar (Lev 17.11), the same principle of substitution seems to be assumed in the dimension of priests, a point which has not been emphasized by scholars.

At this point the importance of Lev 10.16-20 for the *hattat* problem should be underlined in view of the fact that the section has long been enigmatic to exegetes or has been misinterpreted by modern critics. For the section affords clues not only to the basic function of the *hattat* as described above, but also to the rationale of various ritual types as will be set out presently. Furthermore the section is significant in two respects. Firstly, since the section presupposes Lev 6.17-23 (and perhaps Lev 4 as well) and is presupposed by atonement theology in Lev 16, there is a strong possibility that the *hattat* rituals in Leviticus have a coherent system. Secondly, though the section is narrative, it is inseparably united, at least in content, with the laws in Lev 10 and Lev 16. This calls for a reconsideration of sections in the Pentateuch, where narrative alternates with laws.

2. The variety of the *hattat* ritual is marked prominently by two factors: blood manipulation, and the disposal of the *hattat* flesh.

Both the *hizzāh* and *nātan* gestures symbolize purification of sancta. Apparently the *hizzāh* gesture is more potent than the *nātan* gesture. The mode of blood manipulation is basically dependent upon the nature of the occasion (cp. Lev 16.14 with Lev 9.8ff., Lev 16.15 with Lev 9.7).

Eating the *hattat* is the priestly privilege and duty, yet it has no direct bearing on the atoning process (*kipper*). Nor is it part of the *hattat* ceremony. By contrast Lev 10.17 and 16.26-28 suggest that the burning of the *hattat* symbolizes the removal of guilt just as the Azazel goat does. These two modes of disposal of the *hattat* are not invariably combined with a definite mode of blood manipulation. They are determined by whether Aaron bears his own guilt (including the guilt arising out of his capacity as the high priest).

The rituals in Lev 4.3-21 and Lev 9 are related each in its own way to the ritual on the day of Atonement. The *hizzāh* gesture in Lev 4.6-7, 17-18 foreshadows the one in Lev 16.14ff. Furthermore, the two rituals in Lev 4.3-21 form a distinctive type of atonement ceremony over against those in Lev 4.22ff. The difference between the two types of atonement ceremony largely parallels that between the eighth-day service and the day of Atonement ceremony. The latter is illuminated by the incidents in Lev 10 of Nadab and Abihu and the *hattat* flesh, which show that the sin of Aaron's house is not adequately atoned for by the atonement ceremony in the forecourt and the shrine. They demand a fuller ceremony in Lev 16.

Incorporating Lev 15.31 as well as the above two strands (Lev 4.3-21 → Lev 16, Lev 9 → Lev 16), the atonement ceremony in Lev 16 deals with all the sins (חטאת) of the Israelites including Aaron and the priests.

The central problem of the day of Atonement ritual lies in the relationship between the *hattat* which makes purification of sancta, and the Azazel goat which carries the guilt of all the Israelites away into the wilderness. On the assumption that the concept of *kipper* includes both 'purification' and 'bearing guilt' it is possible to hold that by purifying sancta Aaron bears the guilt associated with uncleanness, and that he lays it on the head of the Azazel goat when he confesses the sins of all the Israelites. On this interpretation the Azazel-goat ritual can be seen to meet the demand in Lev 10.16-20 that the guilt Aaron bears as the head of the house must be removed.

Lastly, over against the usual scholarly tendency to see the Azazel-goat ritual as separate from the rest of the day of Atonement ceremony it is proposed that the Azazel goat itself is the *hattat*, and that the ritual is the special form of the burning of the *hattat*, designed to eliminate the guilt that Aaron bears. In view of all the above, the Azazel goat ritual constitutes the climax of the Israelite system of atonement ceremonies.

NOTES

Notes to Introduction

1. Exod 29.10-14, 36; 30.10. Lev 4.1-35; 5.1-13; 6.10, 17-23; 7.7, 37; 8.2, 14-15; 9.2-3, 7-15, 22; 10.16-20; 12.6-8; 14.13, 22, 31; 15.15, 30; 16.3, 5, 6, 9, 11, 14-15, 18-19, 25, 27-28; 23.19. Num 6.11, 14, 16; 7.16, 22, 28, 34, 40, 46, 52, 58, 64, 70, 76, 82, 87; 8.7, 8, 12; 15.24, 25, 27; 18.9; 19.9, 17; 28.15, 22; 29.5, 11, 16, 19, 22, 25, 28, 31, 34, 38.

2. J. H. Kurtz, *Sacrificial Worship* (1863) pp. 182ff.; C.F. Keil, *Archäologie* (1875) pp. 230ff.; G.B. Gray, *Sacrifice* (1925) pp. 55ff.; D. Schötz, *Schuld- und Sündopfer* (1930) pp. 32-52; A. Medebielle, 'expiation' *DBS* (1938) col. 57ff.; P.P. Saydon, *CBQ* 8 (1946) pp. 393-98; R. de Vaux, *Studies* (1964) pp. 98ff.; N.H. Snaith, *VT* (1965) pp. 73-78.

3. S. Daniel, *Recherches sur le vocabulaire du culte dans la Septante* (1966), pp. 299-316, here p. 306. Cf. G. Stählin, 'ἁμαρτάνω', *TDNT*, I, pp. 293-96.

4. J. Milgrom, *Cultic Theology*, p. 68. Cf. further A. Büchler, *Sin and Atonement*, pp. 270ff.

5. Cf. 2 Cor 5.21 and R.J. Daly, *Christian Sacrifice*, pp. 237-40; S. Lyonnet-L. Sabourin, *Sin*, pp. 185ff.

6. Keil, p. 377.

7. Kurtz, *op. cit.*, p. 416. Cp. J. Köberle, *Sünde und Gnade* (1905), p. 333.

8. Cf. for instance, I. Benzinger, *Archäologie* (1927), pp. 367-68; J. Pedersen, *Israel*, vols. III-IV (1940), pp. 369ff.; R. Dussaud, *Origines* (1941), pp. 117-29; de Vaux, *op. cit.*, pp. 91-95; W. Eichrodt, *Theology*, I (1961), pp. 161-62; G. von Rad, *Theology*, I (1962), pp. 251, 258ff.; K. Elliger (1966), p. 69; N.H. Snaith (1967), p. 40; W. Kornfeld (1983), p. 20. Porter (1976) (p. 37), says 'sin- and guilt-offerings are made on occasions where "sin", in our usual understanding of the word, is hardly involved (cp. 5.1-3; 14.1-20; 16.16)'.

9. L. Moraldi, *Espiazione*, p. 154.

10. *Ibid.* Cp. Daniel, *op. cit.*, pp. 306ff.

11. J. Barr, 'Sacrifice and Offering', *DB* (1963), p. 874.

12. *Ibid.*

13. B. Levine, *Presence* (1974) pp. 103ff.

14. Milgrom, *op. cit.*, p. 72.

15. Milgrom, *Tarbiz* 40 (1970), pp. 1-8; *idem, Cultic Theology*, pp. 67-95.

16. *Cultic Theology*, pp. 67-69.

17. *Ibid*. p. 75.

18. *Cult*, (1976) pp. 3-12.

19. *Cultic Theology*, pp. 76-77.

20. *Ibid*. pp. 77-79.

21. *Ibid*. pp. 70-74.

22. *Ibid*. pp. 96-103.

23. Z. Weinberg, *BM* 55 (1973), pp. 524ff.

24. A.M. Rodriguez, in his *Substitution* (1979), has examined in some detail Milgrom's view of the *hattat* as part of his argument for 'substitution'. On the whole he agrees with Milgrom only partially. However his view of the basic function of the *hattat* appears obscure; for on the one hand he holds that 'in cultic legislation sin and impurity are synonyms' (p. 82 n. 3), but on the other he observes that the *hattat* is prescribed for 'situations in which the idea of sin seems to be absent' (p. 101), referring to contexts like Lev 12–15.

25. B. Janowski, *Sühne* (1982), p. 241 n. 287, p. 230 n. 226, p. 236 n. 251 (especially p. 241 n. 287).

26. *Ibid*. p. 185 n. 5.

27. *Ibid*. p. 241 n. 287, pp. 218ff., 247. Milgrom's review of Janowski's work is found in *JBL* 104 (1985), pp. 302-304, in which Milgrom reemphasizes his own standpoint.

28. See G. Wenham, *Numbers* (1981), pp. 29ff.

29. G. von Rad, *Priesterschrift* (1934); K. Koch *Priesterschrift* (1959); R. Rendtorff, *Gesetze* (1963); *idem, Studien* (1967); K. Elliger, *Leviticus* (1966); B. Janowski, *op. cit.*

30. Milgrom, *Levitical Terminology*, pp. 1-2; *idem, Cultic Theology*, p. 101 n. 28. See the review of the first fascicle of R. Rendtorff's *Leviticus* (1985), in *Old Testament Abstracts*, 9/1 (1986), p. 101.

31. Cf. R. Knierim, *Interpretation* 27 (1973), pp. 435-68; Wenham, *op. cit.* pp. 18-21; J. Barton, *Reading the Old Testament* (1984).

32. See Wenham, *ibid*. pp. 32-39.

33. Milgrom, *Levitical Terminology* (1970); *idem, Cult* (1976); *idem, Cultic Theology* (1983).

Notes to Chapter 1

1. On the problem of Lev 5.6-7 see B. Janowski, *Sühne*, pp. 256-57.

2. The 'commandments' include not only cultic but ethical ones. See Dillmann, p. 414; A.M. Rodriguez, *Substitution*, pp. 87, 100; R. Knierim, *Hauptbegriffe*, p. 62. However cp. Porter, p. 37.

3. I.e. the high priest, with most commentators. See J.H. Kurtz, *Sacrificial Worship*, p. 329 n. 1; G.J. Wenham, *Leviticus*, pp. 96-97. We thus

assume that Lev 4 does not deal with expiation of the sin of ordinary priests.
See n. 5 below.

4. Cf. J. Liver *EM*, *s.v.* עדה; J. Milgrom, *Cultic Theology*, pp. 1-18 esp.
pp. 2-12; Wenham, *op. cit.*, p. 98.

5. The phrase עם הארץ does not appear to include ordinary priests. Cp.
P. Heinisch, p. 29.

6. The assumption is that if the ritual is different, it must be prescribed as
in Lev. 5.8-9.

7. See Dillmann, p. 425.

8. So assumed explicitly and implicitly, to my knowledge, by all
commentators.

9. See Rashi, *ad loc.* and D. Hoffmann, p. 124.

10. Shadal, *ad loc.*; K. Elliger, p. 53.

11. Cp. *GK*, p. 382 n. 2.

12. Cp. Elliger, *ibid.*

13. Cp. Num 15.22; Ezek 18.10-11 (with M. Greenberg, *Ezekiel* (AB), *ad.
loc.*); James 2.10.

14. A. Spiro, *PAAJR* 28 (1959), pp. 95-101.

15. M. Noth, p. 44.

16. Spiro, *op. cit.*, p. 95.

17. *Ibid.* p. 99 n. 6.

18. *Ibid.* p. 100.

19. Cf. F. Andersen, *Sentence*, p. 145.

20. See Chapman-Streane, p. 21. Also N. Snaith, p. 48; Orlinsky, *Notes*,
ad loc.

21. E.g. Heinisch, p. 30; Elliger, p. 57. For the whole issue see A.
Bertholet, p. 11 and W.H. Gispen, p. 86.

22. Milgrom, *EM*, *s.v.* קרבן, p. 241; *idem*, 'Sacrifice and offerings', *IDBsup*,
p. 768; *idem*, *JAOS* 103 (1983), pp. 249-50.

23. Cf. *BDB*; Knierim, 'שגג', *THAT*, col.870ff.; Milgrom, *Cultic Theology*,
p. 123 n. 5. However, B. Jackson (in *Essays in Jewish and Comparative Legal
History*, p. 91), assumes 'lack of premeditation' rather than 'unintentionality'
in a case of murder. Cf. also G. Quell, 'ἁμαρτάνω', *TDNT*, I, pp. 267-86, esp.
pp. 274ff.; D. Daube, *RIDA* 2 (1949), pp. 189-213. It appears that both error
and accident are related to שגג.

24. *Op. cit.*, pp. 122ff. Cf. Noordtzij, p. 55.

25. *Ibid.*, pp. 124-25 with nn. 11, 13.

26. *Ibid.*

27. Knierim, *op. cit.*, col. 871, followed by Rodriguez (*op. cit.*, p. 84), and
others.

28. Janowski, *op. cit.*, p. 255 n. 378.

29. *Ibid.* So D. Schötz, *Schuld-und Sündopfer*, p. 46. He equates נעלם מן
with בשגגה.

30. The problem of או will be discussed later.

31. The same is noted by Rodriguez, *op. cit.*, p. 84 n. 7.

32. With Noordtzij, who comments 'this lack of awareness or "being hidden" naturally does not mean that the party in question was unconscious of his deed, but only that it did not dawn on him that this deed constituted a sin' (*op. cit.*, p. 55).

33. For the rabbinic view of this section cf. Rashi, *ad loc.*; Hoffmann, pp. 148-50; Milgrom, *Cult*, nn. 268, 269.

34. See Rashi, *ad loc.*; Hoffmann, p. 148.

35. Ibn Ezra, Shadal, *ad loc.*

36. It is not clear whether Milgrom makes a distinction between consciousness of an act and that of a sin. Cp. *Cult*, p. 9 and *Cultic Theology*, p. 123 n. 7 with *Cult*, p. 76. He assumes that the sin remains unknown forever. This position is adopted by Dillmann, p. 437; Gispen, pp. 95-97; Chapman-Streane, p. 24; Wenham, pp. 107-108 and others.

37. Thus the phrase does not speak of 'an accidental act performed unconsciously' as Milgrom assumes in *Cultic Theology*, p. 123 n. 7.

38. E.g. Kurtz. *op. cit.*, p. 199; Bertholet, p. 17; Schötz, *op. cit.*, pp. 10-11; cf. Hoffmann, p. 148 n. 1.

39. Thus the position in n. 36 above should be excluded.

40. *BDB*: 'be hidden'; *KBL*: 'verborgen sein'. Cp. H. Orlinsky, *Notes, ad loc.*

41. See *BDB*, p. 183.

42. Wenham, pp. 86, 93.

43. F. Keil, pp. 310-11; Heinisch, pp. 30-31; S.R. Driver-H.A. White, p. 67. Cf. further Ibn Ezra, *ad loc.*; Hoffmann, pp. 141-42; Chapman-Streane, p. 21; Elliger, p. 55; Noordtzij, p. 65. AV, RSV; Schötz, *op. cit.*, p. 47.

44. Milgrom, *Cultic Theology*, p. 124 n. 13; *idem*, *Cult*, p. 109 with nn. 406, 408. But in *JAOS* 103 (1983), p. 250, Milgrom translates 'and, though he has known it, the fact escapes him but (thereafter) he feels guilt'.

45. For the inchoative force of the Hebrew verbs see Orlinsky, *op. cit.*, p. 34.

46. Cp. Milgrom's translation in n. 44 above.

47. Dillmann, p. 428; Bertholet, p. 14; Heinisch, p. 30; Elliger, pp. 55-56.

48. With F. Andersen, *op. cit.*, p. 85 and Milgrom, *JAOS* 103 (1983), p. 250 n. 15. Anderson, however, gives a stative meaning to ידע.

49. Spiro, *op. cit.*, pp. 95-96.

50. *Ibid.*, p. 96. But some commentators remark that the very act of a rash oath is sinful in view of Exod 20.7. See Chapman-Streane, p. 21; Noordtzij, p. 66.

51. *Ibid.*

52. *Ibid.*, p. 97.

53. Section A above.

54. See n. 44 above.

55. Milgrom, 'Sacrifice and Offerings' *IDBsup.*, p. 768; *idem*, קרבן, *EM* 7 col. 241.

56. *JAOS* 103 (1983), pp. 250ff.

57. Rodriguez, *op. cit.*, pp. 95-96. Cf. NEB 'concealed by him' and Orlinsky, *op. cit.*, on Lev 4.13.

58. R. Porter (p. 41) sees this passage as out of context of the sin offering because 'it is concerned with an offence with which the sacrificial system could not deal'. But sins which are not inadvertent are also expiable in Lev 5.21ff. Cf. A. Phillips, *JThS* 36 (1985), pp. 146-50.

59. Noth, p. 44.

60. E.g. H.C. Brichto, *The Problem of 'Curse' in the Hebrew Bible*, (Philadelphia, 1968), pp. 42-43.

61. A. Phillips, *'Ancient Israel's Criminal Law'* (Oxford, 1970), p. 138 n. 46.

62. *Ibid.*, p. 138. It is not clear as he claims, though, that the אלה is restricted to cases of theft, but the latter seems to be envisaged by the term. See *ibid.*, p. 139 and *idem*, *JThS* 36, (1985), pp. 146-50.

63. See n. 44 above.

64. Knierim, 'שגג', *THAT*, II col. 871.

65. *BDB* s.v.; *KBL*, 'sich verschulden'.

66. *Cult*, pp. 3-12.

67. *Ibid.*, pp. 11-12.

68. *Ibid.*, pp. 8-9.

69. Rodriguez admits the meaning 'feel guilt' only in four passages: Lev 5.5, 17, 23; Num 5.6 in *op cit.*, p. 156 n. 1, p. 167 n. 4. However his view that נשא עון in Lev 5.1 is synonymous with *'āšēm* (*ibid.*, p. 90) cannot be accepted. See Lev 5.17. H. Jagersma, on Num 5.6, comments that if 'feel guilt' is the right meaning here, the offender who does not feel guilty will not have to make reparation (p. 100). Both Rodriguez and Jagersma, however, seem to fail to present convincing reasons why *'āšēm* should not be 'feel guilty'.

70. *Cultic Theology*, p. 124 n. 11; *Cult*, pp. 9-10.

71. Cf. D. Daube, *Ancient Jewish Law* (Leiden, 1981), pp. 123ff.

72. *Cult*, p. 10.

73. *Ibid.*, p. 9.

74. Dillmann, p. 437: Heinisch, p. 34.

75. The situation was assumed by the traditional Jewish interpretation but the attention was paid more to ידע than to *'āšēm*.

76. Dillmann, *ibid.* Actually he combines the two imaginable situations.

77. Milgrom, *op. cit.*, p. 76.

78. *Ibid.*

79. See Shadal, *ad loc.* In our view an actual case for this law is found in Gen 20. Cp. Gen 12.17; 26.10ff.; and see Knierim, *Hauptbegriffe*, p. 68 with n. 132.

80. Bertholet, p. 13; Elliger, p. 56. Cf. Rodriguez, *op. cit.*, p. 156 n. 3. According to Ehrlich (*Randglossen*, on v. 23) and K. van der Toorn (*Sin and Sanction in Israel and Mesopotamia*, 1985, p. 92) או indicates two possibilities; in one the sinner suffers the punishment of sin (ואשם) and in the other he is forgiven after the *hattat* ritual. However *'āšēm* is unlikely to be synonymous with נשא עון. See Lev 5.17.

81. So Milgrom, *Cultic Theology*, p. 124. As Dillmann (p. 425) correctly remarks, או here does not mean 'if' but 'or if'. From this he infers that 'durch ועשה בשגגה ואשם V. 22 ein Wissen um den Fehltritt nicht aussondern eingeschlossen ist. . . ' (*ibid.*).

82. Milgrom (*op. cit.*, p. 124 n. 10) translates, 'and they suffer guilt when the error is discovered'.

83. With Orlinsky, *op. cit.*, on 4.13.

84. *ZThK* 52 (1955), pp. 1-42.

85. See M. Weiss, *Tarbiz* 31 (1962), pp. 236-63, esp. p. 245 n. 43. and cf. literature referred to in Rodriguez, *op. cit.*, p. 223 n. 1.

86. *Op. cit.*, pp. 77-91.

87. Section C above. But note that Milgrom (*Cult*, p. 6) translates Lev 5.6 'He shall bring his penalty to the Lord. . . as a *hattat*'.

88. *Cultic Theology*, p. 77.

89. *Cult*, p. 4.

90. Cp. Lev 5.1; 7.18; 17.16; 19.8.

91. See Gen 42.21. Cp. Milgrom, *op. cit.*, p. 5 n. 17.

92. Cp. Jer 17.1

93. Cf. Rodriguez, *op. cit.*, p. 144.

94. P. 41. See also Janowski, *op. cit.*, p. 251 n. 349.

95. B. Maarsingh, p. 41. Cp. J.J. Stamm, *Erlösen*, pp. 128-29.

96. Elliger, p. 71; Porter, p. 39; Milgrom, *Tarbiz* 40 (1970), pp. 3-4; *idem*, *Cult*, p. 13 n. 44; Rodriguez, *op. cit.*, p. 86 n. 2; Janowski, *op. cit.*, p. 251.

97. Note that all the ritual is instituted by God himself. See Janowski, *op. cit.*, p. 252.

98. J. Barr, in *DB*, p. 875, holds that 'terms like "validity", "efficacy" and "*ex opere operato*" are inappropriate to OT thinking'.

99. Cp. the corresponding formulaic expression כפר עליו וטהר and Isa 53.5.

Notes to Chapter 2

1. For the following see Introduction.

2. Rodriguez, *Substitution*, pp. 104-105.

3. Kurtz, *Sacrificial Worship*, pp. 144, 147. See also Porter, p. 66; Rodriguez, *ibid.*, pp. 110, 123. Cp. D. Schötz, *Schuld- und Sündopfer*, pp. 20-21.

4. Elliger, p. 113. See Gispen, p. 145.

5. Cf. Wenham, *Num*, p. 38.

6. Cf. Wenham, *Lev*, p. 70; Kurtz, *op. cit.*, pp. 289-92.

7. So Wenham, *ibid.*, p. 144.

8. J. Wellhausen, *Prolegomena*, pp. 65-66; *idem, Composition*, pp. 137-39. See also Chapman-Streane, pp. xii-xiii. Archaeologically this view seems to have been disproved. See M. Haran, 'מזבח', *EM* IV, cols. 778-79; Milgrom, 'Altar', *EJ* II, cols. 760-67; Wenham, *Lev*, p. 68 n. 1. Only the literary problem of Exod 30.1ff. seems to remain unsolved. Cf. D.W. Gooding, *The Account of the Tabernacle* (1959) esp. pp. 66ff.; A.H. Finn, *JThS* 16 (1915), pp. 449-82; V. Hurowitz, *JAOS* 105 (1985), pp. 21-30.

9. Noth, pp. 70.78.

10. Elliger, p. 118

11. P. 46.

12. P. 65

13. Pp. 97-98, 114.

14. Milgrom, 'קרבן', *EM* VII, col. 250.

15. Rodriguez, *op. cit.*, p. 112.

16. Exod 19.21; 20.19; 33.20; Judg 13.22; Isa 6.5-7.

17. Elliger, p. 125; Kennedy, p. 75. Cp. Gispen, p. 155.

18. Keil, p. 346; Dillmann, p. 469.

19. So Ehrlich, *Randglossen, ad loc.*

20. Rodriguez, *op. cit.*, pp.111-12.

21. Porter, p. 73; Wenham, p. 149.

22. Wellhausen, *Composition*, p. 147; Chapman-Streane, p. 57; Noth, p. 88. On כראשון see Ehrlich, *Randglossen, ad loc.*

23. See Dillmann, p. 422.

24. Siphra, cited in Hoffmann, p. 208; Keil, p. 355; R. Smith, *The Religion of the Semites*, p. 349. Cp. Dillmann, pp. 473-74.

25. Von Rad, *Theology*, I, p. 248; R. Rendtorff, *op. cit.*, pp. 215f. Cp. Chapman-Streane p. 57. Most recently Rodriguez has even argued (*op. cit.*, pp. 130-36) that 'the ritual of the eating of flesh can take the place of the ritual of the sprinkling of blood' (p. 135).

26. Kurtz, *op. cit.*, pp. 228ff.

27. Ehrlich, *Randglossen, ad loc.*

28. Milgrom, *Cultic Theology*, p. 70; *idem*, 'קרבן', *EM*, VII, p. 237.

29. Milgrom, *Cultic Theology*, p. 70.

30. *Ibid.*, p. 71. But see D.P. Wright, *Disposal*, p. 344 n. 22.

31. Janowski, *Sühne*, p. 239 n. 272. He concurs with J. Scharbert's view in *idem, Heilsmittler im Alten Testament und im Alten Orient*, p. 104 n. 15.

32. Elliger, p. 139.

33. Cf. also our remark on Lev 9.15 above.

34. Linguistically the phrase אכל חטאת parallels a modern metonymical usage such as 'repair a car'.

35. See Knierim, *Hauptbegriffe*, pp. 237ff., 252ff.; *idem*, 'עון' *THAT*, II, cols. 243-49.

36. With Rodriguez, *op. cit.*, p. 132.

37. So Knierim, *Hauptbegriffe*, pp. 221-22; Rodriguez, *op. cit.*, pp. 133ff. Cf. von Rad, *op. cit.*, pp. 270-71. For Exod 28.38 cp. Dillmann, p. 310; Elliger, p. 229 n. 33; Rodriguez, *op. cit.*, pp. 133-34. For Num 18.1, 23 cp. Ibn Ezra, Shadal, *ad loc.*; Dillmann, p. 99; Gray, p. 219; Knierim, *op. cit.*, p. 242; Levine, *Presence*, pp. 76-77; Milgrom, *Levitical Terminology*, pp. 22ff. It seems to me that Milgrom's interpretation of the phrase in Num 18.1 (=encroachment on sacred objects) is too narrow in the light of v. 7. The phrase in Lev 16.22 will be discussed in Chapter 6.

38. Ehrlich, *Randglossen*, *ad loc.*

39. Milgrom, *Cultic Theology*, p. 70. Cp. C.A. Ben-Mordecai, *JBL* 60 (1941), pp. 311-14.

40. Knierim, *op. cit.*, p. 220 n. 88. See Rodriguez, *op. cit.*, p. 134 n. 2.

41. W. Zimmerli, *ZAW* 66 (1954), p. 10.

42. See Introduction. On עדה (='congregation') representing all Israel, see Wenham, *Lev*, pp. 98-99.

43. Knierim, *op. cit.*, p. 241.

44. See further our observations made in A (2) above.
   In view of these considerations, נתן in v. 17b could be best translated 'assign'. Cf. Milgrom, *Cultic Theology*, p. 97. For the sequence כפר—נתן cp. Lev 17.11; Exod 30.15.

45. Hos 4.8 appears to describe the avarice of the children of the chief priest in their abuse of the *hattat* flesh. It is unnecessary to take חטאת and עונם as synonymous as Rendtorff (*op. cit.*, pp. 62, 63, 241) and F. Andersen/ D.N. Freedman (Hosea [*AB*] *ad loc.*) assume. As noted by Medebielle ('expiation', *DBS*, col. 68), the passage seems to presume the practice in Lev 10.7. The sons of the chief priest 'lift up their throat' because the more the people sinned the more they could partake of the flesh. It is obvious that in v. 8b the prophet is insinuating the proper function of the priests, i.e. נשא עון.

46. With Rodriguez, *op. cit.*, pp. 101-102.

47. *Ibid.*, pp. 104-105.

48. With Rodriguez, *ibid*.

49. Ramban, *ad loc.*

50. See Milgrom, *Levitical Terminology*, n. 103.

51. We presume the exposition of this chapter by Wenham (pp. 85-89).

52. Keil, p. 37; Milgrom, *Cult*, p. 68. Milgrom notes (*Cult*, nn. 246, 250) that the requirement of sacrificial expiation in this case contradicts P's system which requires only sprinkling of מי הנדה (Num 19.14ff.). But the latter law is unlikely to be addressed to the high priest with whom the Nazirite's holiness is comparable. Cp. Dillmann, p. 36.

53. See Kurtz, *op. cit.*, p. 446.

54. Noth, p. 51; Milgrom, *op. cit.*, p. 68; Rodriguez, *op. cit.*, p. 121.

55. For instance, see Wenham's exposition of the שלמים (p. 88).

56. Cp. Lev 8.33; 12.4, 6; Num 6.5, 13 where מלאת occurs.

57. Keil, p. 39; Dillmann, p. 36.

58. Milgrom, 'קרבן' *EM*, VII, col. 249. See also Introduction. *Sifre Num* 6.11; Ramban, *ad loc.*

59. Authors cited in n. 54 above and Milgrom, *ibid.*

60. See references in Milgrom, 'Purification', p. 215.

61. E.g. Rashi, *ad loc.*

62. See Elliger, p. 349 n. 1.

63. Cf. Josh 5.11-12. It may also be noted that the חרם in Josh 6-7 has a character of first fruits. See M. Greenberg, 'Herem', *EJ*, VIII, cols. 347-48.

64. Milgrom (*op. cit.*, pp. 211-14) does not decide on this matter.

65. See Chapter 1 (A).

66. Cf. Wenham, *Numbers*, p. 93.

67. Mishnah, *Sheb* 1.4.

68. Rodriguez, *op. cit.*, p. 108.

69. *Cultic Theology*, p. 75. As far as Lev 15.8 and the similar passages are concerned, the ablution does not purify the unclean person in a material sense since he is unclean until evening.

70. Cp. Schötz, *op. cit.*, p. 20.

71. E.g. Janowski, *op. cit.*, p. 225 n. 204.

72. These passages will be discussed more fully in Chapter 6.

73. See Elliger, p. 192.

74. With Milgrom, *op. cit.*, p. 78. See further Büchler, *Sin and Atonement*, pp. 264-65.

75. See above, p. 16.

76. Cf. J. Neusner, *The Idea of Purity in Ancient Judaism*, p. 1. See also M. Douglas's critique on Neusner's method on pp. 138ff. of the same work.

77. Wenham, pp. 165-68; *idem*, 'Christ's Healing Ministry and His attitude to the Law', in *D. Guthrie Festschrift*, pp. 117-18.

78. Dillmann, *Exodus und Leviticus*, p. 479; W. Kornfeld, *Kairos* 7 (1965), pp. 146-47; W. Paschen, *Rein und Unrein* (1970), p. 63; N. Füglister, 'Sühne', pp. 157-60; E. Feldman, *Biblical and Post-Biblical Defilement and Mourning* (1977).

79. See Wenham, p. 200.

80. Wenham, *ZAW* 95 (1983), pp. 432-34.

81. *Ibid.*, p. 434.

82. With Wenham, who postulates, 'Uncleanness establishes boundaries of action but as long as these are not transgressed no guilt is incurred' (*The Book of Leviticus*, p. 220). Yet this 'guilt' should be replaced by 'sin' for two reasons: (1) as Lev 10.17 has shown, עון (guilt) is present even when sin in our sense is absent; (2) as will be discussed in Chapter 4, *kipper* seems to include נשא עון as its semantic component even in a context like Lev 12.7.

83. See Introduction.

84. Cp. Lev 16.30b.

Notes to Chapter 3

1. We assume that Lev 10 follows Lev 9 not only literarily but chronologically: the Nadab and Abihu incident took place *after* atonement was made for Aaron and the people, and the divine glory manifested.

2. See Chapter 2B above.

3. For instance, Elliger believes that only vv. 1-9 belong to Pg (= priesterliche Grundschrift) (vv. 1-7=Pg^1, vv. 8-9=Pg^2), and that the rest of Lev 10 consists of various additions which presuppose Lev 1-7 and Lev 11-15. See *idem*, pp. 11-12, 132-36. Similar judgments are found in Baentsch, pp. 349-53; Bertholet, pp. 31ff.; Noth, p. 83; Chapman–Streane, pp. 160ff.; von Rad, *Priesterschrift*, p. 84; Koch, *Priesterschrift*, pp. 72-73; Kornfeld p. 42.

4. Chapman–Streane, pp. 57-58; Noth, pp. 87-88; Elliger, pp. 135-36; Porter, pp. 80-81. The former three exegetes assume that the *hattat* flesh was burned outside the camp in Lev 9.15, which we have held to be erroneous on p. 45 above. According to Milgrom this episode (Lev 10.16-20) echoes a conflict between magical belief in the potential power of the *hattat* flesh and the official Israelite belief that the *hattat* flesh should be eaten. See *idem*, *Cultic Theology*, p. 74. Other views of this episode will be mentioned in the course of the discussion.

5. Dillmann, p. 471. But there is the possibility that אִשֶּׁה has nothing to do with 'fire'. See Wenham, p. 56 n. 8. For other views concerning Lev 10.1 see Dillmann, *ibid*.

6. J.C.H. Laughlin, *JBL* 95 (1976), p. 561; Milgrom, 'קטרת', *EM*, VII, col. 113; Haran, *Temples*, p. 232.

7. So Ehrlich, *Randglossen, ad loc.*

8. Ehrlich, *ibid., ad loc.*

9. Dillmann, pp. 471-72.

10. With Dillmann, p. 471 and *contra* Elliger who supposes that קרבים refers to 'all the people', assuming the couplet to be *parallelismus membrorum* (p. 133). See Num 16.5; Ezek 42.13; 43.19.

11. Verse 7 involves two major issues which cannot be discussed here: (1) its relationship with Lev 8.33-35, and (2) the problem of anointing; Aaron's sons are said to be anointed in Lev 10.7 whereas only Aaron is anointed in Lev 8.12. Cp. Hoffmann, pp. 205-206; Chapman–Streane, pp. 55, 160; Gispen, pp. 165-66. Nevertheless as regards (2) it should be noted in the light of the ensuing discussion that perhaps Aaron's sons are regarded as anointed in Lev 10.7 not because they were actually anointed but because they are included, as it were, in the person of Aaron.

12. So Rashbam, *ad loc.*; Hoffmann, p. 205; Chapman–Streane, p. 55; Noth, p. 86; Wenham, p. 157; Maarsingh, p. 85.

13. It is natural to wonder why there was no outburst of divine wrath (קצף) in the wake of the sin of Nadab and Abihu (cf. Ehrlich, *Randglossen* on

v. 6). However, it should be noted that while in Lev 4.3 and Lev 10.6 divine prohibitions are assumed to be known, in Lev 10.1-2 there is as yet no direction from God about burning the incense. Since on our interpretation the direction is implicitly given in Lev 16.12-13, we assume that this circumstance makes the divine punishment lenient.

If Lev 10.6 is comparable with Lev 4.3, it follows that the *hattat* offering is propitiatory rather than expiatory in a narrow sense.

14. Yet it is uncertain how Lev 10 is related to Num 19 where the defilement of death contamination is dealt with.

15. Ehrlich, *Randglossen, ad loc.* One would expect הַשְּׂרֻפִּים as in Num 17.4

16. This implies that Moses admits the correctness of the ritual procedure, particularly the burning of the priests' *hattat* outside the camp, in Lev 9.11. Cp. Noth, p. 88.

17. With Rashbam, *ad loc.*; Dillmann, pp. 473-74.

18. *Ibid.*

19. Chapter 2B above.

20. See Rashi *ad loc.*

21. Dillmann, p. 474.

22. Ehrlich, מקרא כפשוטו, *ad loc.*

23. *Ibid.*

24. See n. 13 above.

25. If not 'mourning', some commentators have assumed some emotional cause in Aaron which prevented him from eating the *hattat.* See for instance, Rashbam *ad loc.*; Baentsch, p. 353; Kornfeld, p. 43. In my judgment, any attempt to attribute emotional cause to Aaron's not eating the *hattat* is possible by itself but, as Shadal correctly remarks, it fails to explain why Aaron said הן היום הקריבו את חטאתם ואת עלתם. Perhaps the major reason why exegetes could not read v. 19 meaningfully is that they have assumed the ritual of the חטאת and עולה simply to be external acts with no theological meaning. See Shadal, *ad loc.*

26. Two additional notes are in order. First, the term 'guilty' should be taken in its widest sense in view of the meaning of עון in Lev. 10.17. Second, the fact that Aaron and his sons are anointed and holy does not mean that they have no need to be atoned for. This is best demonstrated by the fact that Aaron, having been anointed in Lev 8, still needs to be atoned for in order to enter into his regular duty.

27. Cf. Wenham, p. 132.

28. Therefore it seems wrong to assume that Aaron made a ritual mistake.

29. See K. Aartun, *ST* 34 (1980), pp. 73ff. for a survey of the literature.

30. Von Rad, *op. cit.*, p. 85; Koch, *op. cit.*, p. 92.

31. Elliger, pp. 202-203.

32. *Ibid.* Cf. *Joüon*, § 177 j.

33. Dillman, pp. 523-25.

34. I. Benzinger, *ZAW* 9 (1899), pp. 67-68.

35. *Ibid.*, p. 68 n. 1.

36. Ehrlich, *Randglossen, ad loc.*

37. J.R. Wilch, *Time and Event* (1969), pp. 32-33, 43-44, 162.

38. The translation 'at all times' is unlikely since עת is singular.

39. For the connection between Lev 10.1-2 and Lev 16.1 see further below.

40. Dillmann, p. 527; Elliger, pp. 200, 203.

41. See Ibn Ezra, *ad loc.* Snaith (p. 111), and Noordtzij (p. 159) assume that the ram is to be sacrificed for the preparatory cleansing of Aaron. Cp. Benzinger, *op. cit.*, pp. 75-76.

42. Porter, p. 124.

43. See F. Andersen, *Sentence*, pp. 170ff.

44. So Ibn Ezra on v. 1; Dillmann, p. 471. N. Messel (*ZAW* 27 [1907], pp. 1-150 denies the connection between Lev 10.1-7 and Lev 16.1, pointing out that לפני ה' (Lev 10.12) or קדש (v. 4) is unlikely to refer to the inner sancta, and suggests that Lev 16.1 is either 'blosse Übergangsformel' or 'redaktionelle Glosse'. However, as he himself admits these Hebrew terms are ambiguous, and it seems unnecessary to determine, from the context of Lev 10.1-7, whether Nadab and Abihu really entered the adytum. Cp. Haran, *op. cit.*, p. 172 n. 50.

45. So Gispen, pp. 162, 166; Harrison, p. 114. Cf. Rashi on Lev 10.2.

46. Haran's assertion, in *op. cit.*, p. 206, that only Aaron, and not his sons, could enter the tent of meeting seems forced. See Lev 21.23 and Num 18.7.

47. ולא ימות ff. in Lev 16.2 is indeed a crux and needs separate discussion. Cp. Elliger, pp. 203, 210; Janowski, *Sühne*, p. 268 n. 442.

48. The verse will be discussed in Chapter 6.

Notes to Chapter 4

1. See the exhaustive work by Janowski, *Sühne*, esp. pp. 1-26 and bibliography listed there.

2. Cp. Elliger, pp. 70ff.; F. Maass, 'כפר', *THAT*, I, cols. 842-57; Janowski, *op. cit.*, pp. 186-89.

3. To be discussed in C below.

4. See n. 13 below.

5. See Janowski, *op. cit.*, p. 187 n. 11.

6. To be discussed in Chapter 6.

7. Milgrom, *Leshonenu* 35 (1970), pp. 16-17.

8. *Ibid.*, p. 17.

9. *Op. cit.*, p. 188 n. 23.

10. Although *kipper* does not appear in Ezek 45.22 as Janowski points out, it should be noted that עשה in ritual contexts refers not only to bringing of sacrifices but also to blood manipulation. Cf. Milgrom, 'Purification', pp. 212-13.

11. Milgrom, *Cultic Theology*, p. 76; *idem, Tarbiz* 40 (1970), pp. 2-3.

12. *Ibid.*

13. Entry into הקרש or אהל מועד is expressed by בא אל. See Exod 28.29, 35, 43; 29.30; 30.20; 40.32, 35; Lev 6.23; 10.9, 18; 16.2, 3, 23 (bis). Thus בבאו לכפר בקרש in Lev 16.17a means 'from the time of his entering to make atonement in the adytum' and not 'from the time of his entering the adytum to make atonement' (*contra* Rendtorff, *Studien*, p. 232 n. 1).

14. Cp. Lev 14.53. As we shall argue it is artificial to distinguish between *kipper* in the *hattat* context and *kipper* in other contexts.

15. Regarding Lev 16.18-19, B. Levine adopts the view that על means 'on, over', but without argumentation. See Levine, *Presence*, pp. 65, 80.

16. *Op. cit.*, p. 185 n. 5. However it does not seem that Janowski has substantiated this translation. Cp. Milgrom, *JBL* 104 (1985), pp. 302-304.

17. *Op. cit.*, pp. 231-32.

18. As will be shown below, in Exod 29.36 חטא על is not parallel in meaning to כפר על.

19. Janowski, *ibid.*

20. Cf. Porter, pp. 116, 66.

21. *Op. cit.*, p. 303.

22. See II in the table above.

23. *Ibid.*

24. For a possible idea behind this cf. Mettinger, *ZAW* 86 (1974), pp. 403-424.

25. See Janowski, *op. cit.*, pp. 1-26 for a thorough presentation of the history of the investigation of *kipper*, and p. 252 for his view.

26. Cf. Janowski, *op. cit.*, pp. 1-26.

27. E. Jenni, *Das hebräische Pi'el*, Zürich (1968), p. 241; G. Gerleman, 'Die Wurzel kpr im Hebräischen', in *idem, Studien zur alttestamentlichen Theologie*, Heidelberg (1980), pp. 11-23; Janowski, *op.cit.*, pp. 252-53.

28. Authors in n. 27.

29. H. Ch. Brichto, *HUCA* 47 (1976), p. 29 n. 22.

30. Cf. Janowski, *op. cit.*, pp. 22f.

31. This examination appears to be missing in Janowski's work.

32. This passage will be discussed in Chapter 5.

33. Cf. Wenham, *Leviticus*, p. 19.

34. See the conclusion of A above.

35. *Contra* Janowski, *op. cit.*, p. 230 n. 226.

36. AV.

37. Janowski, *op. cit.*, p. 231.

38. Rashi, Ibn Ezra, AV, RSV.

39. Ehrlich, מקרא כפשוטו, *ad loc.*; Gispen, p. 145; Wenham, p. 135; Janowski, *op. cit.*, p.230.

40. *Op. cit.*, p. 231.

41. For '*supernym*' and '*hyponym*' see B. Kedar, *Biblische Semantik*, p. 76.

42. See Chapter 2 B.

43. Cp. Rodriguez, *Substitution*, p. 144.

44. Milgrom, *Levitical Terminology*, pp. 28-29.

45. For conceptual affinity between נשא עון and '*āšēm*, see further Lev 22.16 with Milgrom, *Cult*, p. 65 and n. 230.

46. This may be supported if, as we have proposed, לכפר in Lev 10.17 expresses the result of נשא עון.

47. Cp. Janowski, *op. cit.*, pp. 190ff.

48. For the sacrificial aspect of the Levites see Milgrom, *Levitical Terminology*, pp. 28-29.

49. Janowski, *ibid.*, p. 187. We cannot accept Janowski's tendency to exclude Exod 30.15-16; Num 8.19; 31.50 in the consideration of the concept of *kipper* (see *ibid.*, p. 186 n. 6). These passages may not belong to the theme of 'kultische Sühne' but are relevant to the concept of *kipper*.

50. Milgrom, 'kipper', *EJ*, vol. X, cols. 1039-44; *idem*, 'Atonement in the OT', *IDB Sup.*, pp. 78-80.

51. *Ibid.*

52. Another important issue whether *kipper* is expiatory or propitiatory cannot be discussed here. Provisionally refer to S.R. Driver, 'Propitiation', *HDB*, IV, pp. 128-32; J. Barr, 'Propitiation', *DB*, p. 810; L. Morris, *The Apostolic Preaching of the Cross*, pp. 144-78; B. Lang, 'כפר', *TWAT*, IV cols. 308ff.; Janowski, *op. cit.*, pp. 1ff.; D. Kidner, *TB* 33 (1982), pp. 119-36.

53. Milgrom, *Cultic Theology*, pp. 96-103 followed by H.Ch. Brichto, *HUCA* 47 (1976), p. 27 and D.J. Wold, *SBL Seminar Papers* (1979), p. 9. Cp. Rodriguez, *op. cit.*, pp. 238ff.; A. Schenker, *MTZ* 34 (1983), pp. 195-213, esp. 207ff.

54. *Ibid.*, p.102.

55. *Ibid.*

56. *Ibid.*, p. 103 n. 34.

57. Cf. N. Füglister, 'Sühne durch Blut', in *Studien zum Pentateuch*, p. 147 n. 17; Janowski, *op. cit.*, p. 243 n. 298. Both reject Milgrom's view without much discussion.

58. Cf. R. Soncino, *Motive Clause in Hebrew Law*, California (1980), pp. 104-17.

59. *Op. cit.*, p. 100 with n. 22. Cp. Janowski, *op. cit.* p. 191 n. 30.

60. Certainly it may be admitted that v. 11 can apply to the pouring of blood mentioned in v. 6. In this case, expiation in covenantal contexts could be assumed. See v. 7 and n. 64 below.

61. Cf. for instance, the substitutionary and non-substitutionary meanings of נשא עון.

62. Rodriguez, *op. cit.*, pp. 226-29. Cp. Milgrom and Janowski in n. 59 above.

63. *Ibid.*, p. 227.

64. Kurtz, *Sacrificial Worship*, p. 74. So Benzinger, *Archäologie*, p. 336. Milgrom has pointed out (*JBL* 104 [1985], p. 303) that the joyous character of the שלמים cannot match 'a death sentence' envisaged in Lev 17.11. In response to this it may be argued: (1) Joyous character is the major character of the sacrifice and does not exclude the idea of expiation, just as, conversely, the *hattat* can have a joyous element (see Lev 4.31). (2) Expiation is required in the contexts of consecration and dedication as well. (3) As will be clarified, the term 'a death sentence' is misleading.

65. With Milgrom, *Cultic Theology*, p. 97.

66. Thus it can be inferred that כרת (v. 10) constitutes the antonym of *kipper*. See Num 15.27ff. and Janowski, *op. cit.*, p. 255.

67. With Rodriguez, *op. cit.*, p. 245.

68. Cf. A. Metzinger, *Biblica* 21 (1940), pp. 267-68; Daly, *Christian Sacrifice*, p. 118.

69. See Elliger, p. 228 n. 32. T. Muraoka, *Emphatic Words and Structures in Biblical Hebrew*, Jerusalem and Leiden (1985), pp. 47ff.

70. So Janowski, *op. cit.*, p. 246.

71. *Contra* Daly (*op. cit.*, p. 129 n. 97), who assumes the subject is impersonal.

72. See B (2) above.

73. *Op. cit.*, p. 245.

74. This is the most common view. See Janowski, *op. cit.*, p. 244 n. 301.

75. E.g. Milgrom, *op. cit.*, p. 96.

76. E.g. Levine, *op. cit.*, pp. 67ff.

77. E.g. Rodriguez, *op. cit.*, pp. 248ff. For the LXX translation ἀντὶ τῆς ψυχῆς see Daly, *op. cit.*, pp. 127ff.; Rodriguez, *op. cit.*, pp. 251-57; Janowski, *op. cit.*, p. 244 n. 303.

78. Janowski, following H. Gese (*Zur Biblischen Theologie*, pp. 97ff.), takes ב as a *beth instrumenti* and assumes that the נפש of the offerer is already identified with the sacrificial animal, particularly because the blood manipulation comes after the imposition of hand, which symbolizes the identification of the offerer with the animal. See Janowski, *op. cit.*, pp. 245-46. We prefer, however, to take a more exegetical approach to Lev 17.11.

79. Rodriguez, *op. cit.*, p. 247; Janowski, *ibid.*, p. 245.

80. Levine, *op. cit.*, p. 68 n. 37; Rodriguez, *ibid.*, p. 249. Other arguments by Rodriguez against the *beth-instrumenti* approach (*ibid.*, pp. 247-48) seem to be of minor importance.

81. Brichto, *op. cit.*, p. 27 followed by Janowski, *op. cit.*, p. 244 n. 303.

82. Cf. Muraoka, *op. cit.*, p. 66.

83. Milgrom, *Levitical Terminology*, pp. 28-33: *idem. Cultic Theology*, p. 98 nn. 11, 15. On כפר see Janowski, *op. cit.*, pp. 153-74; A. Schenker, *Biblica* 63

(1982), pp. 32-46. For other possible etymologies of *kipper* see Janowski, *op. cit.*, pp. 15-22.

84. *Cultic Theology*, p. 98 n.15.

85. *Ibid.*, p. 101.

86. E.g. W. Eichrodt, *Theology*, I p. 165 n. 2; Milgrom, *op. cit.*, p. 103 n. 34.

87. *Op. cit.*, p. 148.

88. *Op. cit.*, p. 103.

89. *JBL* 104 (1985), p. 303.

90. With L. Morris, *op. cit.*, p. 117.

Notes to Chapter 5

1. Cf. Kurtz, *Sacrificial Worship*, pp. 101-49. On the term ריח ניחוח cf. J. Hoftijzer, *SVT* 16 (1967), pp. 114-34; A. Hurvitz, *Linguistic Study*, pp. 53-63. On ריח ניחוח in Lev 4.31 see Moraldi, *Espiazione*, pp. 155-56; Noordtzij, p. 63; Noth, p. 43; Rendtorff, *Studien*, pp. 220-21; Janowski, *Sühne*, p. 217; Dillmann, p. 427.

2. Cp. Janowski, *op. cit.*, p. 199. It is not clear to me why Janowski thinks the imposition of hand(s) is important for the *hattat* ritual.

3. It is not mentioned in connection with the אשם offering and the reason for this has been the subject of various speculations. Cf. B.D. Eerdmans, *Alttestamentliche Studien* IV, p. 12; Chapman–Streane, p. 3; Noordtzij, p. 33 n. 8; Milgrom, *Cult*, n. 48; Kidner, *TB* 33 (1982), pp. 134-35. It must also be borne in mind that the mention of the rite may be omitted, being presumed. For instance, see Lev 1.10-11, 15; 5.8; 9.8.

4. Thus an exposition of Lev 24.14; Num 8.10; 27.18, 23; Deut 34.9 will not be offered here. On the whole we concur with Janowski. See *idem*, *op. cit.*, pp. 201-205.

5. See Janowski, *ibid.*, pp. 205ff. Various suggestions to the meaning of the imposition of hand(s) are classified also by Rodriguez under the headings of 1. Transfer and/or substitution theory; 2. The identification theory; 3. The consecration/dedication theory; 4. The appropriation and/or designation theory; 5. The manumissio theory (*Substitution*, pp. 201-208). The essential question is on which biblical passage these theories are based.

6. R. Péter, *VT* 27 (1977), pp. 48-55 followed by Janowski, *ibid.*, p. 201. The same direction is suggested by Milgrom in קרבן, *EM*, p. 235.

7. Keil (p. 404 n. 1) and Elliger (pp. 215-16) adopt the view that the distinction is the matter of emphasis, while Snaith (p. 115) and Kornfeld (p. 64) see it as signifying 'certainty'. Cf. M.C. Sansom, *ET* 94 (1983), p. 326.

8. Cf. Hoffmann on Lev 1.4.

9. Authors cited in Janowski, *op. cit.*, pp. 205ff.; Wenham, p. 62.

10. *Ibid.*, pp. 209-16, esp. p. 215.

11. *Ibid.*, p. 210. Furthermore, according to Janowski the ritual does not belong to what he calls 'Sühne' (*ibid.*, pp. 219-20).

12. See note 9 above.

13. See Janowski, *op. cit.*, p. 219 n. 183.

14. J.C. Matthes, *ZAW* 23 (1903), pp. 97-119.

15. The assumption is shared further by Snaith, p. 42; van der Merwe, *OTWSA* 5 (1962), p. 39.

16. Rodriguez, *op. cit.*, pp. 216ff., anticipated by Medebielle, 'Expiation', *DBS*, col.80.

17. *Ibid.*, p. 218.

18. See Chapter 4.

19. See Chapter 1.

20. This point will be taken up in the next Chapter.

21. Cf. Janowski, *op. cit.*, p. 216 n. 174; Gerleman, 'רצה', *THAT*, II, col. 811.

22. AV; Ibn Ezra, *ad loc.*

23. Elliger, p. 26; Janowski; *op. cit.*, p. 216.

24. RSV.

25. Benzinger, *Archäologie*, p. 372; Baentsch, p. 311; Elliger, p. 26; Maarsingh, p. 19; Janowski, *op. cit.*, p. 216. Cf. GK § 114 o; Joüon § 124 o.

26. NEB; Gispen, p. 39; Cazelles, p. 22; Wenham, p. 48; Kornfeld, p. 14 Cf. GK § 114 f.; Joüon § 124 o.

27. Benzinger (*op. cit.*, p. 372) and Baentsch (*ibid.*) explicitly favour the possibility.

28. Matthes, *ZAW* 23 (1903), p. 107 followed by Janowski, *op. cit.*, pp. 217-18. Facing the alleged contradiction with Lev 17.11, where blood is said to make atonement, Matthes (*ibid.*) points out that (1) in Exod 29.33 and Lev 10.17 atonement is dependent on eating the *hattat* flesh, and that (2) Lev 1.5 shows the blood manipulation plays a major role in the whole ceremony. Both points are, however, fallacious. In Exod 29.33 the priests are assumed to have been atoned for when they eat (note כֻּפַּר). On Lev 10.17 see our discussion in Chapter 2 (B). Thus to render לכפר in Lev 1.4b by '*by* making atonement' cannot be justified.

29. With Ehrlich, מקרא כפשוטו, *ad loc.*

30. If the agent of לכפר is the sacrifice, as we have assumed thus far, then it might be more appropriate to translate כפר 'ransom' rather than 'make atonement'. See Ibn Ezra on Lev 1.4; Cazelles, p. 22 n. (b); Wenham, pp. 59-61.

31. With Noth, p. 22; Kornfeld, p. 14, *et al.*

32. Janowski, *op. cit.*, p. 210.

33. See n. 28 above.

34. Gese, *Zur biblischen Theologie*, pp. 95-96; Janowski, *ibid.*

35. For the religio-historical relationship between the two passages, cf.

Noth, p. 22; Elliger, pp. 34, 37; Janowski, *op. cit.*, p. 218 n. 181.

36. Cp. the formulaic expression כפר עליו ונסלח לו in Lev. 4–5 and our comment on p. 37 above.

37. Dillmann, p. 391. Cp. Hoffmann, p. 89; Levine, *EI*, vol. IX, p. 94.

38. The question will be tackled in the next chapter. Cf. Cazelles, p. 81 n. (b).

39. Thus the *hizzāh* and *nātan* rites in Exod 29.20ff.; Lev 8.23ff.; 14.14ff. are excluded, while Num 19 is included because the ashes of the heifer are called *hattat* (vv. 9, 17).

40. See Eichrodt, *Theology*, I, p. 163 n. 2.

41. Th. C. Vriezen, *OTS* 7 (1950), pp. 201-35 Cf. also Snaith, *ET* 82 (1970-71), p. 23.

42. *Ibid.*

43. Noth, p. 39; Elliger, p. 69; Rodriguez, *op. cit.*, p. 124; Kornfeld, p. 21.

44. Janowski, *op. cit.*, pp. 226-27.

45. For the following see Janowski, *ibid.*, pp. 227ff.

46. *Ibid.*, pp. 232-33.

47. *Ibid.*, p. 233.

48. *Ibid.*, pp. 234-36.

49. *Ibid.*, p. 240.

50. See pp. 41-42 above.

51. See Chapter 2 A.

52. The large majority of commentators assume that the sprinkling of blood on the wall of the altar is necessitated by the practical circumstance that the blood is not sufficient. Rashi, *ad loc.*; Dillmann, p. 430; Elliger, p. 75; Kornfeld, p. 25. However, even the bird *hattat* seems to have sufficient amount of blood to be poured because it reads 'while the rest of the blood shall be drained out at the base of the altar' (RSV Lev 5.9aβ).

53. This is not to say that the order in Lev 4.6-7 was reversed in Lev 16.18-19. As will be discussed below, the section comparable to Lev 4.6-7, 17-18 is Lev 16.14-16 and not Lev 16.18-19.

54. See Janowski, *op. cit.*, p. 227 n. 211.

55. See Gispen, p. 306. Cf. Rodriguez, *op. cit.*, p. 124.

56. As far as I know, no exegete has suggested it.

57. Cp. Lev 15.31, and our discussion in Chapter 2 D.

58. Cp. Rendtorff, *op. cit.*, pp. 218-19; Rodriguez, *op. cit.*, pp. 127-30.

59. For instance, Elliger, p. 69; Milgrom, *Cultic Theology*, p. 78.

60. *Ibid.*

61. Haran, *Temples*, p. 161. Cp. 'פרכת הערות' in Lev 24.3.

62. 'Before'—Gispen, p. 73; 'in the direction of'—Harrison, p. 61; Noordtzij, p. 57; Porter, p. 38; 'against'—Kurtz, *op. cit.*, p. 215; Kornfeld, p. 21. Cf. S. Izre'el, ''el = "to, towards" in Biblical Hebrew', *Shnaton* III (1978), pp. 204-12, esp. 211-12.

63. Kurtz, *op. cit.*, p. 216. The notion of 'direct-indirect' purification is also adopted by Kornfeld (p. 63).

64. Koch, *Priesterschrift*, p. 56; Janowski, *op. cit.*, p. 235.

65. *Ad loc.*

66. If not נסלח, כפר should be expected.

67. *Ad loc.*

68. Noth, p. 41.

69. See Ehrlich, *Randglossen, ad loc.*

70. With Hoffmann, p. 125; Gispen, pp. 71f.; Wenham, p. 97.

71. See Chapter 2 A.

72. See Chapter 3 A.

73. See Hoffmann, p. 309.

74. See Kurtz, *op. cit.*, pp. 392-93; Landersdorfer, *Versöhnungstag*, pp. 30-36.

75. Thus the widespread view that the incense altar is unknown in Lev 16 is unlikely.

76. So Baentsch, p. 385; Orlinsky, *Notes, ad loc.*

77. Wenham, p. 232.

78. As will be shown, our approach does not follow Janowski's. See *idem, op. cit.*, p. 237.

79. *Ibid.*, pp. 236-38.

80. See B above.

81. *Contra* Elliger, p. 135.

82. *Op. cit.*, pp. 70-74.

83. *Ibid.*, p. 70.

84. *Ibid.*, p. 73.

85. *Ibid.* That the burnt *hattat* represents a higher degree of holiness is also assumed by Noordtzij (p. 80).

86. Chapter 2 B.

87. We use the terms 'the eaten *hattat*' and 'the burnt *hattat*' only for convenience's sake. However, one should not be misled to assume that the distinction is invariable; there are two kinds of *hattat from the viewpoint* of the disposal of the *hattat* flesh.

88. Commentators have hardly been systematic on this matter.

89. See Dillmann, p. 422. Cp. Rodriguez, *op. cit.*, p. 218 n. 1.

90. Cf. Rodriguez, *ibid.*; Wenham, p. 158.

91. Keil, p. 307; Noordtzij, p. 59; Gispen, p. 77; Snaith, p. 44; Levine, *Presence*, p. 105. Milgrom, *op. cit.*, pp. 73, 87; D.P. Wright, *Disposal*, pp. 128ff. 'The blood becomes impure because of its use in stripping away these impurities. Since the blood is used pars pro toto for the entire animal, the carcass by extension becomes likewise infected with these impurities' (*ibid.*, pp. 128-29).

92. See the discussion below.

93. In connection with the *hattat* for the priestly consecration (Exod

29.14; Lev 8.17) and the eighth-day service (Lev 9.11) Milgrom has postulated that 'priests are not to eat their own expiatory sacrifices' (*op. cit.*, p. 74). In our opinion, this rationale is correct and should be applied to the burning of the *hattat* in other contexts, though it is not specific enough. The same rationale is anticipated by Dillmann (p. 422).

94. Noted by Lyonnet-Sabourin, *Sin*, p. 183 n. 4; M. Löhr, *Das Ritual von Lev 16*, p. 4.

95. So Lyonnet-Sabourin, *ibid.*

96. Above (A).

97. Heinisch, p. 37; Porter, p. 51; Kornfeld, p. 30; Snaith, p. 57.

98. *Op. cit.*, p. 87 followed by D.P. Wright, *op. cit.*, pp. 143ff.; *idem*, *VT* 35 (1985), p. 216 n. 9.

99. Hoffmann, p. 168.

100. Nevertheless, Hoffmann is surely right in seeing v. 21 as the continuation of v. 20a, and v. 20b as parenthetic. In view of this observation vv. 18b-22 can be viewed as chiastic.

101. See Milgrom, *SVT* 32 (1981), pp. 278-91.

102. Sabourin, *Sciences ecclésiastiques* 18 (1966), p. 37; Lyonnet-Sabourin, *Sin*, p. 182; Cazelles, pp. 82 n. (a), 81 n. (e); Benzinger, *op. cit.*, p. 371; Levine, *EI*, IX, p. 94.

103. Cp. Matthes, *ZAW* 23 (1903), p. 113.

104. With Porter, p. 131; Baentsch, pp. 385-86.

105. For the following refer to Milgrom, *op. cit.*, pp. 85-95.

106. Noordtzij, p. 170.

107. Kurtz, *op. cit.*, pp. 422-32, esp. p. 431.

108. Lyonnet-Sabourin, *Sin*, p. 278 nn. 37, 38; S. Loewenstamm, 'פרה אדמה' *EM* VI, p. 580. Cf. G.B. Gray, p. 255; I.E. Tooms, 'red heifer', *IDB*, IV, pp. 18-19.

109. It appears that the contagiousness of the heifer begins when the blood of the heifer is brought into connection with the sanctuary (v. 4). Cp. Milgrom, *op. cit.*, p. 90.

110. Cp. Baentsch, p. 564. The different degrees of defilement have been noticed by some commentators: Rashi on v. 21; Noordtzij, p. 170; Gispen, pp. 311, 318. Cf. Wenham, p. 147.

111. Note that Aaron does not participate in the ritual of Num 19, presumably because he is the high priest and cannot be defiled (Lev 21.11). See Dillmann, p. 107.

112. Noted by Dillmann, p. 444; Baentsch, p. 355.

Notes to Chapter 6

1. The term 'the day of Atonement' is used conventionally in the following discussion.

2. Pp. 77f. above.

3. The 'distinctness' of the two rites does not necessarily mean that they have nothing to do with each other, as will be discussed below.

4. See pp. 77f. above.

5. Elliger, p. 215. See further Koch, *Priesterschrift*, pp. 92ff.; Janowski, *Sühne*, pp. 210ff., 219ff.

6. See Janowski, *ibid.*, p. 268 n. 447; Wenham, pp. 234-35. The etymology of עזאזל is uncertain. However, we prefer to follow the view suggested by Hoffmann, Hertz and Wenham that it means 'total destruction', assuming ארץ גזרה in v. 22 as interpretive of עזאזל (see Wenham, p. 235).

7. *Mishnah Sheb* 1.4-7. 1.6 states, 'For uncleanness that befalls the temple and its Hallowed things through wantonness, atonement is made by the goat whose blood is sprinkled within (the Holy of Holies) and by the Day of Atonement; for all other transgressions spoken of in the Law—venial or grave, wanton or unwitting, conscious or unconscious, sins of omission or of commission, sins punishable by Extirpation or by death at the hand of the court, the scapegoat makes atonement' (Danby, p. 410).

8. Milgrom, *EJ*, V, cols. 1384-87; *idem, IDB Sup.*, pp. 82-83; *idem, Cultic Theology*, p. 81.

9. Nevertheless, it should be noted that Milgrom and the rabbinic tradition hold the unity of the two rites. Cp. further D.P. Wright, *Disposal*, p. 16.

10. See Chapter 2 B.

11. Dillmann, p. 531.

12. Knobel, cited in Kurtz, *Sacrificial Worship*, pp. 411-12. So Driver-White, *HDB*, p. 202; Cazelles, p. 79; Kornfeld, p. 64; Rodriguez, *Substitution*, p. 118.

13. Kurtz, *ibid.*, p. 412.

14. S. Landersdorfer, *Versöhnungstag*, p. 14. So Y. Kaufmann, תולדות, I, pp. 571-72; Noordtzij, p. 161; C.L. Feinberg, *BS* 115 (1958), p. 324.

15. *Op. cit.*, pp. 385-411.

16. *Ibid.*, pp. 405ff.

17. *Ibid.*, p. 411.

18. *Ibid.*, p. 410.

19. Pp. 115f. above.

20. Another plausible explanation is given by A. Bonar: 'Aaron alone had witnessed atonement in the innermost sanctuary; now he must set it forth in another manner. In order to leave no doubt that sin had been taken away, there must be a removal of it which all Israel could witness'. This is followed by Feinberg (*op. cit.*, p. 332). Though we admit that the purification of sancta is done (not 'witnessed') by Aaron and that the Azazel-goat ritual is witnessed by the people, it seems to us that this has no direct bearing on the symbolism of the two rites.

21. P. 109 above.

22. Cp. Porter, p. 127.

23. Dillmann, p. 527. Similarly Bertholet, p. 54.

24. That חטאת offering can be a collective noun is noted by Kurtz, *op. cit.*, p. 395.

25. Rodriguez, *op. cit.*, p. 113.

26. Note the sequence of the topics in Lev 16: the *hattat* (vv. 14-19) → the Azazel goat (vv. 21-22) → the Azazel goat (v. 26) → the *hattat* (vv. 27, 28). That the *hattat* ritual on the day of Atonement is a remoulded form of the normal burnt *hattat* ritual (Lev 4.3-21) can be inferred from the circumstance that the first and last symbolic acts in the normal ceremony, i.e. the imposition of a hand and the burning of the *hattat*, are combined in the Azazel-goat ritual while the blood manipulation, which normally follows the imposition of a hand, comes first on the day of Atonement.

27. Levine, *Presence*, p. 80.

28. *Ibid.*, p. 65.

29. *Ibid.*, p. 80.

30. See our discussion in Chapter 4 A.

31. Keil, p. 398.

32. Noth, p. 121; Elliger, p. 201; Aartun, *ST* 34 (1980), pp. 77-78; Maass, 'כפר', *THAT*, I, cols. 845, 849; Janowski, *op. cit.*, p. 185 n. 5.

33. Dillmann, p. 528; Driver-White, p. 81; Gispen, p. 245. See Kurtz, *op. cit.*, p. 409.

34. Rashi *ad loc.*; Hoffmann, p. 306; Milgrom, *Cultic Theology*, p. 76 n. 10; Kurtz, *op. cit.*, p. 410; Chapman-Streane, p. 90; Cazelles, p. 79; Noordtzij, p. 163; Maarsingh, pp. 135, 277 n. 19.

35. Chapter 4 A.

36. In this case כפר בעד is not expected, because here Aaron is the object, and not the subject, of atonement. See our discussion in Chapter 4 A.

37. Ehrlich, *Randglossen, ad loc.* Cf. R. Weiss, *Studies*, p. 148 n. 400.

38. See p. 98.

39. Cp. Num 8.10, 19; 18.23.

40. See v. 26. Elliger takes the repetitiveness between ושלח . . . המדברה (v. 21) and ושלח . . . במדבר (v. 22) as indicating two literary layers (p. 206). However, the two sentences are not the same. Not only are the subjects of שלח different but the construction in v. 22 is a pregnant one. See Williams, *Syntax*, §253.

41. See Chapter 5 A above.

42. See p. 129 above.

43. Cf. Elliger, p. 214 n. 11.

44. In other instances of בני ישראל it may or may not include Aaron (and priests). See Lev 1.2; 7.23, 29; 11.2; 12.2; 15.2; 18.2; 20.2; 23.2, 10, 24, 34; 24.2; 25.2; 27.2; 19.2 כל עדת בני ישראל.

45. Cp. עדת בני ישראל (v. 5).

46. Also in v. 21a כל is attached to all the three sin terms. Cf. J.L. Kugel, *The Idea of Biblical Poetry* (1981), pp. 47-48.

47. With D.P. Wright, *op. cit.*, p. 20. Cp. Elliger, pp. 208-209.

48. There is, in fact, another question whether *waw* before מפשעיהם is explanatory as Levine (*Presence*, p. 76) and Kornfeld (pp. 64-65) understand. However, this seems to be unlikely in the light of the following discussion.

49. Although vv. 16a, 21a concern the scope of purgation on the day of Atonement this issue requires separate treatment. The following five approaches show how diversely the scope of purgation has been viewed by scholars; (1) Keil believes that the atonement ceremony deals with sins which have not been atoned for in the course of the year (pp. 394-95). So Baentsch, p. 385. (2) Opposing Keil's view Kurtz argues that the language of Lev 16.16a implies the universality of the scope of purgation, and that therefore the ceremony deals with 'all the sins of the whole nation without exception, known or unknown, atoned for or not atoned for ' (*op. cit.*, p. 386). (3) According to Milgrom the ceremony purges the uncleanness produced by the wanton, unrepented sin (*op. cit.*, pp. 78, 81). (4) In response to Milgrom's view Rodriguez holds that the ceremony deals with 'the iniquities, rebellions, and sins of the sons of Israel, not of the wanton sinners' (*op. cit.*, pp. 116, 148). (5) Most scholars seem to assume that the ceremony deals with 'inadvertent sins' as opposed to presumptuous sins. So Hoffmann, p. 308; S.R. Driver–H.A. White, *HDB*, II, p. 201; Gispen, p. 248. Cp. Ezek 45.20; Heb 9.7.

It seems that Keil's view has no clear support in the text. But it is not easy to decide which of the other four views is most adequate. Undoubtedly, part of the problem lies in the meaning of פשע and חטאת. Firstly, that פשע does not denote 'rebellion' let alone 'wanton sin', has been carefully worked out by Knierim, in *Hauptbegriffe*, pp. 176ff. and in פשע, *THAT*, *II*, cols 488-95. According to him the basic concept of פשע denotes 'Verbrechen', rather than an attitude which is reflected in the translation 'rebellion'. It appears that since פשע is associated with crimes, פשעים in Lev 16.16 can include sins which the אשם offering deals with. Secondly, at least it seems possible to construe the meaning of חטאת in the light of חטאת in the context of the *hattat* offering (Lev 4.3, 14, 23, 28; 5.6, 13). However, whether כל חטאתם in Lev 16.16 can include 'wanton sin' (Num 15.30-31) seems debatable. Cp. Porter, p. 37.

50. לכל basically means 'with respect to all' (cf. BDB, p. 514; Orlinsky, *Notes*, p. 30). The *lamed* functions to specify what precedes it (see *Williams*, *op. cit.*, §271) while כל expresses the totality of what follows it. In other words, לכל as a whole functions to specify what precedes it from a different viewpoint. Cp. Exod 28.38; Lev 5.3-4; 22.18; Num 5.9; 18.8. It seems to me that the common translation 'whatever their sins' is inexact. Cp. Milgrom, *Levitical Terminology*, n. 237.

51 So Dillmann, p. 530; Porter, p. 130.

52. This standpoint seems to be taken by Milgrom. See note 8 above. It seems that commentators have not tackled this syntactical question despite its crucial importance.

The Purification Offering

53. Elliger, p. 196.
54. P. 61 above.
55. Eg. Lev 17.4. See the index in Haran, *Temples*, p. 364.
56. *Contra* Haran (*ibid.*, p. 179 n. 10), who equates אהל מועד in these passages with the tabernacle.
57. Pp. 65-66 above. On this interpretation v. 16a virtually says: וכפר על הקרש מכל חמאת בני ישראל. Cp. Lev 16.30, 34. For the relationship between טמא and פשע see Ezek 14.11; 37.23.
58. Chapter 5 B and Chapter 3 A respectively.
59. Pp. 59-60.
60. Section B.
61. See Chapter 2 C.

BIBLIOGRAPHY

Aartun, K, 'Studien zum Gesetz über den grossen Versöhnungstag: Lev 16 mit Varianten', *ST* 34 (1980), pp. 73-109.

Abarbanel, Don Isaac, פרוש על התורה, new edn; Jerusalem, 1979.

Andersen, F.I., *The Sentence in Biblical Hebrew*, The Hague and Paris, 1974 [cited as *Sentence*].

Baentsch, B., *Exodus, Leviticus, Numeri*, Göttingen, 1903.

Barr, J., 'Propitiation', *DB*, p. 810.

—'Sacrifice and Offering', *DB*, pp. 868-76.

—'Atonement', *DB*, pp. 76-78.

Barton, J., *Reading the Old Testament*, London, 1984.

Beauchamp, E., 'Péché', *DBS*, VII (1966), cols. 407-71.

Ben-Mordecai, C.A., 'The Iniquity of Sanctuary', *JBL* 60 (1941), pp. 311-14.

Benzinger, I., *Hebräische Archäologie*, 3rd edn; Hildesheim, 1974.

—'Das Gesetz über den grossen Versöhnungstag Lev XVI', *ZAW* 9 (1889), pp. 65-89.

Bertholet, A., *Leviticus*, Tübingen, 1901.

—'Zum Verständnis des alttestamentlichen Opfergedankens', *JBL* 49 (1930), pp. 218-33.

—*Der Sinn des kultischen Opfers*, Berlin, 1942.

Blau, J., 'The Red Heifer; A Biblical Purification Rite in Rabbinic Literature ', *Numen* 14 (1967), pp. 70-78.

Brandt, W., 'Zur Bestreichung mit Blut', *ZAW* 33 (1913), pp. 80-81.

Brawer, A.J., 'ע', השעיר לעזאזל וצפור המצורע, *BM* 12 (1967), pp. 32-33.

Brichto, H.C., *The Problem of 'Curse' in the Hebrew Bible*, Philadelphia, 1968.

—'On Slaughter and Sacrifice, Blood and Atonement', *HUCA* 47 (1976), pp. 19-55.

Büchler, A., *Studies in Sin and Atonement in the Rabbinic Literature of the First Century*, reprint; New York, 1967 [cited as *Sin and Atonement*].

Cazelles, H., *Le Lévitique*, Paris, 1958.

—'Pureté et impureté', *DBS* IX (1979), cols. 491-508.

Chapman, A.T., and Streane, A.W., *The Book of Leviticus*, Cambridge, 1914.

Christ, H., *Blutvergiessen im Alten Testament*, Basel, 1977.

Daly, R.J., *Christian Sacrifice*, Washington, 1978.

Danby, H., *The Mishnah*, Oxford, 1933.

Daniel, S., *Recherches sur le vocabulaire du culte dans la Septante*, Paris, 1966.

Daube, D., 'Error and Accident in the Bible', *RIDA* 2 (1949), pp. 189-213.

—*Ancient Jewish Law*, Leiden, 1981.

Davies, D.J., 'An Interpretation of Sacrifice in Leviticus', *ZAW* 89 (1977), pp. 387-99.

Dillmann, A., *Exodus und Leviticus*, 2nd edn; Leipzig, 1880.

—*Numeri, Deuteronomium und Josua*, 2nd edn; Leipzig 1886.

Douglas, M., *Purity and Danger*, London, 1966.

—*Natural Symbols*, London, 1970.

—*Implicit Meanings*, London, 1975.

Driver, G.R., 'Three Technical Terms in the Pentateuch', *JSS* 1 (1956), pp. 97-105.
Driver, S.R., 'Propitiation', *HDB*, IV, pp. 128-32.
Driver, S.R., and White, H.A., *The Book of Leviticus*, Leipzig, 1894.
Dussaud, R., *Les Origines cananéennes du sacrifice israelite*, 3rd edn; Paris 1941 [cited as *Origines*].
Eerdmans, B.D., *Alttestamentliche Studien*, IV: *Das Buch Leviticus*, Giessen, 1912.
Ehrlich, A., *Randglossen zur hebräischen Bibel*, 7 vols; Leipzig, 1908-1914 [cited as *Randglossen*].
—מקרא כפשוטו, 3 vols.; reprint; New York, 1969 (1st edn, 1899).
Eichrodt, W., *Theology of the Old Testament*, 2 vols. trans. from German; Philadelphia, 1961, 1967.
Elliger, K., *Leviticus*, Tübingen, 1966.
Feinberg, C.L., 'The Scapegoat of Lev 16', *BS* 115 (1958), pp. 320-33.
Feldman, E., *Biblical & Post-Biblical Defilement and Mourning: Law as Theology*, New York, 1977.
Ferguson, E., 'Laying on of Hands: Its Significance in Ordination', *JThS* 26 (1975), pp. 1-12.
Finn, A.H., 'The Tabernacle Chapters', *JThS* 16 (1915), pp. 449-82.
Frymer-Kensky, T., 'Pollution, Purification, and Purgation in Biblical Israel', in *The Word of the Lord Shall Go Forth* (FS, D.N. Freedman), ed. by C.L. Meyers and M. O'Connor, Philadelphia (1983), pp. 399-414.
Füglister, N., 'Sühne durch Blut—Zur Bedeutung von Lev 17.11', in *Studien zum Pentateuch* (FS, W. Kornfeld) ed. by G. Braulik; Wien/Freiburg/Basel (1977), pp. 143-64.
Garnet, P., 'Atonement Constructions in the Old Testament and the Qumran Scrolls', *EQ* 46 (1974), pp. 131-63.
Gayford, S.C., *Sacrifice and Priesthood*, London, 1924.
Gerleman, G., 'Die Wurzel *kpr* im Hebräischen', in *idem*, *Studien zur alttestamentlichen Theologie*, Heidelberg (1980), pp. 11-23.
—'רצה', *THAT*, II, cols. 810-13.
Gese, H., *Zur biblischen Theologie*, München, 1974.
Gispen, W.H., 'The Distinction between Clean and Unclean', *OTS* 5 (1948), pp. 190-96.
—*Het Boek Leviticus*, Kampen, 1950.
—*Het Boek Numeri*, 2 vols.; Kampen, 1959.
Gooding, D.W., *The Account of the Tabernacle*, Cambridge, 1959.
Gradwohl, R., 'Das "fremde Feuer" von Nadab und Abihu', *ZAW* 75 (1963), pp. 288-96.
Gray, G.B., *Numbers*, New York, 1903.
—*Sacrifice in the Old Testament*, Oxford, 1925 [cited as *Sacrifice*].
Greenberg, M., 'Herem', *EJ*, VIII (1971), pp. 344-50.
—*Ezekiel*, 1-20, New York, 1983.
Haran, M., *Temples and Temple Service in Ancient Israel*, Indiana reprint 1985 (1st edn 1978) [cited as *Temples*].
—'מזבח', *EM*, IV, cols. 763-80.
Harrison, R.K., *Leviticus*, Leicester, 1980.
Heinisch, P., *Das Buch Leviticus*, Bonn, 1935.
Henniger, J., 'Pureté et impureté', *DBS* IX (1979), pp. 399-430.
Herrmann, J., *Die Idee der Sühne im Alten Testament*, Leipzig, 1905.
Hoffmann, D.Z., ספר ויקרא, 2 vols.; trans. from German; Jerusalem, 1976.
Hoftijzer, J., 'Das sogenannte Feueropfer', in *Hebräische Wortforschung* (FS, W. Baumgartner, *VTS* 16), Leiden (1967), pp. 114-34.

Hurowitz, V., 'Priestly Account of Building the Tabernacle', *JAOS* 105, pp. 21-30.

Hurvitz, A., *A Linguistic Study of the Relationship between the Priestly Source and the Book of Ezekiel*, Paris, 1982 [cited as *Linguistic Study*].

Ibn Ezra, Abraham, אבן עזרא על התורה, ed. by A. Weiser; Jerusalem, 1977.

Izre'el, S., ' 'el = "to, towards" in Biblical Hebrew', *Shnaton* III (1978), pp. 204-12.

Jackson, B.S., *Essays in Jewish and Comparative Legal History*, Leiden, 1975.

Jagersma, H., *Numeri*, deel I, Nijkerk 1983.

Janowski, B., *Sühne als Heilsgeschehen*, Neukirchen-Vluyn, 1982 [cited as *Sühne*].

Jenni, E., *Das hebräische Pi'el*, Zürich, 1968.

Kaufmann, Y., תולדות האמונה הישראלית, 4 vols.; 10th edn; Tel-Aviv, 1976 [cited as תולדות].

Kedar, B., *Biblische Semantik*, Stuttgart, 1981.

Keil, C.F., *The Pentateuch* II–III (*Biblical Commentary on the OT*) reprint; Grand Rapids, 1968.

—*Handbuch der biblischen Archäologie*, 2nd edn; Frankfurt, 1875 [cited as *Archäologie*].

Kennedy, A.R.S., *Leviticus and Numbers*, Edinburgh, 1910.

Kidner, D., *Sacrifice in the Old Testament*, London, 1952.

—'Sacrifice—Metaphors and Meaning', *TB* 33 (1982), pp. 119-36.

Knierim, R., *Die Hauptbegriffe für Sünde im Alten Testament*, Gütersloh, 2nd edn; 1967 [cited as *Hauptbegriffe*].

—'Old Testament Form Criticism Reconsidered', *Interpretation* 27 (1973), pp. 435-68.

—'אשם', *THAT*, I, cols. 251-57.

—'חטא', *THAT*, I, cols. 541-49.

—'עון', *THAT*, II, cols. 243-49.

—'פשע', *THAT*, II, cols. 488-95.

—'שגג', *THAT*, II, cols. 869-72.

Köberle, J., *Sünde und Gnade im religiösen Leben des Volkes Israel bis auf Christum*, München, 1905 [cited as *Sünde und Gnade*].

Koch, K., *Die Priesterschrift von Exodus 25 bis Leviticus 16*, Göttingen, 1959 [cited as *Priesterschrift*].

—'Gibt es ein Vergeltungsdogma im Alten Testament?', *ZThK* 52 (1955), pp. 1-42.

Kornfeld, W., *Leviticus*, Würzburg, 1983.

— 'Reine und unreine Tiere im AT', *Kairos* 7 (1965), pp. 134-47.

Kugel, J.L., *The Idea of Biblical Poetry*, New Haven and London, 1981.

Kurtz, J.H., *Sacrificial Worship of the Old Testament*, Grand Rapids, 1980 (reprint of the 1863 edn) [cited as *Sacrificial Worship*].

Lang, B., 'כפר', *TWAT*, IV, cols. 303-18.

—ed. *Anthropological Approaches to the Old Testament*, Philadelphia/London, 1985.

Landersdorfer, S., *Studien zum biblischen Versöhnungstag*, Münster, 1924 [cited as *Versöhnungstag*].

Laughlin, J.C.H. 'The "Strange Fire" of Nadab and Abihu', *JBL* 95 (1976), pp. 559-65.

Levin, B., 'כפורים', *EI*, IX (1969), pp. 88-95.

— *In the Presence of the Lord*, Leiden, 1974 (cited as *Presence*].

Liver, J., 'עדה', *EM* VI, cols. 83-89.

Lods, A., 'Israelitische Opfervorstellungen und -bräuche', *Theologische Rundschau* 3 (1931), pp. 347-66.

Loewenstamm, S.A., 'פרה אדמה', *EM* VI, cols. 579-81.

Löhr, M., *Das Ritual von Lev 16*, Berlin, 1925.

—*Das Räucheropfer im Alten Testament*, Halle, 1927.

Loss, N.M., 'La terminologia e il tema del peccato in Lev 4–5', *Salesianum* 3 (1968), pp. 437-61.

Lyonnet, S. - Sabourin, L., *Sin, Redemption and Sacrifice*, Rome, 1970 [cited as *Sin*].

Maarsingh, B., *Leviticus*, Nijkerk, 1980.

Maass, F., 'כפר', *THAT*, I, cols. 842-57.

Matthes, J.C., 'Der Sühnegedanke bei den Sündopfern', *ZAW* 23 (1903), pp. 97-119.

Medebielle, A., 'Expiation dans l'Ancien Testament', *DBS* III (1938), pp. 48-112.

—'Le symbolisme du sacrifice expiatoire en Israël', *Biblica* 2 (1921), pp. 146-69, 273-302.

van der Merwe, B.J., 'The Laying on of Hands in the OT', *OTWSA* 5 (1962), pp. 34-43.

Messel, N., 'Die Komposition von Lev 16', *ZAW* 27 (1907), pp. 1-15.

Mettinger, T.N.D., 'Abbild oder Urbild "Imago Dei" in traditionsgeschichtlicher Sicht', *ZAW* 86 (1974), pp. 403-24.

Metzinger, A., 'Die Substitutionstheorie und das alttestamentliche Opfer mit besonderer Berücksichtigung von Lev 17, 11', *Biblica* 21 (1940), pp. 159-87, 247-72, 353-77.

Milgrom, J., *Studies in Levitical Terminology*, I, Berkeley, 1970 [cited as *Levitical Terminology*].

—'כפר על/בעד', *Leshonenu* 35 (1970), pp. 16-17.

—'תפקיד קרבן חטאת', *Tarbiz* 40 (1970), pp. 1-8.

—*Cult and Conscience*, Leiden, 1976 [cited as *Cult*].

—*Studies in Cultic Theology and Terminology*, Leiden, 1983 [cited as *Cultic Theology*].

—'Sin-offering or Purification-offering?', *VT* 21 (1971), pp. 237-39, and in *idem*, *Cultic Theology*, pp. 67-69.

—'Two Kinds of Hatta't', *VT* 26 (1976), pp. 333-37, and in *idem*, *Cultic Theology*, pp. 70-74.

—'Israel's Sanctuary: The Priestly "Picture of Dorian Gray"', *RB* 83 (1976), pp. 390-99, and in *idem*, *Cultic Theology*, pp. 75-84.

—'The Paradox of the Red Cow (Num xix)', *VT* 31 (1981), pp. 62-72, and in *idem*, *Cultic Theology*, pp. 85-95.

—'A Prolegomena to Lev 17.11', *JBL* 90 (1971) pp. 149-56, and in *idem*, *Cultic Theology*, pp. 96-103.

—'The Cultic šggh and its Influence in Psalms and Job', *JQR* 58 (1967), pp. 115-25, and in *idem*, *Cultic Theology*, pp. 122-32.

—'Altar', *EJ* II, cols. 760-67.

—'Day of Atonement', *EJ*, V, cols. 1384-87.

—'kipper' *EJ* X, cols. 1039-44.

—קטרת, *EM* VII, cols. 111-18.

—'קרבן', *EM* VII, cols. 233-51.

—'Atonement in the OT', *IDBSup*, pp. 78-82.

—'Atonement, Day of' *IDBSup*, pp. 82-83.

—'Sacrifice and Offerings, OT', *IDBSup*, pp. 763-71.

—'Sancta Contagion and Altar/City Asylum', *SVT* 32 (1981), pp. 278-310.

—'The Graduated ḤAṬṬA'T of Leviticus 5.1-13', *JAOS* 103 (1983), pp. 249-54.

—'The Two Pericopes on the Purification Offering', in *The Word of the Lord Shall Go Forth* (FS D.N. Freedman), Philadelphia (1983), pp. 211-15 [cited as 'Purification'].

—Review of B. Janowski, *Sühne als Heilsgeschehen*, *JBL* 104 (1985), pp. 302-304.

Moraldi, L., *Espiazione sacrificale e riti espiatori nell'ambiente biblico e nell'Antico Testament*, Rome, 1956.

Morris, L., *The Apostolic Preaching of the Cross*, London, 1972.

Muraoka, T., *Emphatic Words and Structures in Biblical Hebrew*, Jerusalem/Leiden, 1985.

Neusner, J., *The Idea of Purity in Ancient Judaism*, Leiden, 1973.

Noth, M., *Leviticus*, Philadelphia, 1962.

—*Numbers*, Philadelphia, 1968.

Orlinsky, H.M., *Notes on the New Translation of the Torah*, Philadelphia, 1969 [cited as *Notes*].

Paschen, W., *Rein und unrein*, München, 1970.

Pedersen, J., *Israel: Its Life and Culture*, III-IV, London, 1940.

Péter, R., 'L'imposition des mains dans l'Ancien Testament' *VT* 27 (1977), pp. 48-55.

Phillips, A., *Ancient Israel's Criminal Law*, Oxford, 1970.

—'The Undetectable Offender and the Priestly Legislators', *JThS* 36 (1985), pp. 146-50.

Porter, J.R., *Leviticus*, Cambridge, 1976.

Quell, G., 'ἁμαρτάνω', *TDNT*, I, pp. 267-86.

von Rad, G., *Old Testament Theology* I-II, New York, 1962, 1965.

Rashi (שלמה בר יצחק 'ר), *The Pentateuch with Rashi's Commentary*, translated by M. Rosenbaum and A.M. Silbermann; New York, 1973.

Rashbam (שמואל בר מאיר 'ר), פרוש התורה, ed. by D. Rosin; Breslau, 1842.

Ramban (משה בר נחמן 'ר), פירושי התורה, ed. by C.B. Chavel; Jerusalem, 1959.

Rendtorff, R., *Die Gesetze in der Priesterschrift*, 2nd edn; Göttingen, 1963 [cited as *Gesetze*].

—*Studien zur Geschichte des Opfers im Alten Israel*, Neukirchen-Vluyn, 1967 [cited as *Studien*].

Rigby, P., 'A Structural Analysis of Israelite Sacrifice and Its Other Institutions', *Église et théologie* 11 (1980), pp. 299-351.

Rivière, J., 'Satisfactio Vicaria', *Revue des sciences religieuses* 26 (1952), pp. 221-57.

Rodriguez, A.M., *Substitution in the Hebrew Cultus*, Berrien Springs, 1979 [cited as *Substitution*].

Saalschütz, J.L., *Das Mosäische Recht*, Berlin, 1853.

Sabourin, S.J., 'Nefesh, sang et expiation (Lev 17.11.14)', *Sciences ecclésiastiques* 18 (1966), pp. 25-45.

Saggs, H.W.F., Review of Milgrom's, *Cult and Conscience*, *JSS* 24 (1979), pp. 129-30.

Sansom, M.C., 'Laying on of Hands in the Old Testament', *ET* 94 (1983), pp. 323-26.

Saydon, P.P., 'Sin-offering and Trespass-offering', *CBQ* 8 (1946), pp. 393-98.

Schenker, A., 'koper et expiation', *Biblica* 63 (1982), pp. 32-46.

—'Das Zeichen des Blutes und die Gewissheit der Vergebung im Alten Testament', *MTZ* 34 (1983), pp. 195-213.

Schötz, D., *Schuld- und Sündopfer im Alten Testament*, Breslau, 1930 [cited as *Schuld- und Sündopfer*].

Schur, I., *Versöhnungstag und Sündenbock*, Helsingfors/Leipzig 1934.

Shadal (Luzzatto, S.D.), פירוש שד"ל על חמישה חומשי תורה, ed. by P. Schlesinger; Tel-Aviv, 1965.

Smith, R. *The Religion of the Semites*, New York, 1972.

Snaith, N., 'Sacrifices in the OT', *VT* 7 (1957), pp. 308-17.

—'The Sin-Offering and the Guilt-Offering', *VT* 15 (1965), pp. 73-80.

—*Leviticus and Numbers*, London, 1967.

—'The Sprinkling of Blood', *ET* 82 (1970/71), pp. 23-24.

Sonsino, R., *Motive Clause in Hebrew Law*, Chico, 1980.

Spiro, A., 'A Law on the Sharing of Information', *PAAJR* 28 (1959), pp. 95-101.

Stamm, J.J., *Erlösen und Vergeben im Alten Testament*, Bern, 1940 [cited as *Erlösen*].

Steinmueller, J.E., 'Sacrificial Blood in the Bible', *Biblica* 40 (1959), pp. 56-67.

Tooms, I.E., 'Clean and Unclean', *IDB*, I, pp. 641-48.

—'Red Heifer', *IDB*, IV, pp. 18-19.

van der Toorn, K., *Sin and Sanction in Israel and Mesopotamia*, Assen/Maastricht, 1985.

de Vaux, R., *Studies in Old Testament Sacrifice*, Cardiff, 1964 [cited as *Studies*].

Volz, P., 'Handauflegung beim Opfer', *ZAW* 21 (1901), pp. 93-100.

Vriezen, Th.C., 'Hizza: Lustration and Consecration', *OTS* 7 (1950), pp. 201-35.

Wefing, S., 'Beobachtung zum Ritual mit der roten Kuh (Num 19, 1-10a)', *ZAW* 93 (1981), pp. 341-64.

Weinberg, Z., 'חטאת ואשם', *BM* 55 (1973), pp. 524-30.

Weiss, M., 'מבעיות תורת הגמול המקראית', *Tarbiz* 31 (1962), pp.236-63.

Weiss, R., מחקרי מקרא, Jerusalem, 1981 [cited as *Studies*].

Wellhausen, J., *Die Composition des Hexateuchs und der Historischen Bücher des Alten Testaments*, 4th edn; Berlin, 1963 [cited as *Composition*].

—*Prolegomena to the History of Ancient Israel* (Meridian reprint), Cleveland, 1961 (German original 1878) [cited as *Prolegomena*].

Wenham, G.J., *The Book of Leviticus*, Grand Rapids, 1979.

—*Numbers*, Leicester, 1981.

—'Christ's Healing Ministry and his Attitude to the Law', in *Christ the Lord* (FS D. Guthrie) Leicester (1982), pp. 115-26.

—'Why Does Sexual Intercourse Defile (Lev 15.18)?', *ZAW* 95 (1983), pp. 432-34.

Wilch, J.R., *Time and Event*, Leiden, 1969.

Williams, R.J., *Hebrew Syntax*, Toronto/Buffalo/London, 1967 [cited as *Syntax*].

Wold, D.J., 'The Karet Penalty in P; Rationale and Cases', *SBL* seminar papers (1979), pp. 1-45.

Wright, D.P., *The Disposal of Impurity in the Priestly Writings of the Bible with Reference to Similar Phenomena in Hittite and Mesopotamian Cultures*, Ann Arbor: University Microfilms, 1984 [cited as *Disposal*].

—'Purification from Corpse-contamination in Numbers xxxi 19-24', *VT* 35 (1985), pp. 213-23.

Zimmerli, W., 'Die Eigenart der prophetischen Rede des Ezekiel', *ZAW* 66 (1954), pp. 1-26.

INDEX

INDEX OF BIBLICAL REFERENCES

INDEX OF AUTHORS

JOURNAL FOR THE STUDY OF THE OLD TESTAMENT

Supplement Series

*   Out of print